Modern Rwanda

Rwanda has been the subject of much research following the genocide against the Tutsi ethnic group in 1994. Moving beyond recent histories which examine Rwanda's past predominantly through the lens of this tragic event, Filip Reyntjens utilises a *longue durée* framework to provide new insights into historical developments over the last 150 years. Tracking the foundations of modern Rwanda from the mid nineteenth century to the present day, this book offers the first comprehensive examination of both the political continuities and ruptures which have shaped the country. Reyntjens examines the nineteenth-century precolonial polity; colonisation from the end of the nineteenth century; the revolution of 1959–1961, followed by independence in 1962; and the 1994 genocide, followed by the seizure of power by the Rwandan Patriotic Front. Across these periods of dramatic transition, this study demonstrates the role of both political constancy and change, allowing readers to reshape their understanding of Rwanda's political history.

Filip Reyntjens is Professor Emeritus of Law and Politics at the University of Antwerp. He has specialised in the law and politics of Sub-Saharan Africa, particularly the Great Lakes Region, for over forty years. Previous publications include *The Great African War: Congo and Regional Geopolitics, 1996–2006* (Cambridge University Press, 2009), *Political Governance in Post-genocide Rwanda* (Cambridge University Press, 2013) and *Le génocide des Tutsi au Rwanda* (Presses universitaires de France, 2017, 2021).

Modern Rwanda
A Political History

Filip Reyntjens
University of Antwerp

CAMBRIDGE
UNIVERSITY PRESS

CAMBRIDGE
UNIVERSITY PRESS

Shaftesbury Road, Cambridge CB2 8EA, United Kingdom

One Liberty Plaza, 20th Floor, New York, NY 10006, USA

477 Williamstown Road, Port Melbourne, VIC 3207, Australia

314–321, 3rd Floor, Plot 3, Splendor Forum, Jasola District Centre, New Delhi – 110025, India

103 Penang Road, #05–06/07, Visioncrest Commercial, Singapore 238467

Cambridge University Press is part of Cambridge University Press & Assessment, a department of the University of Cambridge.

We share the University's mission to contribute to society through the pursuit of education, learning and research at the highest international levels of excellence.

www.cambridge.org
Information on this title: www.cambridge.org/9781009284479

DOI: 10.1017/9781009284493

© Filip Reyntjens 2024

This publication is in copyright. Subject to statutory exception and to the provisions of relevant collective licensing agreements, no reproduction of any part may take place without the written permission of Cambridge University Press & Assessment.

When citing this work, please include a reference to the DOI 10.1017/9781009284493

First published 2024

A catalogue record for this publication is available from the British Library

Library of Congress Cataloging-in-Publication Data
Names: Reyntjens, Filip, author.
Title: Modern Rwanda : a political history / Filip Reyntjens, University of Antwerp.
Description: Cambridge ; New York, NY : Cambridge University Press, 2024. | Includes bibliographical references and index.
Identifiers: LCCN 2024011980 | ISBN 9781009284479 (hardback) | ISBN 9781009284493 (ebook)
Subjects: LCSH: Rwanda – Politics and government.
Classification: LCC DT450.3 .R49 2024 | DDC 967.571–dc23/eng/20240725
LC record available at https://lccn.loc.gov/2024011980

ISBN 978-1-009-28447-9 Hardback
ISBN 978-1-009-28448-6 Paperback

Cambridge University Press & Assessment has no responsibility for the persistence or accuracy of URLs for external or third-party internet websites referred to in this publication and does not guarantee that any content on such websites is, or will remain, accurate or appropriate.

Contents

Acknowledgements	*page* vii
List of Abbreviations	viii

	Introduction	1
	I.1 Methodology	1
	I.2 A Brief Look at Pre-mid Nineteenth-Century History	6
1	**From Old to New Kings**	**13**
	1.1 Political Organisation	13
	1.2 Military Campaigns	16
	1.3 Terror inside the Court and across Society	17
	1.4 Ethnicity	20
	1.5 The Arrival of New Kings	23
	1.6 Other Kings: The Missions	25
	1.7 German Policy	26
	1.8 International Status	28
	1.9 Conclusion	29
2	**Early Belgian Colonialism**	**32**
	2.1 Military Campaign and Occupation	32
	2.2 International Status	33
	2.3 Colonial Public Law	35
	2.4 Indirect Rule Belgian Style	36
	2.5 Early Political Measures	41
	2.6 Conclusion	50
3	**Consolidating Colonial Rule**	**52**
	3.1 Destitution and Relegation of Musinga, Accession of Rudahigwa	52
	3.2 Consolidation of Tutsi Political Monopoly	54
	3.3 Bureaucratisation of the Chiefly Function	56
	3.4 The Situation of the Hutu Masses	63
	3.5 The Consolidation of the Indigenous Political Organisation	67
	3.6 The Dual Administration	68
	3.7 Conclusion	69
4	**Revolutionary Change**	**73**
	4.1 Conditions for Revolution	73
	4.2 Premises of the Revolution	74

	4.3	The Revolution	80
	4.4	From Absolute Tutsi Monarchy to 'Democratic' Hutu Republic	90
	4.5	Conclusion	93
5	The 'Hutu Republics'	94
	5.1	An Autochthonous Constitution	94
	5.2	From De Jure Multi-party to De Facto Single-Party Rule	98
	5.3	*Inyenzi* Attacks and Massacres of Tutsi	100
	5.4	Internal Conflicts	105
	5.5	Regional Conflicts	108
	5.6	The End of the First Republic	109
	5.7	The Birth of the Second Republic	112
	5.8	Civilianisation	113
	5.9	Elections	115
	5.10	Internal Conflicts, Again	116
	5.11	The Situation of the Tutsi: A Festering Wound	119
	5.12	The Two Republics Compared	121
	5.13	A Looming Political Crisis	123
	5.14	Conclusion	126
6	The Abyss: Political Transition, Civil War and Genocide	128
	6.1	Political Transition and Civil War	128
	6.2	The Genocide	137
	6.3	Crimes Committed by the RPF	146
	6.4	Sequels	149
	6.5	Conclusion	154
7	Post-genocide Political Governance	155
	7.1	Two Rwandas	155
	7.2	Elections as a Means of Regime Consolidation	156
	7.3	Managing Political Space	162
	7.4	Law as a Tool of Control	164
	7.5	The RPF Challenged from Within	165
	7.6	Human Rights and Impunity, a Dismal Record	167
	7.7	A Regional Powerhouse	170
	7.8	Information and Communication Management	172
	7.9	Engineering a New Society	178
	7.10	Conclusion	180
	Conclusion	184
Bibliography			194
Index			208

Acknowledgements

It is a pleasure to express my gratitude to those who have generously given their precious time to comment on the draft of this book: Klaus Bachmann, Marie-Ève Desrosiers, René Lemarchand, David Newbury, Susan Thomson and four anonymous reviewers for Cambridge University Press. Of course, remaining errors of fact and analysis are my responsibility.

Abbreviations

ANT	Assemblée nationale de transition
Aprosoma	Association pour la promotion sociale de la masse
CDR	Coalition pour la défense de la République
CEPGL	Communauté économique des pays des grands lacs
CPUN	Comité pour la paix et l'unité nationale
DSP	Division spéciale présidentielle (Zaire)
FAR	Forces armées rwandaises
FARDC	Forces armées de la République Démocratique du Congo
FIB	Force Intervention Brigade
GTBE	Gouvernement de transition à base élargie
ICTR	International Criminal Tribunal for Rwanda
IDPs	Internally displaced person(s)
Liprodhor	Ligue pour la promotion et la défense des droits de l'homme au Rwanda
MDR	Mouvement démocratique républicain
MICT	International Residual Mechanism for Criminal Tribunals
MRND	Mouvement révolutionnaire national pour le développement
NRA	National Resistance Army (Uganda)
NURC	National Unity and Reconciliation Commission
OBK	Organisation pour l'aménagement et le développement du bassin de la rivière Kagera
OCAM	Organisation commune africaine et malgache
OIF	Organisation internationale de la Francophonie
OTP	Office of the Prosecutor (ICTR)
Parmehutu	Parti du mouvement de l'émancipation hutu
PDC	Parti démocrate-chrétien
PL	Parti libéral
PSD	Parti social-démocrate
RADER	Rassemblement démocratique ruandais

RDF	Rwanda Defence Force
RPA	Rwandan Patriotic Army
RPF	Rwandan Patriotic Front
RSF	Reporters sans frontières
RTLM	Radio Télévision Libre des Mille Collines
SCR	Service central des renseignements
UNAMIR	United Nations Assistance Mission for Rwanda
UNAR	Union nationale rwandaise
UNHCR	United Nations High Commission for Refugees
UNMIS	United Nations Mission in Sudan

Introduction

I.1 Methodology

Although Rwanda had been a widely researched country before the 1994 genocide against the Tutsi,[1] scholarship exploded after this catastrophic event. As researchers, many of them young and 'newcomers' to Rwanda studies, flocked to the country, both the quantity and quality of publications steadily increased. Most research centred on understanding the causes and the unravelling of the genocide, its sequels, such as transitional justice and the regional wars, and the new regime's governance – both political and bureaucratic/technocratic. Much of the scholarship was doctoral research, often involving long and thick fieldwork in challenging circumstances caused by a traumatic environment and the limitations imposed by an authoritarian and touchy government. One of the consequences of the massive arrival of the newcomer academics who discovered Rwanda after – and indeed as a result of – the genocide is that the past was looked at predominantly through its lens. This led to 'presentism', that is the hindsight affecting the writing of the country's history. However, veteran researchers Catharine and David Newbury have argued that the genocide should be analysed through an understanding of Rwandan history rather than looking at the past through the lens of the genocide.[2] Likewise, and more generally, Desrosiers and Russell observe that 'the past is understood

---

[1] A bibliography until the 1980s is offered in M. d'Hertefelt, D. de Lame, *Société, culture et histoire du Rwanda: Encyclopédie bibliographique 1863–1980/87*, Tervuren, Musée royal de l'Afrique centrale, 1987, 2 vols. A commented bibliography on the period of the Belgian trusteeship can be found in F. Lagarde, *Colonialisme et révolution: Histoire du Rwanda sous la Tutelle*, Paris, L'Harmattan, 2017, 2 vols; Lagarde also updates *Bibliographies sur le Rwanda* from 1990 onwards on the website of the University of Paris 1 Panthéon Sorbonne (https://recherche-afriquedesgrandslacs.pantheonsorbonne.fr/publications-recensions/bibliographies-rwanda-f-lagarde).

[2] D. Newbury, C. Newbury, 'Bringing the Peasants Back In: Agrarian Themes in the Construction and Corrosion of Statist Historiography in Rwanda', *The American Historical Review*, Vol. 105, No. 3, 2000, pp. 832–833.

through the prism of the present' and note the 'tendency to "write history backwards" from present concerns'.[3]

This is what this book sets out to avoid, by attempting to address the past without prior knowledge of the genocide until it occurred. Indeed, contrary to what is often claimed or suggested, the genocide was not inscribed as an inexorable event in the *longue durée* of Rwanda's history. I will show that some of these historical evolutions have been path dependent, while others occurred at critical junctures. Sometimes they were a combination of both. As shown by Capoccia and Kelemen,[4] periods of path-dependent institutional stability and reproduction are occasionally punctuated by brief phases of institutional flux – referred to as critical junctures – during which more dramatic change is possible. They define critical junctures as '*relatively* short periods of time during which there is a *substantially* heightened probability that agents' choices will affect the outcome'.[5] A key element of the analysis of critical junctures is contingency, which addresses the question of 'what happened in the context of what could have happened'.[6] The combination of path dependency and critical junctures will be highlighted throughout this book.

As can be seen elsewhere as well, history writing in Rwanda is not merely about the past but it also very much constitutes a contemporary political stake. To quote Desrosiers and Russell again, 'the past is not only a prologue but is a very lively part of the present'.[7] It is even more than that, having become an oft-exploited ideological tool. At crucial critical junctures – such as the 1959 revolution and the 1990–1994 civil war, which ended with the genocide and the seizure of power by the Rwanda Patriotic Front (RPF) – history has been produced by conflict parties in very different, even opposite, fashions as it suited their respective positions. Examples of divergent readings will be given later in this book, but one instance of 'Hutu' versus 'Tutsi' presentations is useful at this stage.[8] In the early 1990s, one could read on the 'Hutu' side that 'Rwandan society [...] has always presented itself under the form of three distinct ethnic groups. Since the existence of centralised state structures of power, the Tutsi ethnic group has dominated

---

[3] M.-E. Desrosiers, A. Russell, 'Histories of Authority in the African Great Lakes: Trajectories and Transactions', *Africa*, Vol. 90, No. 5, 2020, pp. 952, 954.
[4] G. Capoccia, R. D. Kelemen, 'The Study of Critical Junctures: Theory, Narrative, and Counterfactual in Historical Institutionalism', *World Politics*, Vol. 59, 2007, p. 341.
[5] Ibid., p. 348. Italics in the original text.
[6] Ibid., p. 355.
[7] Desrosiers, Russell, 'Histories of Authority', p. 967.
[8] 'Hutu' and 'Tutsi' are put between inverted commas as this generalisation hides the fact that the ethnic categories (on which more later) are not monolithic and that other identities are present. That said, 'Hutu' and 'Tutsi' discourses are articulated by elites, particularly in periods of crisis, and they are recognisable as such.

I.1 Methodology

the two other groups, the Hutu and the Twa.'[9] The 'Tutsi' reading was that 'these three groups constitute a single and same ethnic group rather than three different ethnicities'.[10] Both these positions are ideological and, as is often the case, they are in part true and in part false.

Competing and politicised historical narratives have engendered a great deal of polarisation in the political world, civil society, the media and even in academia.[11] This has led to those expressing themselves on Rwandan history to be placed in 'camps', generally in favour of or against the RPF or pro or anti Tutsi or Hutu. This book will attempt to avoid that pitfall, by only adhering to facts around which there is a large scholarly consensus or, when that is not the case, by presenting competing narratives (while taking or not taking a position on them). In so doing, facts and their interpretation will be distinguished.

What differentiates this book from earlier Rwandan historiography is its attempt to cover the entire approximately 150-year period during which modern Rwanda became what it is today. The work that comes the closest to this endeavour is René Lemarchand's seminal *Rwanda and Burundi*,[12] which, however, after a historical survey, mainly addresses the revolution and the first years of independence. Also seminal is Jan Vansina's *Antecedents to Modern Rwanda*,[13] which covers precolonial Rwanda, as does David Newbury's *The Land beyond the Mists*,[14] for the lands on both sides of Lake Kivu. Like this book, Alexis Kagame's *Abrégé* starts in the mid nineteenth century but ends with the first republic,[15] and his writing is strongly influenced by the author's proximity to the royal court. My own *Pouvoir et droit au Rwanda* addresses the period from the Belgian presence to the end of the first republic.[16] Bernard

---

[9] Extract of the political programme of the Coalition pour la Défense de la République (CDR), extremist Hutu party, March 1992.
[10] Communauté rwandaise de France, 'Mémorandum sur le crise politique actuelle au Rwanda', December 1990, p. 4.
[11] On polarisation in academia, see J. Fisher, 'Writing about Rwanda since the Genocide: Knowledge, Power and "Truth"', *Journal of Intervention and Statebuilding*, Vol. 9, No. 1, 2015, pp. 134–145; B. Chemouni, 'La recherche sur l'État rwandais en débat', *Politique africaine*, No. 160, 2020, pp. 17–22.
[12] R. Lemarchand, *Rwanda and Burundi*, London, Pall Mall Press, 1970.
[13] J. Vansina, *Antecedents to Modern Rwanda: The Nyiginya Kingdom*, Madison, University of Wisconsin Press, 2004.
[14] D. Newbury, *The Land beyond the Mists: Essays on Identity and Authority in Precolonial Congo and Rwanda*, Athens, Ohio University Press, 2009.
[15] A. Kagame, *Un abrégé de l'histoire du Rwanda de 1853 à 1972*, Butare, Editions universitaires du Rwanda, 1975. This volume followed A. Kagame, *Un abrégé de l'ethnohistoire du Rwanda*, Butare, Editions universitaires du Rwanda, 1972, which covers the years up to the accession of Rwabugiri.
[16] F. Reyntjens, *Pouvoir et droit au Rwanda: Droit public et évolution politique, 1916–1973*, Tervuren, Musée royal de l'Afrique centrale, 1985.

Lugan's *Histoire du Rwanda*,[17] as its subtitle suggests, covers a very long period from prehistory to the 1990s and for that reason remains very general and descriptive. The *History of Rwanda*, written on behalf of the governmental National Unity and Reconciliation Commission (NURC), is an extensive (726 pages) treatment of Rwanda's entire history.[18] While granting some concessions to the regime's narrative, it is a useful source. Bachmann's recent *History of Rwanda* tends to render the current regime's 'soft' version of some controversial issues.[19] Other works cover specific and limited historical periods, such as the reign of King Musinga,[20] the German period,[21] the run-up to, unravelling and sequels of the 1959 revolution,[22] the period of the Belgian mandate,[23] or the 'Hutu Republics',[24] to quote just a few, in addition to histories written from a missionary or administrative perspective.[25]

Given both its broad temporal scope and its analytical dimension, this book therefore aspires to cover ground hitherto uncovered in the literature on Rwanda. Many of the facts presented here are known, and most are uncontested. Presenting them in an orderly and succinct fashion is useful in itself, but what this book adds to the existing literature is the presentation and analysis of events in a *longue durée* framework, with a focus on continuities and breaks, whereby constancy outnumbers change, even at moments of dramatic transition. The ambition is nevertheless limited. By presenting facts and analysing them, the book aims at proposing a rational understanding of a historical evolution marked by a great deal of violence, both in a distant past and contemporaneously, and that has given rise to considerable debate. It is hoped that this presentation offers material for more detached conversations and further exploration of Rwanda's political journey based on common ground.

---

[17] B. Lugan, *Histoire du Rwanda: De la préhistoire à nos jours*, s.l., Bartillat, 1997.
[18] National Unity and Reconciliation Commission, *History of Rwanda: From the Beginning to the End of the Twentieth Century*, Kigali, 2016.
[19] K. Bachmann, *A History of Rwanda: From the Monarchy to Post-genocidal Justice*, London–New York, Routledge, 2023.
[20] A. Des Forges, *Defeat Is the Only Bad News: Rwanda under Musinga, 1896–1931*, Madison, University of Wisconsin Press, 2011.
[21] W. R. Louis, *Ruanda-Urundi 1884–1919*, Oxford, Clarendon Press, 1963.
[22] D. Murego, *La révolution rwandaise 1959–1962: Essai d'interprétation*, Louvain, Publications de l'Institut des sciences politiques et sociales, 1976.
[23] J. Rumiya, *Le Rwanda sous le régime du mandat belge (1916–1931)*, Paris, L'Harmattan, 1992.
[24] M.-E. Desrosiers, *Trajectories of Authoritarianism in Rwanda: Elusive Control before the Genocide*, Cambridge, Cambridge University Press, 2023.
[25] For a missionary perspective, see L. de Lacger, *Ruanda*, Kabgayi, 1959; for an administrative perspective, see *Historique et chronologie du Ruanda*, s.l., s.d. (1955).

I.1 Methodology

This book has (at least) two limitations. First, in line with Rwandan historiography in the past, it focuses on the central political level. Referring to the writing of precolonial history, David Newbury noted that this bias towards central institutions leads to a skewed presentation of a more complex reality: 'Central court allegiance and local cultural affinities were seldom aligned.'[26] As information came predominantly from court sources, '[o]fficial accounts present Rwandan history as exclusively the history of kings'.[27] Newbury could have issued a similar warning with regard to Rwanda's colonial and postcolonial historiography where the periphery is largely absent. Noting that 'politics have often been removed from rural life and agricultural practices separated from political life',[28] he and Cathy Newbury proposed 'a reunion of [central politics and rural experiences], too long separated: providing a rural dimension to conventional history and a historical dimension to rural studies, bringing politics into the understanding of peasants'.[29] Given that the vast majority of Rwandans have been, and still are today, rural dwellers, one cannot but agree with the Newburys. However, precisely because of the bias they observe and denounce, only very limited research is available on local, rural, dynamics.[30] Only after the genocide did a wealth of field scholarship conducted on Rwanda's thousand hills become available, quite paradoxically in a very constrained research environment. However, this does not offer the material needed for the comparative presentation necessary in the *longue durée* approach attempted here. This book therefore privileges the central political arena, with only some inroads in peripheral experiences.

The second limitation is in a way linked to the first one. This is first and foremost a political history, with only occasional attention for socio-economic issues. It is a choice made on the basis of both my expertise and the limited availability of information on that topic.

---

[26] Newbury, *The Land beyond the Mists*, p. 5.
[27] Ibid., p. 15.
[28] Newbury, Newbury, 'Bringing the Peasants Back In', p. 833.
[29] Ibid., p. 876.
[30] There are exceptions though, such as, in addition to journal articles, P. Leurquin, *Le niveau de vie des populations rurales au Ruanda-Urundi*, Louvain-Paris, Nauwelaerts, 1960; P. B. Gravel, *Remera: A Community in Eastern Rwanda*, The Hague, Mouton, 1968; C. Newbury, *The Cohesion of Oppression: Clientship and Ethnicity in Rwanda, 1860–1960*, New York, Columbia University Press, 1988; A. Hanssen, *Le désenchantement de la coopération: Enquête au pays des mille coopérants*, Paris, L'Harmattan, 1989; F. Bézy, *Rwanda 1962–1989, bilan socio-économique d'un régime*, Louvain, Institut d'Etudes du Développement, 1990; D. de Lame, *A Hill among a Thousand: Transformations and Ruptures in Rural Rwanda*, Madison, University of Wisconsin Press, 2005, and, by addressing popular oral culture, P. Smith, *Le récit populaire au Rwanda*, Paris, Armand Collin, 1975.

Apart from macro technical data on economic output, educational and health facilities, and physical infrastructure, there is little analysis of socio-economic data during the colonial period and the two 'Hutu' republics. Again, this changed to some extent after the genocide, when for instance land and agricultural policies, as well as poverty, health and education, were more closely studied. Like with regard to local dynamics, this however does not allow for the drawing of lines along the *longue durée* pursued in this book.

A last preliminary remark concerns the organisation of this book. While its broad construction is chronological and proceeds from one period to the next, within chapters it is predominantly thematic. Chapter 7, which deals with the post-genocide period, is exclusively thematic. Dealing with the present, it takes the form of a contemporary chronicle. A thematic feature along the entire book is the attention for continuities and breaks in this 150-year history. Continuities can be found in authoritarianism and the concentration of power, intra-regime conflict, the salience of ethnicity, the nature of the state, and the role of ideology and historical narrative. A continuity that bridges the precolonial period and the post-genocide era is the strong elite belief in exceptionalism, invincibility, political power, military might and excellence. Breaks are apparent in the role of the military, both as an organisation and a producer and disseminator of ethical values and norms, and the role and use of ethnicity as a political tool.

I.2　A Brief Look at Pre-mid Nineteenth-Century History

As this book starts in the middle of the nineteenth century, a brief outline of what preceded is necessary. Much of Rwanda's history is mythical, from the first king (*mwami*) Kigwa, who descended from heaven and started organising the realm. Gihanga, one of Kigwa's successors known as the creator, is said to have had three sons, Gahutu, Gatutsi and Gatwa. He entrusted each of them with a jar of milk for safekeeping. Gatwa drank the milk, Gahutu spilled it during his sleep, Gatutsi kept it intact. The next morning, Gihanga rewarded Gatutsi for his performance by making him the ruler over his brothers.[31] Thus the three ethnic groups, Tutsi, Hutu and Twa, were born.[32] In the Rwandan mythico-history, the

---

[31] A similar myth of origin exists in Ankole; see M. Doornbos, *Not All the King's Men: Inequality as a Political Instrument in Ankole, Uganda*, The Hague, Mouton Publishers, 1978, p. 20.

[32] A brief explanation of the notion of 'ethnic group' is in order here. The usual anthropological definition refers to groupings of people sharing attributes that distinguish them from other groups. Attributes commonly proposed include common traditions,

genealogy of kings proposed by those who trace the dynasty back to the eleventh century is 'purely imaginary', a 'fairy tale'.[33]

The reality is that, despite many publications during the colonial period, little is known about Rwanda's precolonial history. D'Hertefelt noted that most of the ethno-historical literature 'contains interpretations of sources, their reinterpretation, or reinterpretations of reinterpretations'.[34] For his part, Rennie warned against the concordant views of influential authors like Pagès, Kagame or de Lacger: the unity of their interpretation can be explained by the fact that their works were all 'based on court traditions and the fact that there was a certain "intellectual consensus" among missionary historians'.[35] The warning of Claudine Vidal against oral historiography, which is in reality an ideological literature of the royal court, is worth reminding: 'Rather than the history of a state born out of successively resolved contradictions, this knowledge appears as the expression of a pre-established model which events only incarnate and confirm. Everything happens as if (...) the only sense the guardians of oral traditions find in history is its correspondence with the model that is theirs.'[36] As will be made clear later, this idealised official historiography explains the references to an eternal 'Rwanda' as if it were one homogeneous political and social format throughout the area associated with the contemporary state. However, this vision hides the diversity and contingency that marked political institutions and social relationships before 1900, and even well into the colonial period. The court ideology, as reflected in the writings until the 1960s and presenting an image of a 'unitary Rwanda', indeed deviated from the reality of most of the area now known as Rwanda.

This summary therefore starts with an era on which some reliable information is available. After a dynastic break, the Nyiginya kingdom

---

ancestry, language, history, society, nation, religion, custom and area of residence. Under that definition, Hutu, Tutsi and Twa do not qualify as ethnic groups as they share most of these characteristics. As will be seen later, this was a problem faced by international justice when legally qualifying the extermination of the Tutsi in 1994 as genocide. Though the terms 'ethnicity' and 'ethnic group' are used in this book, they could be translated more broadly as 'identity groups'.

[33] Vansina, *Antecedents to Modern Rwanda*, pp. 44, 217. For works tracing the dynasty back to the eleventh century, see Kagame, *Un abrégé de l'ethno-histoire*; B. Muzungu, *Histoire du Rwanda pré-colonial*, Paris, L'Harmattan, 2003; F. Rusagara, *Resilience of a Nation: A History of the Military in Rwanda*, Kigali, Fountain Publishers Rwanda, 2009.

[34] M. d'Hertefelt, *Les clans du Rwanda ancien*, Tervuren, Musée royal de l'Afrique centrale, 1971, p. 22.

[35] J. K. Rennie, 'The Precolonial Kingdom of Rwanda: A Reinterpretation', *Transafrican Journal of History*, Vol. 2, No. 2, 1972, p. 12.

[36] C. Vidal, 'Anthropologie et histoire; le cas du Ruanda', *Cahiers internationaux de sociologie*, Vol. 43, 1967, pp. 147–148.

emerged in the seventeenth century with the reign of *mwami* Ruganzu Ndori, a conqueror probably coming from Karagwe in current-day Tanzania. Although the official historiography hid the dynastic interruption, Ruganzu Ndori was a usurper from abroad, who created a new dynasty and a new drum, *Kalinga*, to replace the old one, *Rwoga*, which was seized by *mwami* Ntsibura from Bushi (Bunyabungo), who occupied the country for eleven years, and was destroyed.[37] This was the beginning of a centuries-long evolution, but reliable and detailed information on Rwanda's history became available only from the mid eighteenth century.[38] However, enough is known about the previous period to allow Vansina to write that under *mwami* Ruganzu Ndori the army – an innovation that he created – along with the *ubuhake* clientship system (discussed later in the chapter), became the foundation of power in the kingdom. While the Nyiginya kingdom was but one of the many that emerged in the Great Lakes region during the seventeenth century, in the course of the eighteenth century it became very different from its neighbours when non-territorial, multiple and permanent armies were put in place under the authority of a single military commander.[39] The monarchy then took shape, linking military expansion with political centralisation. King Rujugira (reign ca. 1770–ca. 1786) structured the armies by installing them in permanent camps near the most threatened borders. Two thirds of these armies were created during his reign and that of Rwabugiri, roughly between 1770 and 1895.[40] This was the period of the 'great expansion'.[41]

The deepest effect of this new military organisation was 'the institutionalisation of a glorification of militarism and martial violence that finally permeated the whole of Nyiginya culture as the armies became the foundation of the administrative structure of the realm. (...) [U]ltimately, all the inhabitants of the realm were incorporated in the military organisation.'[42] The army constituted the administrative

---

[37] E. Mworoha, *Peuples et rois de l'Afrique des Lacs*, Dakar–Abidjan, Les Nouvelles Editions Africaines, 1977, p. 94; L. de Heusch, *Le Rwanda et la civilisation interlacustre*, Brussels, Université Libre de Bruxelles, Institut de Sociologie, 1966, pp. 118–120.
[38] Vansina, *Antecedents to Modern Rwanda*, p. 52; J.-P. Chrétien, *The Great Lakes of Africa: Two Thousand Years of History*, New York, Zone Books, 2003, p. 159.
[39] Vansina, *Antecedents to Modern Rwanda*, p. 196; de Heusch, *Le Rwanda*, p. 127.
[40] Chrétien, *The Great Lakes of Africa*, pp. 160–161.
[41] National Unity and Reconciliation Commission, *History of Rwanda*, pp. 81–98.
[42] Vansina, *Antecedents to Modern Rwanda*, pp. 61–62. However, most people in the territory now defined as 'Rwanda' were either outside the domain of court power or only intermittently subjected to military requisitions. Many regions resisted court intrusions until well into the colonial period (as shown later).

I.2 A Brief Look at Pre-mid Nineteenth-Century History 9

framework of royal court rule, and the concentration of power in the hands of the military commanders was an essential step in the consolidation of court power.[43] The RPF military historian Rusagara noted that 'it is the military that played the most central socio-political role in what became of Rwanda'.[44]

Vansina also finds that the recruitment and indoctrination of *intore* (chosen young men serving as soldiers) from about ten years of age 'favoured [the] exaltation of violence, imposture, and the right of the strongest that became the universal theme of all literary and choreographic artistic forms'.[45] Although his book is replete with the 'fairy tales' denounced by Vansina, Sebasoni, an early RPF ideologue, states that *itorero*, where the *intore* were trained, was the 'crucible of chiefs and warriors', 'a military school of sorts'.[46] By the end of the eighteenth century, the part of Rwanda under the reach of central court power was characterised by 'utter militarisation': the military machine included some thirty armies with about 12,000 combatants.[47] While state making has been violent in many places across the world,[48] the role played by the armies in Rwanda had been unique among the kingdoms in the region.

Under these cultural, logistical and institutional conditions it is not surprising that the history of the kingdom is coterminous with war and violence, at least for those areas targeted by the Nyiginya court or administered by its delegates. The current official historical narrative is based on the notion of continuous war and conquest, *ku-aanda* ('from which Rwanda derives its name'[49]), literally 'expansion or spreading out from the centre': 'the principle of *ku-aanda*, which involved annexation and subsequent integration of neighbouring territories, informed the continued expansion and growth of pre-colonial Rwanda'.[50] All the kings mentioned by Rusagara are warrior kings, and the 'Map of *Ku-aanda*' includes large parts of present-day Uganda and the Democratic Republic

---

[43] Ibid., p. 78.
[44] Rusagara, *Resilience of a Nation*, back cover. I must make it clear that I do not quote Rusagara on a par with scientific historians but because he articulates the historical narrative of the current regime.
[45] Vansina, *Antecedents to Modern Rwanda*, p. 62. Vansina adds in a footnote: 'Today this literary glorification of violence persists, and it is a particularly nefarious legacy of the ancestral heritage' (p. 246).
[46] S. Sebasoni, *Les origines du Rwanda*, Paris, L'Harmattan, 2000, pp. 59–60.
[47] Vansina, *Antecedents to Modern Rwanda*, p. 123.
[48] C. Tilly, 'War Making and State Making as Organized Crime', in P. B. Evans, D. Rueschemeyer, T. Skocpol (Eds.), *Bringing the State Back In*, New York, Cambridge University Press, 1985, pp. 169–191.
[49] Rusagara, *Resilience of a Nation*, p. xvi.
[50] Ibid., p. 1.

of Congo (DRC).⁵¹ Kagame quotes the saying 'Rwanda attacks, it cannot be attacked' (*Urwanda ruratera, ntiruterwa*) attributed to King Rujugira.⁵² More recent Rwandan scholarship insists on the need for the kingdom to conquer and expand in order to politically and socially increase the number of subjects, who became taxpayers, economic producers and army members. Power was associated with reigning over a large number of people.⁵³

Even the largely mythical narrative proposed by Kagame is a long litany of wars against neighbours, conquests, punitive expeditions against unruly regions, reprisal attacks, insurrections and their repression, and civil wars. Violence was not only directed towards external enemies and internal opposition, it was also a frequent occurrence within the court and among ruling circles. Kagame's list of royal succession struggles, massacres of entire princely families and those of chiefs whose loyalty was in doubt, rumour mongering and revenge, poisoning and cruel torture, executions, score settling and so on is near endless.⁵⁴ Struggles at the top of the state were by no means exceptional, as most successions in Rwanda's history have been violent and sometimes led to outright civil war. An uncontested accession to the drum was such a rare event that when it occurred in 1786, with Ndabarasa succeeding his father Rujugira in an orderly fashion, the latter's sons were called *Abatangana*, 'those who agree with each other'.⁵⁵ However, after Ndabarasa's death in 1796, civil war again broke out when his sons violently clashed over the succession.⁵⁶ Vansina notes that from the reign of Rujugira in the late eighteenth century onwards 'the country was almost continually in a state of war'.⁵⁷

Despite the internal and external violence, or perhaps due to it, the political organisation of the country had stabilised by the mid nineteenth century, considered here as the beginning of 'modern' Rwanda.

---

⁵¹ Ibid., p. 208. In November 1996, at the beginning of the first Congo war, Rwandan president Bizimungu showed a map to the media. On it, 'Greater Rwanda' included large parts of eastern DRC. However, at the end of the nineteenth century, Rwanda was smaller rather than larger than it is today (see e.g. G. Mathys, 'Bringing History Back In: Past, Present, and Conflict in Rwanda and the Eastern Democratic Republic of Congo', *Journal of African History*, Vol. 58, No. 3, 2017, pp. 470–475).

⁵² Kagame, *Un abrégé de l'ethno-histoire*, p. 137. A former holder of high office told me that this saying is regularly recited in conversations between President Kagame and top military officers.

⁵³ C. Kabwete Mulinda, R. Nkaka, 'The Political Vision of the Rwandan Kingdom', *Rwanda Journal of Arts and Humanities*, Vol. 2, No. 2, 2017, p. 64.

⁵⁴ Kagame, *Un abrégé de l'ethno-histoire*.

⁵⁵ Vansina, *Antecedents to Modern Rwanda*, p. 107.

⁵⁶ Ibid., p. 109.

⁵⁷ Ibid., p. 75.

I.2 A Brief Look at Pre-mid Nineteenth-Century History

The military organisation had given rise to an administrative structure that went beyond army matters. In the areas under central court control, officials were appointed in each district in a three-layered structure. Those who were originally army commanders, called *abatware b'ingabo*, received powers of taxation (*ikoro*). The *abanyabutaka* were entrusted with the management of agricultural land and the people living on it. The *abanyamukenke* were put in charge of pastureland and the cattle holders. This complex structure allowed the king to maintain control by playing one delegate against another, but it also to some extent protected the population against abuse as it could seek the support of one official against another.

At the personal level, this structure of authority was supported by *ubuhake*, a clientship system whose description was strongly influenced by the court's ideology promoted by Jacques-Jean Maquet and Kagame (see Chapter 1). According to this portrayal, *ubuhake* entailed a person seeking protection and wishing to enjoy the prestige of possessing cattle to offer his allegiance to a person of higher status owning cattle. If the latter accepted the former as his client (*umugaragu*), he gave him one or more cows in usufruct and thus became his patron (*shebuja*). The client performed certain services for the patron, who in turn protected the client and assisted him, mainly in case of political or judicial problems. The *ubuhake* relationship did not end with the death of the parties but was inherited by the male descendants of the *shebuja* and the *umugaragu*. The contract could be terminated by either party, in which case the cattle returned to the patron and the client was liberated from his obligations towards the patron. Although *ubuhake* was strictly speaking a private relationship, it was also a political asset to protect the position of the ruling class. By allotting but a precarious usufruct to the *abagaragu*, who could be Hutu or Tutsi, the *shebuja*, who all were Tutsi, maintained the ultimate control over cattle, the symbol of political, social and economic power. However, it must be noted that, contrary to a long-held view, *ubuhake* was by no means universal. It involved a minority of the population and was primarily contracted among Tutsi.[58] There were significant regional differences in clientship forms, and patterns changed over time.[59] *Ubuhake* was not 'invented' at a particular moment but grew out of other forms of clientship; its expansion represented the growing power of court actors over their clients.[60]

---

[58] J.-F. Saucier, 'The Patron–Client Relationship in Traditional and Contemporary Southern Rwanda', New York, Columbia University, PhD thesis, 1974.
[59] Newbury, *The Cohesion of Oppression*, pp. 134–140.
[60] Newbury, Newbury, 'Bringing the Peasants Back In', pp. 860–861.

Presented from the central court's vision, at the central level the *mwami* was the eminent owner of the land, the cattle, the harvests and even his subjects. He was considered to be of heavenly origin, not a human being (*'umwami si umuntu'*). The royal drum *Karinga* was the symbol of royalty and was saluted like the king himself. Being at the apex of the administrative, military and clientship structures, the king's powers were in theory unlimited. He however had to consider the interests of powerful lineages and take the advice of influential members of his court. Among them were the *abiru*, the guardians of the royal ritual codified in the *ubwiru*. They played a major role, in particular at the occasion of royal successions. The king chose his successor among his sons and entrusted three *abiru*, called the '*abiru* of the great secret', with his name. This process led to many disputes, violence and even civil wars, as both other sons and the king's wives' lineages often contested this choice and jostled for power. These conflicts were in part due to the prominent role played by the queen mother, who was the king's mother or, if she had died, another women in the royal family designated in accordance with the *ubwiru*. Their influence was considerable, particularly if the king was not yet of age when acceding to the drum, and many were known to be unscrupulous and cruel intrigantes. As an example will show in Chapter 1 the competition between lineages over this position of power was sometimes violent. This description is again, as mentioned earlier, the one proposed by the ideology of the royal court. However, this model was limited in scope for most Rwandans during most of Rwanda's history, and local experiences differed from court ideological norms imposed on them. As will be seen later, the reactions of the people outside royal court culture and the resistance to their inclusion to court power, particularly in peripheral areas, belies such ideology of social uniformity across the entire realm.

The last precolonial *mwami* was to put the final touch to the kingdom as 'discovered' by the European colonisers. It is to the era of king Rwabugiri that I now turn.

1 From Old to New Kings

Kigeri IV Rwabugiri was to be the last *mwami* of independent Rwanda. Before him, three periods, each associated with long reigns,[1] had resulted in major institutional developments: the establishment of a coherent kingdom, the refinement of court institutions (including the army formations and the ritual ideology) and the extension of court power over the population. Each of these periods corresponded with a crisis at the court, as these reigns appear to have been those of usurper kings who came to power by military force.[2] Rwabugiri's accession too was not uncontested and followed intense factional infighting in the court, which left a hecatomb of opponents.[3]

Born around 1855, Rwabugiri became king in 1867,[4] with the queen mother, Murorunkwere, acting as regent until he came of age. This was the third time in a row a queen mother had assumed the function of regent, showing the importance of her position. When he reached the age of around twenty in 1875, Rwabugiri fully acceded to the drum.[5] During his twenty-year reign, Rwanda achieved its maximum territorial extension and its most complete political and administrative organisation. However, the court's control of the realm was uneven. More importantly, Rwabugiri's reign was marked by extreme violence, inside the court and among the aristocracy, as well as across the country.

1.1   Political Organisation

While, like his predecessors, Rwabugiri attempted to centralise power and exercise physical and administrative control over the entire

---

[1] Ruganzu II Ndori (mid seventeenth century), Cyilima II Rujugira (mid eighteenth century) and Yuhi IV Gahindiro (early nineteenth century).
[2] D. Newbury, 'Editor's Introduction', in Des Forges, *Defeat Is the Only Bad News*, p. xxxv.
[3] Vansina, *Antecedents to Modern Rwanda*, p. 166.
[4] Both years are uncertain, as are most dates before the 1890s.
[5] Kagame, *Un abrégé de l'histoire*, p. 21; Vansina, *Antecedents to Modern Rwanda*, pp. 209–211. Actually, Rwabugiri's accession was a very complicated affair (for details see Newbury, *The Land beyond the Mists*, pp. 331–332).

territory considered part of the kingdom, we have seen that the presentation of Rwanda as a centralised, static, uniform, orderly, functional and harmonious polity in the official court history is an ideological fantasy. Under the influence of the work of authors such as Jacques-Jean Maquet,[6] this idealised interpretation remained dominant until the 1960s, but – like Alexis Kagame – Maquet based his research on sources that represented the norms of central Rwanda, more particularly those of the royal court.[7]

The reality was not so tidy. The Newburys note that violent changes – coups d'état and dynastic shifts – were masked by the ideology of unbroken continuity.[8] Likewise, Vansina finds that 'it is false to think that everyone was happy with their station in life and all lived in peace under the shepherd's staff of wise kings'.[9] Indeed Rwabugiri ruled by force. His was a time of significant consolidation of rule by the central court and of the arbitrary power of the king, but also of struggles between important court personalities, army leaders and aristocratic lineages. While war consolidated external power, it also intensified internal conflicts and created a great deal of resentment.[10] Although Mworoha observed that Rwabugiri accentuated the control of the Nyiginya dynasty over Rwanda,[11] in reality the centralised administration was not homogeneous and prevailed only in parts of the realm.[12] Therefore, despite his attempts to concentrate power and his 'despotic tendencies',[13] Rwabugiri was not an omnipotent autocrat, and his

---

[6] After his *Le système des relations sociales dans le Ruanda ancien*, Tervuren, Musée royal de l'Afrique centrale, 1954, was translated in English (*The Premise of Inequality in Ruanda: A Study of Political Relations in a Central African Kingdom*, London, Oxford University Press, 1961) in the heydays of British structuralism–functionalism, it became the main reference on Rwanda in the anglophone research community. This centralised, court-based account can also be found in National Unity and Reconciliation Commission, *History of Rwanda*, pp. 98–106.

[7] For a critique of Maquet, see Newbury, *The Cohesion of Oppression*, pp. 3–6; S. Thomson, *Rwanda: From Genocide to Precarious Peace*, New Haven–London, Yale University Press, 2018, pp. 41–43. A critique of Kagame's rendering of history can be found in C. Vidal, 'Alexis Kagame entre mémoire et histoire', *History in Africa*, Vol. 15, 1988, pp. 493–504. The Newburys point out that Kagame was the single most influential actor in consolidating court historiography and in turning court history into 'Rwandan history' (Newbury, Newbury, 'Bringing the Peasants Back In', p. 854). This is due to the fact that Kagame's vision comes mainly from a handful of courtiers who were the ideologues of the official narrative (Vansina, *Antecedents to Modern Rwanda*, p. 4). Bachmann finds it 'impossible to disentangle his political agenda from his research as a historian' (*A History of Rwanda*, p. 14).

[8] Newbury, Newbury, 'Bringing the Peasants Back In', p. 849.

[9] Vansina, *Antecedents to Modern Rwanda*, p. 198.

[10] Newbury, *The Land beyond the Mists*, p. 332.

[11] Mworoha, *Peuples et rois*, p. 51.

[12] Vansina, *Antecedents to Modern Rwanda*, p. 188.

[13] Mworoha, *Peuples et rois*, p. 223.

1.1 Political Organisation

political and administrative innovations were seldom enduring.[14] Control of outlying regions was incomplete and often ephemeral. Socially and culturally, as well as administratively, these regions were different from the central kingdom. Therefore, rule by the court was effective in the heartland but shaded off elsewhere, especially in the west and the north.[15]

Louis notes that it was not until 1904 that the Germans learned that 'beneath the veneer of absolutism was political turmoil that could lead to civil war'.[16] Both the Hutu and Tutsi of the outlying regions resisted the extension of control by the court and resented the cultural and social arrogance, as well as the political dominance, of the rulers at the centre.[17] The central court indeed displayed a strong sense of superiority and mocked differences ('They don't do these things as well as we do'). Its elitist tendencies and deeply hierarchical nature characterised relations with the periphery.[18] We shall see that this superiority complex became apparent again after 1994.[19] Rule across the country was therefore uneven and lacked uniformity, and many regions in the east, south-east, north, west and south-west were not under permanent court control.[20] As will be seen later, stable and more or less uniform rule was achieved only with German support afforded by Resident Richard Kandt, who saw 'anarchy' in areas not governed by representatives of the court and therefore concluded that he had no alternative but to support the rule of the king and his notables. For instance, the Germans launched four expeditions against Bushiru alone between 1909 and 1914.[21]

Colonial overrule had a paradoxical outcome. While external sovereignty was lost, internal administrative power increased. During the first

---

[14] Newbury, *The Land beyond the Mists*, p. 334.
[15] De Lame noted that references to regional variations can be found in the literature as early as in 1909 (de Lame, *A Hill among a Thousand*, p. 48). The resistance of kingdoms in the north and north-west to the Nyiginya expansion is described in F. Nahimana, *Le Rwanda: Émergence d'un État*, Paris, L'Harmattan, 1993, pp. 230–246.
[16] Louis, *Ruanda-Urundi*, p. 126.
[17] Des Forges, *Defeat Is the Only Bad News*, pp. 12–13. Interestingly, a Burundian historian referred to 'a certain Rwandan "imperialism"' (Mworoha, *Peuples et rois*, p. 92).
[18] David Newbury illustrates this well in the court's relations with Bunyabungo, a loose description of the 'barbarians to the west'. Although the term often referred to Bushi because it was the largest and best-known polity across Lake Kivu, it also applied to the Havu, Hunde, Tembo and Nyanga peoples (Newbury, *The Land beyond the Mists*, pp. 204–228).
[19] An erstwhile funder of the RPF wrote that 'before European penetration, the Banyarwanda were convinced that their country was the centre of the world, and that it was the biggest, most powerful and most civilised kingdom on earth'. He found among his ancestors 'a certain conquering spirit' (V. Kajeguhakwa, *Rwanda: De la terre de paix à la terre de sang, et après?*, Paris, Editions Remi Perrin, 2001, p. 20).
[20] Newbury, 'Editor's Introduction', pp. xxviii–xxxi.
[21] Des Forges, *Defeat Is the Only Bad News*, pp. 106–107. As will be seen later, Bushiru is one of the regions that maintained strong local loyalty until well after independence.

twenty years of European rule the Rwandan kingdom roughly doubled the area under its control. Administrative capacities were consolidated, and the territorial domain of centralised power was expanded, while outlying areas lost their autonomy.[22]

1.2 Military Campaigns

Wars were more frequent under Rwabugiri's personal rule than ever before. He raised eight new armies and waged thirteen military campaigns in under twenty years, meaning the country was at war two years out of every three, not even including the border raids.[23] His operations were of three main types: those resulting in the full incorporation of neighbouring regions, thus aiming at the geographical expansion of the kingdom; those leading to a simple military occupation, often of brief duration; and those consisting of raids.[24] Kagame lists campaigns against Ndorwa (three times), Bushi (three times), Ijwi (twice), Butembo, Gikore, Bushubi and Nkore.[25] David Newbury's survey of Rwabugiri's campaigns mentions Mpororo, Ijwi (twice), Burundi (twice), Ndorwa, Nkore (twice) and Bushi (three times). Some went as far away as Bumpaka, to the east of Lake Edward, Butembo, north-west of Lake Kivu, and Gikore, near present-day Kabale in Uganda.[26]

While Rwabugiri's reign was one long military campaign directed against both neighbouring societies and regions within Rwanda, his operations were often unsuccessful and his victories ephemeral. David Newbury notes that many expeditions led to the acquisition of status and booty, while only some resulted in the conquest of other countries. Overall, 'there were (...) few permanent political annexations'.[27] In Bushi, which he attacked on several occasions, Rwabugiri suffered defeat after defeat: 'his "victories" were few and ephemeral, and they were costly'.[28] Most areas of his attacks did not survive as Rwandan conquest after his death, which occurred as he was leading an expedition against Bushi, west of Lake Kivu.[29] Mworoha also found that his 'foreign enterprises ha[d] not always been successful'.[30]

---

[22] Newbury, *The Land beyond the Mists*, p. 338.
[23] Vansina, *Antecedents to Modern Rwanda*, p. 183.
[24] Newbury, *The Land beyond the Mists*, pp. 332–333.
[25] Kagame, *Un abrégé de l'ethno-histoire*, pp. 21–103.
[26] Newbury, *The Land beyond the Mists*, pp. 133–141.
[27] Ibid., p. 141.
[28] Ibid., p. 138.
[29] Ibid., pp. 332–334. Vansina notes that 'the conquest of new territories ended in failure' (Vansina, *Antecedents to Modern Rwanda*, p. 194).
[30] Mworoha, *Peuples et rois*, p. 52.

Despite his being the 'quintessential military monarch' who embarked on military expeditions virtually every year of his reign, in the end the lasting external effects of Rwabugiri's campaigns were limited.[31] Many areas conquered during his reign were only briefly incorporated into Rwanda and they regained their autonomy after his death.[32] His territorial strategies did not amount to stable annexations. Control was imperfect and indistinct at best, and it was continuously contested.[33] Even inside the kingdom, several enclaves escaped the central power's control, a situation that did not change until German colonisation.[34] Vansina therefore concludes that 'Rwanda as a fully centralised state is a colonial creation'.[35] In Chrétien's words, 'eternal Rwanda' does not exist.[36] Mathys concludes that the perspective promoted by historians such as Kagame that Rwanda existed as a nation-state before colonisation is 'a chimera rather than a reflection of historical realities'. As boundaries between political and cultural zones rarely coincided, she differentiates between being Rwandan culturally – what Ntezimana called *ikinyarwanda* – and being Rwandan politically. Belonging was not exclusive but characterised by liminality – the capacity to inhabit different spheres.[37] In other words, 'what "Rwanda" meant was never static'.[38]

1.3 Terror inside the Court and across Society

Rwabugiri came to power as a result of an internal coup, against a background of intrigue, which had always been pervasive at the court. David Newbury notes that in all but one of the seven successions from Rujugira to Musinga, conflict over the position of queen mother was the critical issue: in naming her, one indirectly named the king and brought the queen mother's kin to the centre of power.[39] This kind of in-court fighting marked Rwabugiri's reign, 'punctuated by successive waves of persecution and executions from which no one was immune'.[40] Internal politics, rather than the external wars, were the driving force shaping the kingdom.

---

[31] Newbury, *The Land beyond the Mists*, pp. 129–141.
[32] Des Forges, *Defeat Is the Only Bad News*, p. 11.
[33] G. Mathys, *Conflicts and Connections: Making the Histories of the Lake Kivu Region*, Cambridge, Cambridge University Press, in press.
[34] Chrétien, *The Great Lakes of Africa*, p. 160.
[35] Vansina, *Antecedents to Modern Rwanda*, p. 195.
[36] Chrétien, *The Great Lakes of Africa*, p. 159.
[37] Mathys, *Conflicts and Connections*.
[38] Mathys, 'Lines through the Lake: Why the Congo-Rwanda Border Can't Be Redrawn', *African Arguments*, 2 May 2023.
[39] Newbury, *The Land beyond the Mists*, p. 331.
[40] Vansina, *Antecedents to Modern Rwanda*, p. 180.

The dynamics at work were characterised by a succession of major upsets presented as follows by Vansina. Soon after Rwabugiri's contested accession to the throne, the new queen mother attacked a competing faction at the court. Its leader was executed, and all the members of his family and his adherents were also tracked down and killed. For the next few years, the queen mother's regime was free of any serious opposition, but after he came of age around 1875, Rwabugiri had her killed. This heralded a five-year period of rumours, plots and revenge, culminating in Rwabugiri ordering the execution of his own father.[41] In 1889 Rwabugiri took the fateful decision to designate Rutarindwa as his successor and to install him as co-ruler. The dramatic consequences of this move will be seen later.

In the meantime, terror continued to rule. Accusations and denunciations were the main tools used by courtiers to eliminate their adversaries. As Rwabugiri was easily convinced of treason, this was often enough for him to immediately condemn the accused and his family to death. His whole reign was characterised by a series of cascading disgraces, often accompanied by executions. These executions triggered consequences that could last for a generation, as they led to vengeance and counter-vengeance, thus giving a cumulative effect to waves of executions. These massacres, even more than the losses during combat, decimated the ranks of the nobility.[42] Vansina's conclusion on Rwabugiri is severe: 'He was first and foremost a warrior, inclined to resolving all difficulties by applying brute force.'[43] Mworoha agreed, and called him a 'fundamentally belligerent *mwami*'.[44]

Although he was the semi-official court historian and tended to paint a rosy picture of precolonial Rwanda, Kagame called Rwabugiri's reign 'bloody': 'It was impossible to find a family in the country of which he had not killed at least one member.'[45] Like Vansina, he details a long list of plots, intrigue, assassinations, executions and exterminations of entire families.[46] In a similar vein, David Newbury notes that, apart from confrontations with the court ritualists, Rwabugiri, like many of

---

[41] It is necessary to specify that the man Rwabugiri had killed was his biological father. First known as Sebizoni (Vansina) or Sezisoni (Kagame), Rwabugiri was an adopted son of his royal predecessor Mutara II Rwogera. Through a complex series of manoeuvres, this allowed to make him king (for more details on this complex story, see Kagame, *Un abrégé de l'ethno-histoire*, pp. 212–214; Newbury, Newbury, 'Bringing the Peasants Back In', pp. 855–856).
[42] Vansina, *Antecedents to Modern Rwanda*, pp. 164–195.
[43] Ibid., p. 195.
[44] Mworoha, *Peuples et rois*, p. 52.
[45] Kagame, *Un abrégé de l'histoire*, p. 108.
[46] Ibid., pp. 26–103.

his predecessors, especially those of doubtful legitimacy, was in constant conflict with the aristocratic elite from the most powerful lineages of the land, indicating his attempt to free the kingship from all political constraint. He dismissed or executed many army leaders and made delegated authority greater than inherited authority, thus undercutting the autonomous power base of influential families.[47] David Newbury concludes that at the end of Rwabugiri's reign the kingdom was marked by an accumulation of frustration among many factions at the court, where a culture of intense calculation reigned, and by a state under duress, as many neighbouring societies, occupied or attacked by the king's armies, sought to reclaim their autonomy.[48]

The instability and conflict proneness of the monarchical regime showed in a dramatic fashion immediately after Rwabugiri's death, at the occasion of his succession. According to Kagame, Rutarindwa's accession to the drum was contrary to the *ubwiru* on several counts: he was but an adopted son of Rwabugiri; a king could not designate his successor as co-ruler and Rwabugiri could not designate his wife Kanjogera as his successor's adopted queen mother. In addition to other infringements, Kanjogera also had a biological son with Rwabugiri, Musinga, who could succeed him. By pushing through his choice of co-ruler and successor, Rwabugiri had opened the door to a war of succession, which, as we have seen, is a frequent feature in Rwandan history.[49] Considered by powerful quarters as a usurper, if only because his biological father was not a king, Rutarindwa's legitimacy was immediately challenged, notably by the designated queen mother Kanjogera, supported by her powerful half-brothers Kabare and Ruhinankiko,[50] who wanted to reign with her own son.[51]

A long and bloody fight ensued between two camps, one supporting Rutarindwa, the other Musinga. The conflict was replete with treason, defections and killings in aristocratic circles,[52] and ended with the massacre of the supporters of Rutarindwa, who was himself killed in 1896 in what is known as the coup d'état of Rucunshu. This was just the start of new conflicts. In the eyes of many, Musinga rather than Rutarindwa was the usurper, and legitimist rebellions were to last for fifteen years, mainly in the north, where Musinga was particularly contested. Infighting inside

---

[47] Newbury, *The Land beyond the Mists*, pp. 333–334.
[48] Newbury, 'Editor's Introduction', p. xxxvi.
[49] Kagame, *Un abrégé de l'histoire*, pp. 75–80.
[50] An interesting detail: President Paul Kagame's great grandfather was the brother of Kanjogera and of both Kabare and Ruhinankiko.
[51] Kagame, *Un abrégé de l'histoire*, p. 107.
[52] Des Forges, *Defeat Is the Only Bad News*, pp. 22–23.

court circles likewise continued, a civil war started, and massacres and revolts continued until 1912. Were it not for the intervention of the Germans in support of Musinga (see later in the chapter), the civil war would have been total and long.[53]

During Rwabugiri's reign, the role of violence grew, not just within the court and among aristocrats but also in society as a whole. Especially in the centre of the kingdom, spoliation was the rule on the hills. Chiefs abused their power and extorted arbitrary tributes and *corvée* labour from their subjects. The king's ceaseless travels throughout the realm caused great suffering among ordinary people because of the constant looting that accompanied these.[54] The bulk of the population suffered most from the politics of violence, in the first place through the devastation caused by the armies even in friendly territory. They pillaged harvests and cattle, a disaster that occurred two years out of every three in the heart of the country. Among many examples, Des Forges mentions a campaign in the north-west where the king's troops, under the guise of re-establishing royal control, pillaged and burned the possessions of all in their path, whether or not they had actually rebelled against the court. The troops, called *Inkemba*, 'The Predators', by the people of Bugoyi so devastated the region that it suffered a grave famine soon after.[55]

Under these circumstances it is not surprising that insurrections had to be continually quelled. When people rose up and attacked the royal retinue, the army intervened in strength and repressed the revolt. The violence inspired millenarian expectations among oppressed farmers, who, particularly in the north and the east, turned to the Nyabingi cult in the hope of liberation from all these ills thanks to the coming of a new king, a legitimate and beneficent ruler who would do away with all calamities.[56] Some of the insurrections against the Nyiginya kingdom even developed distinct ethnic overtones.

1.4 Ethnicity

Although ethnicity and its instrumentalisation as a political resource have played an important role in Rwanda's politics, it is necessary to first stress that identities have been and are plural. Following Amselle and M'Bokolo, Florent Piton refers to 'chameleon identities' made of several belongings: clan, lineage, region, religion, education, gender

---

[53] Kagame, *Un abrégé de l'histoire*, pp. 106–169; Des Forges, *Defeat Is the Only Bad News*, pp. 14–23.
[54] Vansina, *Antecedents to Modern Rwanda*, p. 189.
[55] Des Forges, *Defeat Is the Only Bad News*, p. 20.
[56] Vansina, *Antecedents to Modern Rwanda*, pp. 180–194.

1.4 Ethnicity

and so on.[57] Despite ethnicity therefore not being the sole or even the most important structuring factor of political developments, its emergence must be briefly addressed here.

It is sometimes claimed, especially by Tutsi elites before 1959 and after 1994, that political ethnicity emerged in colonial times, but this is only partly true. There are many indications that it existed earlier and became particularly salient under Rwabugiri's rule. Like others, Vansina shows that the history of the terms Hutu and Tutsi is complex, that their meaning changed over time, and that this distinction spread gradually across the country. Only in the mid-nineteenth century did the introduction of chiefs of cattle and chiefs of land (as mentioned earlier) institutionalise a division between Tutsi herders and Hutu farmers. This division was deeply aggravated by the introduction, around 1870, of a new system of exploitative demands called *uburetwa*, which was imposed only on the Hutu.[58] The obligations to the chiefs included the surrendering of a significant portion of the family's crops and the delivery of services for which two out of every five days of the Rwandan week had to be set aside. So two hierarchised categories emerged, and the awareness of the division between Tutsi herders and Hutu farmers spread all over the country.[59] Vansina therefore sees 'the scission of society into the Tutsi and Hutu social categories as a case of disaggregation between a ruling class and its subjects, at the level of the whole society'.[60] As will be seen later, the consciousness of a great divide between the Hutu and Tutsi expressed itself in rebellions and insurrections at the end of the nineteenth century.

Other historians of precolonial Rwanda arrive at similar findings. Jean-Pierre Chrétien notes that, by the mid nineteenth century, a clear discrimination emerged between the Hutu and Tutsi, which became part of everyday rural life and not just in court functions. Backed by government practices, the Hutu–Tutsi cleavage penetrated social life decisively, the connotation of ethnic membership became hierarchical and the term Tutsi was increasingly perceived as an identity closely related to power. Although wealth and poverty did not correlate with the Tutsi–Hutu divide, government interventions increased privileges

---

[57] F. Piton, 'Dans les plis de l'ethnie: Pouvoirs et société au nord du Rwanda (1930–1961)', doctoral thesis, University of Paris, 2020, pp. 53–65.
[58] Remarkably, the current 'official history' confirms that 'King Rwabugiri imposed *uburetwa* on the Abahutu in order to punish them for their responsibility in his defeat in Nkore' (National Unity and Reconciliation Commission, *History of Rwanda*, p. 121).
[59] Vansina, *Antecedents to Modern Rwanda*, pp. 134–139.
[60] Ibid., pp. 191–192.

benefiting the Tutsi.[61] David Newbury observes that 'virtually all positions of political authority within the Rwandan state were held by Tutsi' and that 'as the state structures expanded and rigidified, Hutu were increasingly excluded from positions of effective power'.[62]

Mathys notes that it probably was the integration into the political structures of the Nyiginya kingdom which made the Hutu and Tutsi labels politically and socially meaningful for the first time.[63] This impact of the extension of the central state is noted in Cathy Newbury's research on the south-western region of Kinyaga, where she notes that, before the introduction of central Rwandan rule during the second half of the nineteenth century, identification as 'Hutu' appears to have had little political importance.[64] However, with the arrival of Rwabugiri and his chiefs, classification into the categories of Hutu or Tutsi tended to become rigidified, and as a result of the introduction to Kinyaga of central Rwandan administrative structures, current ethnic identifications became salient: 'During the period of Tutsi rule, later overlaid by European rule, the advantages of being Tutsi and the disadvantages of being Hutu increased enormously. In this context there occurred a gradual enlargement of "ethnic" awareness among Hutu through realization of common oppression.'[65] The current 'official history' concurs: 'The emergence of the ethnic divide in Kinyaga dates as far back as the second half of the nineteenth century (...). It was the Rwandan royal court and the colonial machine that imposed the predominance of Tutsi chiefs.'[66]

This does not mean that Hutu and Tutsi were monolithic categories. The Newburys note that '[t]he political classes – those who wielded power – accounted for less than ten per cent of the Tutsi'.[67] While finding that the connotation of ethnic membership had become hierarchical, Chrétien similarly observes that 'simple Tutsi were almost invisible'.[68] According to Linden, 'there were perhaps about 50,000 adult male Tutsi

---

[61] Chrétien, *The Great Lakes of Africa*, pp. 187–190.
[62] Newbury, *The Land beyond the Mists*, p. 209.
[63] Mathys, *Conflicts and Connections*.
[64] Newbury, *The Cohesion of Oppression*, p. 10.
[65] Ibid., p. 11.
[66] National Unity and Reconciliation Commission, *History of Rwanda*, pp. 240–241. This observation and the one on the imposition of *uburetwa* on the Hutu only (mentioned earlier) contradict the RPF's assertion that ethnicity was 'created' during the colonial period.
[67] Newbury, Newbury, 'Bringing the Peasants Back In', p. 839, with reference to H. Codère, *The Biography of an African Society: Rwanda, 1900–1960*, Tervuren, Royal Museum for Central Africa, 1973, p. 70.
[68] Chrétien, *The Great Lakes of Africa*, p. 190.

in Rwanda by the end of the nineteenth century for a total of about 2,500 chieftaincies and political offices in the state. Rwandan society was thus ruled by a minority of about five per cent of the Tutsi.'[69] Mworoha has argued that, rather than speaking of 'Tutsi domination', it was more appropriate to point at the control exercised by Tutsi belonging to certain clans, in particular the Banyiginya, Bega and Batsobe.[70]

While insurrections at the end of the nineteenth century were aimed at the royal court or chiefs generally, some expressed clear ethnic animosity. Tensions between Hutu and Tutsi appeared before 1890 and again in 1897–1899. An insurrection aimed against Tutsi in the south in 1892 or 1893 was soon followed by an armed anti-Tutsi movement that engulfed large parts of the north-west in 1897. This insurrection was particularly significant as it showed not only that the population was conscious of a great divide between the Tutsi and Hutu but also that the antagonism had broken into the open.[71] Vansina therefore rejects 'the views of those who attribute the distinction between Tutsi and Hutu as well as the engendering of their mutual hostility to each other to the first Europeans'.[72] I agree with this opinion in general but will show later that interventions by the colonial administration and the Catholic Church have further institutionalised and rigidified the ethnic categories and increased the conflict potential of this divide.

1.5 The Arrival of New Kings

In the second half of the nineteenth century, the regime's main concerns were the continuous expansion of the realm, keeping in check the court and the aristocracy, maintaining control over the entire kingdom by fighting insurrections small and large, and raising the revenue needed to entertain armies and a sizeable administrative/political bureaucracy both at the centre and locally. These needs were generally achieved by the rule of terror exercised in an overall unstable context.

While the kingdom was busy trying to expand its rule and keeping the land under control, it ignored the notion of territorially fixed borders.

---

[69] I. Linden, *Church and Revolution in Rwanda*, Manchester, Manchester University Press, 1977, p. 18.
[70] Mworoha, *Peuples et rois*, pp. 224–225.
[71] Vansina, *Antecedents to Modern Rwanda*, pp. 136–139. As late as in 1912, the Germans were worried about the possibility of 'a revolution of Hutu against Tutsi' and saw indications of 'antagonism' between both groups (Louis, *Ruanda-Urundi*, p. 155). It is also telling that some areas not under central court control, such as Bugoyi and Bushiru in the north-west and Busanza in the south, were regarded as 'country of the Hutu' (Des Forges, *Defeat Is the Only Bad News*, p. 102).
[72] Vansina, *Antecedents to Modern Rwanda*, p. 138.

More importantly, it did not realise that European powers, in Berlin first and other far away European capitals later, were drawing lines on maps. Kagame notes that the Rwandans did not realise that in Berlin the supposedly invincible kingdom had been placed in German East Africa and that some recently conquered territories fell outside Rwanda as defined by the Europeans.[73] Completely different ideas about political control were to clash and to lead to great misunderstandings. Conflicts of a kind different from the ones rulers in Central Africa were familiar with were to be resolved in the European interest as a result of superior firepower.

Europeans arrived late in Rwanda. When H. M. Stanley attempted to enter Gisaka in March 1876, he was threatened with bows and arrows. Faced with this hostile reception, he left Rwanda and returned to Karagwe.[74] It was only from 1892 that explorers, mainly German, started travelling in the country with the authorisation of the *mwami*. Oscar Baumann visited the south of the country in September 1892, followed in May–June 1894 by Count von Götzen, who crossed the kingdom from Gisaka to Bugoyi and visited Rwabugiri.[75] As the country was going through a very unstable period after the Rucunshu coup and just weeks after the contested enthronement of Musinga, the court was visited by Captain Ramsay, who was accompanied by two other German officers and 300 armed soldiers. The reception was suspicious and reserved, and Ramsay forced his way into the royal enclosure, where he thought he met the *mwami*. However, the man who played the role of the king was a notable in charge of the worship of the *Imandwa* spirits at the court. This impersonation was probably staged because the queen mother, Kanjogera, and her brothers assumed that a powerful ritualist was better equipped than young Musinga to face the visitor's mysterious force. Ramsay was fooled and later recounted that after he had explained his mission, 'Juhi [sic], with whom I entered into a blood pact, put himself under German protection and received a German flag and a letter of protection (*Schutzbrief*)'.[76] Des Forges notes that Ramsay left the court highly satisfied with what he called 'the main political success of the expedition', unaware of how the Rwandans must have scorned his naïve acceptance of a mock blood pact ritual with a false *mwami*.[77]

---

[73] Kagame, *Un abrégé de l'histoire*, p. 95.
[74] 'Which compelled us (…) to sheer off and leave them in their ferocious exclusiveness' (H. M. Stanley, *Through the Dark Continent*, London, Sampson Low, Marston, Searl & Rivington, 1878, Vol. I, p. 464).
[75] Vansina, *Antecedents to Modern Rwanda*, p. 176.
[76] Hauptmann Ramsay, 'Uha, Urundi und Ruanda', *Mitteilungen aus den Deutschen Schutzgebieten*, 1897, p. 180.
[77] Des Forges, *Defeat Is the Only Bad News*, p. 18. On Ramsay's visit, also see Kagame, *Un abrégé de l'histoire*, p. 130; Chrétien, *The Great Lakes of Africa*, p. 218.

The Rwandans accepted the German presence on the principle that 'my enemy's enemy is my friend'. Just a year earlier, still under Rutarindwa's short-lived reign, the Rwandan army indeed suffered heavy losses and was defeated by an expeditionary corps of the Congo Free State under the command of Belgian lieutenant Sandrart, who had established a fortified camp on Shangi hill on the shores of Lake Kivu. The battle was a disaster, showing the superiority of European power. As the Belgians had shown in Shangi that they were the enemy, it made sense to make friends with an equally powerful force, in this case the Germans. But their support also became crucial in the internal struggles that followed Musinga's controversial and violent accession to the throne. As will be seen later, without German support, Musinga might well not have survived the civil war that started after the Rucunshu coup d'état. We will also see that German power allowed the royal court to expand its territorial control roughly to the borders that currently define the country. However, while German overrule reinforced royal power internally, it also put an end to its external sovereignty, which was a major development unknown to the court at that time.[78] Indeed, when Ramsay visited the court, Rwanda was in a state of nascent civil war, and young Musinga, or rather the queen mother and her brothers, accepted German protection not realising what the flag and the *Schutzbrief* meant.[79]

1.6 Other Kings: The Missions

The missionaries arrived at around the same time as the Germans. After the creation in 1900 of the first Catholic mission in Save, the White Fathers (officially called the Société des Missionnaires d'Afrique) set up four others by 1904. Just ten years later, missionary work was the most thriving European activity in the country, with nine Catholic and five Protestant missions. The eighty missionaries were a substantial part of the European population of Ruanda-Urundi.[80] While the founder of the White Fathers Cardinal Lavigerie believed that Christianity would be widely accepted in a country only when it was adopted by the rulers, the new faith was met with suspicion at the court. It decreed that religious teaching was to be only for the Hutu and Twa. As they were the men

---

[78] Chrétien notes that the fixing of borders following agreements between European powers blocked nineteenth-century historical dynamics and meant that Rwanda could no longer expand (Chrétien, *The Great Lakes of Africa*, p. 220).
[79] Ibid., p. 248.
[80] Louis, *Ruanda-Urundi*, p. 184.

of the *mwami* and of him alone, the Tutsi were not to be approached.[81] During the years following their arrival, the missionaries were involved in conflicts with the court, and they emerged victorious. The missionary order became a major pillar of colonial rule, and its role will be discussed later in this book.[82]

1.7   German Policy

Not much will be said here about German policy generally, as its effective civilian administration lasted for only ten years, from 1906 to 1916. Despite this limited presence, Germany's impact on Rwanda had been considerable as it put an end to an incipient civil war that could have violently displaced Musinga and made considerable steps towards imposing a central administration throughout the entire Rwandan territory. This was achieved with a minimum of European administrators, which led Louis to conclude that '[t]he most astounding aspect of German rule (…) was that so much was accomplished by so few people'.[83] Although German rule was mainly concerned with establishing law and order in a brutal vein, it created the conditions that later allowed Belgium to put in place an effective administration, as will be seen in the next chapter.

Initially, 'German activity in Ruanda-Urundi was more a military occupation than a colonial administration'.[84] It served a dual purpose: imposing the German order on the 'indigenous' political system and safeguarding the continuously and often violently contested position of Musinga.[85] These were complementary goals, aimed at facilitating the effective colonisation of the country and at ensuring political stability. Given the extreme scarcity of German personnel, indirect rule was the only viable policy, and it was made possible by the presence of what the Germans considered, in part erroneously (as shown later), a well-organised kingdom. What Germany had in mind was well expressed by the Duke of Mecklenburg:

---

[81]   Des Forges, *Defeat Is the Only Bad News*, p. 27–29. This incidentally again shows the political relevance of ethnic identity at the time.
[82]   A history of the early years of the White Fathers' missionary implantation can be found in S. Minnaert, 'The White Fathers and Rwandan Society during the German Colonial Period', in K. Bachmann, J. Bar (Eds.), *German Colonialism in Africa*, Berlin, Peter Lang, 2023, pp. 157–196.
[83]   Louis, *Ruanda-Urundi*, p. 204.
[84]   Ibid., p. 127.
[85]   I put 'indigenous' between inverted commas here as it is an expression with clear colonial overtones. As this was a standard legal expression, I will not use quotation marks in the further text.

1.7 German Policy

It is desired to strengthen and enrich the sultan (*mwami*) and persons in authority, and to increase thereby their interest in the continuance of German rule (...). At the same time, by steadily controlling and directing the sultan and using his powers, civilizing influences would be introduced. (...) (The sultan) eventually would be nothing less than the executive instrument of the (German) Resident.[86]

Relations were to be mutually advantageous, as the Germans used Musinga to establish their authority, while the *mwami* used the Germans to strengthen his own position,[87] or so he thought. The instruction of the governor of German East Africa was to cooperate completely with the *mwami*, whom the local administration was to regard as the ultimate authority in Rwanda. It was not to interfere in Rwandan internal affairs except at Musinga's request.[88] However, the court soon realised that there was now a superior authority, which might not intervene often in internal affairs but *could* intervene when considered necessary. This had become clear already in 1903, when the Germans imposed a fine of forty cows on the king as punishment for executions perpetrated at the court. Kagame notes that this was a supreme humiliation: 'This was the first time in history that a Rwandan monarch endured such an affront.'[89] It was not just an insult but challenged the king's right of life and death which his predecessors had widely used – and on which his reputation of sovereign authority was based.

However, both sides found each other in the need to establish full territorial control and a uniform administration across the entire country. While Musinga resented the expansion of German power, he also used it to his advantage. When faced with the rejection of his authority, he had the Germans execute his opponents. Confronted with notables who openly opposed him, he used German troops to capture and pillage them.[90] This 'consensual couple' operated clearly during an insubordination in the north-west where both the *mwami* and the Germans were rejected. The region had a strong sense of independence of all 'foreigners', both the European occupiers and the Tutsi chiefs from the centre, who had tried to impose new obligations like *uburetwa*. As a lingering consequence of the Rucunshu coup, the region rose up in support of Ndungutse, presented as the true successor to Rwabugiri. The rebellion

---

[86] Duke of Mecklenburg, *In the Heart of Africa*, London, Cassell, 1910, Vol. 1, p. 46. As will be seen later, this was also the philosophy behind Belgium's version of indirect rule.
[87] Louis, *Ruanda-Urundi*, p. 122.
[88] Des Forges, *Defeat Is the Only Bad News*, p. 39.
[89] Kagame, *Un abrégé de l'histoire*, p. 151. Also see Des Forges, *Defeat Is the Only Bad News*, p. 40.
[90] Des Forges, *Defeat Is the Only Bad News*, p. 90.

was brutally suppressed by the Germans who killed many insurgents, destroyed entire hills, and eventually executed Ndungutse.[91] Kagame concluded that '[t]his execution crowned the expedition and put an end to the troubles that had kept Rwanda in turmoil since the events at Rucunshu. The legitimist fever had lasted for 15 years. Were it not for the Germans' intervention in favour of Yuhi V Musinga, nothing would have prevented things to continue their course'.[92]

Although German military occupation was replaced by colonial administration in 1906, it remained rudimentary. In 1914, there were only five civilian administrators in Rwanda, in addition to a few dozen mainly African military. The principal means of maintaining German authority was the 'punitive expedition' (*Strafexpedition*), which was also used elsewhere in the colonial empire. These expeditions were very brutal. Villages and crops were destroyed, cattle was seized and in cases of serious revolt, such as with Ndungutse, the main 'offenders' were hanged.[93] Apart from relative pacification, the only successful colonial measure was the introduction of a one rupee per head tax,[94] the first general tax collection achieved in 1914. It was a success mainly due to the Hutu believing that by paying taxes to the Germans they would be protected from the tyranny of the court and the chiefs.[95] Louis's overall assessment of the German presence is severe: 'Failure characterised German colonialism in Ruanda-Urundi more than success',[96] but this should not surprise in light of the paucity of the human and material means put to task.

1.8 International Status

While the Rwandan royal court was intensely and continuously engaged in expansionary wars and internal settling of scores, far-away Europeans were busy sharing out the continent in the 'scramble for Africa' without those first concerned by these struggles being aware of them. The territorial demarcation of Rwanda has been a complex and drawn out process, which is only summarily presented here.[97] Needless

---

[91] A detailed account of the court's and Germans' alliance in dealing with the northern insurgency can be found in Bachmann, *A History of Rwanda*, pp. 76–83.
[92] Kagame, *Un abrégé de l'histoire*, p. 169. Also see Chrétien, *The Great Lakes of Africa*, p. 255.
[93] Louis, *Ruanda-Urundi*, p. 203.
[94] Currency used in German East Africa.
[95] Louis, *Ruanda-Urundi*, p. 203.
[96] Ibid., p. 200.
[97] A more detailed treatment can be found in Louis, *Ruanda-Urundi*, pp. 3–97; P. Jentgen, *Les frontières du Ruanda-Urundi et le régime international de tutelle*, Brussels, Académie royale des sciences coloniales, 1957, pp. 12–33.

to say that, in the colonial world order of the day, the placement of boundaries was the affair of European powers without the presence of Africans, neither the royal court nor local authorities nor of course the affected populations.

Borders were drawn between Leopold's Congo Free State, the UK's Uganda and German East Africa. Those between the Congo and German East Africa, of which Ruanda-Urundi was part, were fixed in a treaty between Germany and the Association Internationale du Congo in 1884, as later specified in a German–Belgian treaty in 1910. The territory west of the Rusizi river and the largest part of Lake Kivu, including the large Ijwi Island, became Congolese. As seen earlier, at the time of the signing of the 1884 treaty, some of these lands, most prominently Ijwi and Bushi, were the object of Rwabugiri's expansionary expeditions, but he never realised he had lost them on paper (and he did not win them permanently in battle). Rwandan expansion into the west thus became impossible. The border between German East Africa, and therefore Rwanda, and Uganda was fixed in a German–British arrangement signed in Berlin in 1890 and made more precise in a 1909 arrangement, also signed in Berlin. This cut Rwanda off from its territorial ambitions in the north, again without the court realising this had happened.

As both Ruanda-Urundi and the later Tanganyika Territory were part of German East Africa, the delimitation of Rwanda's eastern and southern borders was not necessary at the time, but we will see later that the issue of the eastern border came up after the First World War and that it was again settled at the expense of the Rwandan court's old territorial ambitions. However, those were no longer relevant at the time, and the contenders by then had become the UK and Belgium. This will be discussed in the next chapter.

1.9   Conclusion

Under warrior king Kigeri IV Rwabugiri, Rwanda was a violent society, at both the centre and the periphery. His accession and succession were conflictual, as most of his predecessors' had been in the past. Inside the royal court and among the aristocracy there was continuous infighting, accompanied by executions, killings and even the massacre of entire families, settling of scores through revenge and counter-revenge, rumour mongering and plots, and the constant threat of civil war. Society was profoundly militarised; force and terror served as the main political tools. The saying 'Rwanda attacks, it cannot be attacked' (*Urwanda ruratera, ntiruterwa*) mentioned earlier underscored expansionary projects. Particularly under Rwabugiri, the country was almost constantly at war, either against neighbouring countries or against unruly parts of the realm. Political ethnicity and its pernicious potential came to the fore during this period, particularly as a result of the introduction of the *uburetwa* exactions and the installation by the court of unpopular and exploitative Tutsi notables in outlying regions.[98] The regime became increasingly authoritarian, and its attempts at centralisation only partly succeeded. As noted by David Newbury, the death of Rwabugiri in 1895 marked the end of an era in two respects: eighteen months after his death, his chosen successor was overthrown by the queen mother he himself had chosen and, consequentially and more significantly, Rwanda lost its independence to Germany.[99]

The end of independent Rwanda was marked by a profound political crisis that led to the Rucunshu coup and the beginning of a civil war. The paradox of this period is that it coincided with the beginning of German colonial rule. On the one hand Germany's intervention saved the incumbent monarch Musinga, gradually put an end to the civil war and installed a relatively uniform if extractive and inegalitarian authority over the entire country. On the other hand it profoundly limited the king's and the court's power, as well as ending the previous dynamics of Rwanda's territorial expansion through the fixing of colonial borders. Germany's version of indirect rule, which was necessary due to the scarcity of its resources, was to be made much more interventionist by the Belgians, who 'inherited' Rwanda and Burundi as a result of the outcome of the First World War (as shown in Chapter 2).

While the precolonial political game involved fractions inside the royal court and within the nobility, during German days it gradually was played between three pillars of power: the colonial administration, the indigenous political regime and the Christian – predominantly Catholic – missionary order. The period presented in this chapter was the outcome of the meeting of two histories, that of the Rwandan kingdom and that of European colonisation. The first history was path dependent. Although Rwabugiri's Rwanda was exceptionally militarised, considerable continuity with previous reigns showed in expansionist ambitions, intra-regime conflict and attempts at establishing a uniform administration throughout the realm, as well as in pervasive violence and the emergence of political ethnicity. The second history, the imposition of German overrule, was a crucial critical juncture with

---

[98] This theme is developed in a case study of Buhoma and Rwankeri in the north by Florent Piton (*Dans les plis de l'ethnie*).
[99] Newbury, *The Land beyond the Mists*, pp. 334–335.

1.9 Conclusion

long-lasting effects that went far beyond two other critical junctures that will be addressed later in this book, namely the 1959–1961 revolution and the 1994 genocide. Neither of these would even have taken place had Rwanda not been colonised, as other path-dependent and more organic, indigenous dynamics would have prevailed. While in the context of indirect rule the kingdom and the chiefly structure continued to exist (path dependency), their functioning and meaning were fundamentally altered beyond recognition (critical juncture). These alterations are the subject of the next two chapters.

2 Early Belgian Colonialism

2.1 Military Campaign and Occupation

After the beginning of the First World War, new German colonial ambitions aimed at establishing a great empire in Central Africa (*Das deutsche Kaiserreich Mittelafrika*). However, its military strength in East Africa allowed Germany no more than a defensive campaign.[1] Hostilities started in September 1914, when German troops occupied Ijwi Island, thus giving them control over Lake Kivu. As Ijwi belonged to the Belgian Congo, it was drawn into the war, even though Belgium had no territorial ambitions east of Lakes Kivu and Tanganyika. In application of a British–Belgian agreement of October 1914, troops from the Belgian Congo attacked Ruanda-Urundi in April 1916.[2] Supported by British logistics, they moved quickly: Kigali was taken on 11 May, Bujumbura on 6 June and Tabora on 19 September. At the end of this campaign, Belgian Congolese troops occupied a vast territory of around 200,000 square kilometres, ranging from Lakes Kivu and Tanganyika to Lake Victoria and from the northern Rwandan volcanoes to Tabora on the Dar es Salaam–Kigoma railway line.

This occupation raised the issue of how these territories were to be administered. The Belgian government considered the occupation to be temporary, awaiting a settlement after the war, but – contrary to the position of the UK, which proposed to exercise the full control and administration of all territories occupied by the Allies – it insisted on administering them itself. In a letter of 27 April 1916 to General Tombeur, the commander of the Belgian Congolese corps, Colonial Minister Renkin instructed: 'The country will be submitted to the military regime. (...) Our occupation will limit itself to the maintenance of general order (...), especially the security of lines of communication.'[3] Therefore, the administration of the conquered territories was not an act

---

[1] Louis, *Ruanda-Urundi*, pp. 210–211.
[2] Ibid., pp. 214–216.
[3] Africa Archive (Brussels), AE/II, (3287) 1844.

of sovereignty: awaiting negotiations, the occupation and administration of part of German East Africa were to be precarious.[4]

The administrative measures taken at the beginning of the occupation conformed to this status. Article 9 of law-ordinance 2/5 of 6 April 1917 stipulated that 'the functionaries and officers charged with the administration of the occupied territories will act in conformity with the rules and traditions established by the German administration'. German law remained largely applicable in both civil and criminal matters.

As seen earlier, the administrative organisation the Belgians found in Rwanda was rudimentary, and they soon faced similar problems as the Germans had. At the beginning of 1917, 'most Watusi [sic] chiefs showed (...) independentist tendencies that rapidly threatened Ruanda with total anarchy'.[5] A functional administration was therefore urgent. A high royal commissioner, first posted in Kigoma and later in Usumbura (Bujumbura), was in charge of the occupied territories. The Ruanda residency, created in May 1917, was put under the charge of Major J.-F. De Clerck and divided into four territories (*territoires*) in 1921. Those in charge of the four territories were military officers, and only in 1919 was Major De Clerck replaced by a civilian resident. The political and administrative organisation of the residency as well as its relations with the indigenous authorities will be addressed later.

2.2 International Status

At the end of the war, Belgium occupied a large territory in the west of the German colony. However, it was not interested in the areas east of Lakes Kivu and Tanganyika, and its claims there were a means of attaining another goal, located 2,000 kilometres further west. The idea was to use the occupied territories in East Africa as a pawn at anticipated negotiations aimed at the acquisition of the southern bank of the Congo river, part of the Portuguese possession Angola. Via Britain, Belgium hoped to operate an exchange between the East African territories and the south bank.[6] This was to be a complex operation: Belgium was to cede its East African territories to Britain; Portugal was to cede the south bank to Belgium; and Portugal was to receive a territorial compensation

---

[4] Murego, *La révolution rwandaise*, p. 350.
[5] *Rapport sur l'Administration belge des territoires occupés de l'Est-Africain allemand et spécialement du Ruanda et de l'Urundi pour les années 1920 et 1921*, présenté aux Chambres par M. le ministre des Colonies, Brussels, 1921, p. 11. These reports, renamed *Rapport sur l'administration belge du Ruanda-Urundi pendant l'année* from 1922 onwards, will be quoted as *Rapport* followed by the year (e.g. *Rapport 1922*).
[6] Louis, *Ruanda-Urundi*, pp. 233–234.

from Britain in the south-eastern corner of German East Africa. Portugal did not buy into the proposed deal, and Belgium was left with the need to secure its East African conquests.[7]

This proved no easy task. In the Treaty of Versailles signed on 28 June 1919, Germany renounced all rights to its overseas possessions in favour of the Principal Allied and Associated Powers.[8] Not being one of these powers, Belgium could have been excluded of the share, which it initially was at the first repartition of the German colonies decided by the Supreme Council of Allied and Associated Powers on 6 May 1919.[9] However, negotiations between Britain and Belgium led to the Orts–Milner accord signed on 30 May 1919, barely a month before the Versailles Treaty.[10] In it, Belgium and Britain committed to jointly ask the Supreme Council to give Belgium the right to administer Ruanda-Urundi and to give Britain the right to administer the rest of the former German colony. The Supreme Council accepted this joint proposal on 21 August 1919. While Belgium was thus forced to cede three quarters of the territories it occupied, it narrowly escaped being left empty-handed. On the other hand, 'Belgium's acquisition of Ruanda-Urundi is surely one of the great ironies in the (colonial) history of Africa'.[11] Because of the failure of the negotiations concerning the acquisition of the Congo river south bank, Belgium was left with Ruanda-Urundi, a territory it was not really interested in.

The mandate system agreed in Versailles was established by article 22 of the Covenant of the League of Nations. It emphasises as one of the core principles the well-being and development of peoples living in former colonies as a 'sacred trust of civilization'. The decision of the Supreme Council to entrust Belgium with a mandate over Ruanda-Urundi was confirmed on 20 July 1922 by the Council of the League of Nations. The Belgian mandate was one of category B, deemed to require a greater level of control by the mandatory power than those of category A. The mandatory was made responsible for the administration of the territory under conditions which guaranteed freedom of conscience and religion. In theory, the sovereignty of the mandatory was limited by the obligation to respect the terms of the mandate and to report annually to the League of Nations, the acceptance to

---

[7] Ibid., pp. 245–247.
[8] British Empire, France, Italy and Japan. As it did not ratify the treaty, the US was not part of this group of countries.
[9] T. Heyse, *Le mandat belge sur le Ruanda-Urundi*, Brussels, La Renaissance de l'Occident, 1930, p. 5.
[10] On the negotiations and the accord, see Louis, *Ruanda-Urundi*, pp. 238–251.
[11] Ibid., p. 255.

2.3 Colonial Public Law

submit disputes on the application of the provisions of the mandate to the Permanent Court of International Justice and the respect of the right of inhabitants of the territory to address petitions to the League of Nations.

The first two articles of the mandate addressed the territorial delimitation, which raised the thorny 'Gisaka affair'. Following the Orts–Milner accord, Belgium had to cede to Britain a territory inside Rwanda of around 5,000 square kilometres to the west of the Akagera river, in order to allow the construction of the Cape to Cairo railway projected by the British. This severed part of Musinga's kingdom, depriving him of one of his principal riches, namely the many cattle herds in this region. This amputation threatened administrative stability, as some local chiefs who owed allegiance to the *mwami* would fall under British jurisdiction. Both Belgian and British governments realised that a revision of the map was necessary, and they concluded a new accord retroceding Gisaka and other regions to the west of the Akagera to Belgium.[12]

Articles 4–8 contained clauses related to peace, the indigenous populations, freedom of trade and equality between nationals of member states of the League of Nations and freedom of conscience and religion. Article 10 defined the principles of administration. Belgium was given the power to legislate for the territory, which could be linked through customs, fiscal or administrative unions or federations with neighbouring Belgian Congo. Belgium thus received a general power of administration covering the three branches of government: legislative, executive and judicial. We will now see how these principles were translated in internal public law.

2.3 Colonial Public Law

Only on 26 March 1926, when the Act of 21 August 1925 on the government of Ruanda-Urundi entered into force, did Belgium legally end the occupation regime put in place almost ten years earlier. As seen, a royal commissioner was charged in November 1916 with provisionally administering the German East African territories occupied by the colonial troops. He received a delegation of power formulated in very general terms by the law-ordinance of 5 December 1916: 'With regard to the troops and the civilian, military and judicial personnel, the Royal Commissioner exercises all rights delegated to the governor general and the general prosecutor by the legislation of the colony

---

[12] On the Gisaka affair, see Murego, *La revolution rwandaise*, pp. 422–475.

(of Belgian Congo).' An ordinance-law of 6 April 1917 later determined the territorial and administrative organisation of the occupied territories. As will be seen later, this text also, for the first time, formulated the essential principle of indigenous policy, very much in line with that of the Germans.

When tabling its bill on the government of Ruanda-Urundi, the Belgian government was of the opinion that it was not enough to simply confirm the war time organisation. While it had rendered good services for the daily management of the occupied territories, it was considered too rudimentary for their veritable 'valorisation'. The Act of 21 August 1925,[13] with barely seven articles, and the Royal Decree of 11 January 1926 were to be the essential sources of constitutional law for Rwanda until its independence in 1962.[14] To these needed to be added the *Charte coloniale* on the Belgian Congo,[15] which was also applicable to Ruanda-Urundi, as the 1925 Act placed the mandate territory under the regime of Congolese laws voted by the Belgian parliament.

Using the right conferred by the mandate to link the mandate territories in administrative unions or federations with neighbouring possessions, a Belgian law established an administrative union between Ruanda-Urundi and the Belgian Congo, in addition to the customs union already put in place during the occupation. However, the 1925 Act made Ruanda-Urundi into a distinct legal entity, thus meeting the explicit desire of the Society of Nations, which, among its other aims, wanted to allow the Permanent Mandates Commission to exercise its oversight. In order to exclude provisions of the colonial legislation that were inappropriate for the mandate territory, the Act also stipulated that the decrees (*décrets*) and law-ordinances (*ordonnances législatives*) of the governor general of the Belgian Congo were applicable to Ruanda-Urundi only when declared in force there by an ordinance (*ordonnance*) of the vice governor general, governor of Ruanda-Urundi. The Act finally excluded from Ruanda-Urundi the provisions of Congolese legislation that were contrary to those of the mandate.

2.4 Indirect Rule Belgian Style

Until 1944, the legal foundation of the indigenous policy applied in Rwanda remained very limited and only consisted of the law-ordinance

---

[13] *Moniteur belge*, 9 September 1925, p. 4544.
[14] *Moniteur belge*, 15–16 February 1926, pp. 731–732.
[15] 'Loi du 18 octobre 1908 sur le gouvernement du Congo belge', *Moniteur belge*, 19–20 October 1908, pp. 5887–5894.

2.4 Indirect Rule Belgian Style

of 6 April 1917 mentioned earlier. The basic principle was set out in article 4 as follows: 'Under the direction of the resident, the Sultans exercise their political and judicial powers to the extent and in the way determined by indigenous custom and the instructions of the royal commissioner.'[16] This text shows considerable continuity with the line adopted by the Germans. As seen in Chapter 1, Musinga had put Rwanda under German protection, without however realising the extent of his loss of sovereignty. After the occupation of Rwanda by Belgium, resident Major De Clerck was given a draft protection treaty to be signed between the Belgian government and the *mwami*. The draft outlined 'the conduct to be followed in different areas of the administration'.[17] On political matters it stipulated

6. The European authorities will not directly intervene in the affairs of the Sultanate. This mission is left to the delegates of the Sultan. The latter must conform to the instructions given by the resident in this domain. The Sultan ensures the police of the territories under his administration. He must ensure the security of roads of communication and prevent internal wars among his subjects. If he were incapable to assume these missions, the European authority will take the appropriate measures.

While this 'treaty' was never signed, it is interesting as it outlines the Belgian administration's conceptions on its relations with the indigenous political authorities at the beginning of the occupation.

In the absence of a formal treaty, Belgium tried to find other arguments in the perspective of international negotiations influenced by US president Woodrow Wilson's ideas on the self-determination of peoples. Already in October 1916, the minister of the colonies, Renkin, had suggested to 'receive' or even 'provoke' 'statements of obedience and fidelity' by indigenous authorities.[18] It is in this context that the Belgian occupying authorities organised a 'referendum' among the *mwami* and his notables. After a visit to Musinga in September 1918, the royal commissioner announced in a cable to Renkin that 'if Ruanda asked choice of protectorate, king will insistently ask that of the Belgians. Neither English nor Germans are desired.'[19] In a letter of 27 December 1918, Musinga formally confirmed his allegiance:

---

[16] As seen earlier, Sultan was already the term used to designate the king under German rule.
[17] 'Note sur le Rapport politique du Ruanda', 3 January 1919, Africa Archive, AE/II, (3288) 1847.
[18] Letter of October 1916 by Minister Renkin to General Tombeur, Africa Archive, AE/II, (3287) 1844.
[19] Cable No. 68 of 27 September 1918, Africa Archive, AE/II, (3287) 1842.

I immediately write that I and my chiefs want and love the Bula [king Albert] (...) I have great faith in the Belgians and want them to stay! I and mine love him for his justice and do not want anyone else than the Bula Matari. (...) For all that I have written, I want the flag of the Bula Matari to become mine, and that is also what my people wants.[20]

While this letter was of course not a treaty under international law, it was seen as an unequivocal request of the *mwami* to remain under Belgian administration.

This was confirmed during the 'referendum' or 'consultation of the inhabitants of the occupied territories as to their fate after the war' as it was officially called. In order 'to have the absolute conviction that the wishes expressed [in the king's letter] are sincere and express the opinion of all, we have assembled at Nyanza the great Watuzis [Tutsi] of the kingdom. After having read out the request of the sultan, we have proceeded to the interrogation in the presence of the Europeans present in Nyanza'.[21] In all, the royal commissioner was able to collect fifty-four minutes of meetings and letters with the opinion of about 300 chiefs and notables 'given in the name of the population'.[22] The operation was a success. The resident reported that 'one can wonder whether the indigenous are mature and sufficiently conscious to express their wishes on this issue, but the sympathy and confidence they have for us is indisputable. Frankly, an international commission can come and hold a referendum.'[23]

This position favourable to Belgium obviously imposed itself. Musinga and his chiefs probably perceived their collaboration, which was in reality a submission, as a condition for the maintenance of their customary powers.[24] At any rate, the Rwandans had known the Belgians for hardly two years, and the comparison with other colonial powers, except Germany, was impossible. As noted by a missionary who observed the operation, the Rwandans had no choice. The opinion of a notable who stated that he was not interested in knowing which Europeans were to 'advise the court' as long as they were not Christian was probably never registered in Europe.[25]

---

[20] Africa Archive, AE/II, (3290) 1859. The original is in Swahili, and a translation in French is attached. 'Bula Matari' means 'the breaker of rocks', reportedly first used in Congo with regard to Stanley who dynamited rocky terrain to build roads.
[21] Procès-verbal de la réunion tenue à Nyanza le 9.1.1919, Africa Archive, AE/II, (3290) 1859.
[22] Letter No. 4327-J-Polit. of 17 February 1919 by the royal commissioner to the Minister of Colonies, Africa Archive, AE/II, (3290) 1859.
[23] Letter of 17 January 1919 by the resident of Ruanda to the royal commissioner, Africa Archive, AE/II, (3290) 1859.
[24] In this sense, also see Murego, *La revolution rwandaise*, pp. 374–384.
[25] Des Forges, *Defeat Is the Only Bad News*, p. 158.

2.4 Indirect Rule Belgian Style

We have seen earlier how Belgium acquired the mandate over Ruanda-Urundi, including Gisaka and – while not essential for its claims – that it invoked 'the interest and wish of the indigenous populations'.[26] For its administration of the territory, nothing else than the terms of the mandate were binding. Regarding indigenous policy there was no precise obligation other than to govern in the direct interest of the autochthonous populations. In addition, Belgium had not found in the German succession any particular political obligation towards the indigenous authorities.[27] However, from the very beginning Belgium found that, contrary to other colonial territories, Rwanda and Burundi were organised societies well suited for a system of indirect rule.[28] This was already made clear in 1916 in a letter from the minister of the colonies to General Tombeur: 'The only institution that has probably survived the conquest is that of the indigenous chiefs (...). No doubt there would be a political interest in maintaining it and only touching it with a cautious hand.'[29] As seen earlier, this had also been the policy of the Germans.

In early 1920, the minister of the colonies decided that '[in Rwanda] where there exists a strongly established indigenous organisation with a well-established authority, the relations between the metropole and these territories will be those of indirect rule'.[30] The authority over the inhabitants would remain in principle in the hands of the supreme indigenous ruler 'to whom will be added as a councillor and possibly as a tutor a European resident appointed by the government of the metropole'.[31] In a long confidential memorandum, Franck clarified his ideas:

We will practise [...] a policy of colonial protectorate. This policy's basis is the maintenance of the indigenous institutions. It makes the European the guide and educator. It excludes a direct administration. It is perfectly feasible in countries with an old and remarkable organisation, and whose ruling class exhibits obvious political talent.

But this method does not limit itself to *respecting* and using indigenous institutions. It also aims at *developing* them based on their own merit in order to gradually adapt them to the needs of colonisation and of the country's economic progress.

(...)

---

[26] *La position internationale de la Belgique*, Brussels, Imprimerie du Moniteur belge, 1934, p. 27.
[27] G. Lebart, Mupangu, 'La "politique indigène" de la Belgique au Ruanda-Urundi', *La Revue Nouvelle*, 1960, p. 462.
[28] *Rapport 1920–1921*, p. 10.
[29] Letter of October 1916 by Minister Renkin to General Tombeur, Africa Archive, AE/II, (3287) 1844.
[30] Letter No. 303 of 6 January 1920 of Minister Franck to the Governor General of the Belgian Congo at Boma, Africa Archive, AE/II, (3288) 1847.
[31] Ibid.

Our administration will *maintain royal authority* and reinforce it, in conformity with custom, where it has been weakened. But we will ensure, on the one hand, that this authority needs our support, while on the other hand not diminishing too much or annihilating the role of the nobility. (...) Between these elements we will maintain a rational balance, so that both need us and appreciate the value of our action.

Next to our obligations of general policy, we have duties toward the Hutu. We must protect them against arbitrary acts of which they are often victim, and assure them peace, security of their goods and labour, and justice. But we will not go further; there is no question, under the pretext of equality, to touch the foundations of the political institutions; we find the Tutsi established for a long time, intelligent and capable; we will respect this situation.[32]

I have quoted these long extracts because Franck's memorandum reveals the seeds of the problems and the contradictions of the policy of indirect rule applied in Rwanda over the years. The balance proposed is much too subtle and theoretical to be applied in practice: at the same time respecting and developing the indigenous institutions; maintaining royal authority, but not too much; protecting the Hutu without touching the essence of the political regime, and so on. We will later see the practical and political difficulties inherent in the implementation of such ideas. From the outset, the administration itself recognised one of these contradictions: custom was to be respected only 'insofar as it is not contrary to essential principles of morality or incompatible with progress, and to the extent indigenous authorities apply it with justice'.[33]

Only in 1925 were the principles of indirect rule coherently formulated. The report on the Belgian administration described the programme as applied and to be realised in the future. It was based on the notion of legitimacy. The king was to play a central role in the relations between the European authorities and the population. In the eyes of his subjects he always had a power that Europeans would not possess for a long time to come: that of conferring legitimacy to administrative decisions and measures. 'Legitimacy is a moral factor of crucial importance. It gives much more authority than constraint. The legitimate chiefs are the only wheels that can function without creaking between European authority and the indigenous masses. They alone, *because they are legitimate*, will be able to have accepted the necessary innovations that others may not succeed in imposing through force.'[34]

---

[32] 'Memorandum confidentiel du ministre des Colonies L. Franck', Buta, 15 June 1920, Africa Archive, AE/II, (3288) 1849 (italics in the original text).
[33] *Rapport 1922*, p. 6.
[34] *Rapport 1925*, p. 63 (italics in the original text).

The ideas of Pierre Ryckmans, the then governor of Ruanda-Urundi, are clearly visible in the report. While underlining the importance of the presence of kings, he rejected the idea of a mere protectorate dealing only with the kings, without engaging with the chiefs as the Germans had done. To the contrary, 'the only remedy is the real and intense occupation and the intimate, permanent contact of the whites with the chiefs, all of them. (...) We need people [on the ground]. (...) We are either masters or nothing.' Simple advice would be sufficient only when the people were ready to govern itself. 'The real protectorate is the pinnacle of the civilising mission, not its point of departure.'[35] These ideas are quite far from a real policy of indirect rule. Compared to Franck's position just five years earlier, Ryckmans' stance advocated a much more intrusive action that holds the germs of direct rule. As will be seen in a moment, Belgium was to apply an interventionist policy that was indirect in name only. Compared with the British version of indirect rule, it was described as 'both complicated and interfering; it wanted to do everything for the people, without considering the sociological implications of what was being done'.[36] In other words, Belgian rule was paternalistic, as can be seen in the title of a book published by Ryckmans in 1931, *Dominer pour servir*.[37] More than ten years later, the minister of the colonies reasoned in the same vein: 'The natives are children, something of children whom a parent loves and for whose well-being he strives.'[38]

2.5 Early Political Measures

2.5.1 *Domesticating the* Mwami

In Rwanda, the presence of a ruling ethnic minority gave a particular meaning to the policy of indirect rule. Indeed, it structurally involved what d'Hertefelt has called a 'dual consensus':[39] according to him, on the one hand, a traditional consensus linked the majority of the population to its 'natural' autochthonous rulers (the Tutsi-dominated hierarchy); on the other, a colonial consensus was established between these rulers

---

[35] P. Ryckmans, 'Le problème politique du Ruanda-Urundi', *Congo*, 1925, pp. 407–413.
[36] R. E. S. Tanner, 'The Belgian and British Administration in Ruanda-Urundi and Tanganyika', *Journal of Local Administration Overseas*, 1965, p. 205.
[37] P. Ryckmans, *Dominer pour servir*, Brussels, A. Dewit, 1931.
[38] A. De Vleeschauwer, *Belgian Colonial Policy*, New York, Belgian Government Information Center, 1943, p. 36, quoted by J. Gahama, *Le Burundi sous administration belge*, Paris, Karthala, 1983, p. 62.
[39] M. d'Hertefelt, 'Les élections communales et le consensus politique au Rwanda', *Zaïre*, 1960, p. 403.

and the European administering power. However, the term 'consensus' is not appropriate, as in both cases it was to a large extent imposed by the stronger on the weaker. Indeed, we have seen that the traditional consensus was not unchallenged and that it was accompanied by a great deal of violence, which in the nineteenth century even developed ethnic overtones. The colonial consensus, first with Germany and later with Belgium, was the outcome of a show of force between very unequal parties. That said, Belgium did side with an internal power structure that was dominated by the ethnic minority. As will be seen later, it switched sides in the 1950s with dramatic consequences.

'Civilising measures' were taken since the beginning of the military occupation, and some challenged the very symbolic basis on which the *mwami*'s power rested. As seen earlier, the Germans already limited or straightforward forbade some of his attributions, such as his power over life and death of his subjects. Already in 1917, Major De Clerck announced to Musinga that the court was henceforth forbidden to pronounce or execute a death sentence without the resident's authorisation.[40] However, for long the court ignored this prohibition, as it had done with a similar decision imposed by the Germans. The victims, who had generally become fewer in numbers and less noble, were executed during the night, and rumours were spread that they had exiled themselves abroad.[41] It is apparently only around 1922 that executions at the court ceased, and the effect of this loss of power on the king's position was considerable. Alison Des Forges cites a Rwandan observer who opined that 'of course he could [kill as he wished] and besides, he did because it was his country (...) [He killed] until the Europeans arrived and became more powerful than he.'[42]

Other grave limitations to the king's power followed soon. In 1922 it was decided that the *mwami* was to be assisted in his judicial function by the resident's delegate in Nyanza. As the administration realised that grave or important cases were dealt with in the absence of the delegate, sessions that used to be held before the hut of the queen mother, Nyirayuhi, had to take place before Musinga's office and later at the administrative post. Another important challenge to the *mwami*'s authority came about in 1923. In order to ensure some stability in political command functions, the king was forbidden to appoint or revoke territorial governors, and they in turn could no longer appoint or revoke their subaltern officers,

---

[40] *Rapport 1920–1921*, p. 15.
[41] Kagame, *Un abrégé de l'histoire*, pp. 175–176. This explanation of 'disappearances' was used again after 1994.
[42] Des Forges, *Defeat Is the Only Bad News*, p. 175.

without the prior agreement of the residency.[43] By intervening in this way, the Belgian administration increasingly became the final source of authority, as chiefs and sub-chiefs were no longer seen as the subordinates of the king but of the Belgian administration. This evolution will be further discussed in Chapter 3.

As early as in July 1917, the *mwami* was forced to decree the freedom of religion: 'I, Musinga, mwami of Ruanda, decide that from this day on every subject of my kingdom will be free to practice the religion of his choice.'[44] Given the sacred nature of kingship, the impact of this measure was considerable as religion was to rapidly compete with the *mwami*'s supernatural legitimacy and power. However, following Belgian practice, Major De Clerck guaranteed the separation of State and Church, a principle certainly unknown to Musinga. In August, De Clerck issued instructions stating that the missionaries were there to teach religion, not to rule; that it was up to the chiefs to settle disputes; and that the chiefs depended only on the king and could put themselves at the service of the missions only if so ordered by him.[45] Nevertheless, the *mwami* remained concerned. Worried by the fast-rising number of conversions, including among Tutsi notables, when Minister Franck visited Rwanda in 1920, Musinga implored him never to force his subjects to convert to Christianity. Embarrassed by this plea, which he saw as justified, Franck assured him that the negative freedom of religion was guaranteed in 'civilised countries' and that the Belgian administration would never force anyone to abandon their traditional beliefs.[46] In reality, this concession simply respected the provisions of the mandate regarding freedom of conscience and the free exercise of cult.

Rituals that sustained the sacred legitimacy of the court also came under fire. In 1925, the resident informed Musinga that the *umuganura* rite was henceforth forbidden,[47] along with other rites contained in the *ubwiru*. While these intangible elements were as important for royal authority as the right to life and death, the Belgian administration considered them a 'superstitious' impediment on the road to progress.

---

[43] de Lacger, *Ruanda*, p. 490.
[44] Ibid., pp. 466–467.
[45] Ibid., p. 467.
[46] Société des Missionnaires d'Afrique (Pères Blancs), *Rapport annuel 1919–1920*, p. 362.
[47] The preparation and presentation to the *mwami* of the first fruits of the sorghum harvest. This celebration was to ensure the agricultural wealth of the country, but it was more than an agricultural ceremony. This essential annual ritual reasserted the legitimacy of the king (Newbury, *The Land beyond the Mists*, pp. 229–251). *Umuganura* was officially reintroduced in 2011.

Making the *mwami* as European as possible was part of the advent of 'civilisation', as is well illustrated in a report of 30 June 1919 written by a jubilant Monsignor Classe, head of the White Fathers in Rwanda: 'Musinga can see his children, which is prohibited by custom. He presents them. The four oldest are dressed in European style. Who would have predicted a year ago that Musinga would routinely welcome travellers, officers and missionaries, offering them cigarettes and drinks? This is the effect of one year of a good policy by the government of occupation.'[48]

Other measures entailed a gradual but radical shift in authority. In 1925, the administration decided to relegate the great court sorcerer (*umupfumu*), Gashamura, to Burundi. The reason was his 'obstinate opposition to progress and the unlimited and pernicious influence he exercised over Musinga'.[49] The *mwami* was not even consulted on this measure, which made clear who was really in charge. An official report offers a good example of this shift. Before the European occupation, the king or the queen mother often instructed chiefs to cede a hill or part of it to a favourite. When the residence embarked on a territorial reorganisation that will be discussed later, it was decided that the *mwami* could no longer privilege his courtiers in this way without the resident's authorisation. Musinga tried to evade the administration's control, but 'the province chiefs, who felt supported by the European authority, resisted the *mwami*'s whims, giving as pretext for their refusal the fear to contravene an order of the administration'.[50] Unsurprisingly, the *mwami* complained: 'Today I'm no longer the *mwami*. I can no longer kill who I want, nor dispossess people at my discretion. How can one say that I am still the king? For the rest, everything I say, everything I do, everything I think, the Europeans always immediately know.'[51] Other incidents showed that the residency was intent on controlling the distribution of wealth and power.[52] Worse still, the administration's decisions appeared to favour the *mwami*'s opponents and punish those loyal to him.[53] In this way, it had not only captured the king's power but even used it against him. As will be seen later, in 1931 the destitution and relegation of Musinga was the supreme confirmation of this dramatic shift of authority.

[48] de Lacger, *Ruanda*, p. 469.
[49] *Rapport 1925*, p. 66.
[50] *Rapport établi en réponse au Questionnaire adressé en 1929 par M. le Gouverneur du Ruanda-Urundi à l'Administrateur du Territoire de Nyanza*, p. 43, Derscheid Collection.
[51] de Lacger, *Ruanda*, p. 526.
[52] Examples can be found in Reyntjens, *Pouvoir et droit*, pp. 84–85.
[53] Des Forges, *Defeat Is the Only Bad News*, p. 206.

2.5.2 *Extension and Consolidation of the Reach of the Central Kingdom*

We have seen that the territorial control exercised by the central kingdom was historically uneven. Certain parts of Rwanda as defined by the colonial delimitation were not effectively incorporated in the realm, and were often opposed to the court. Even areas governed by Tutsi rulers, such as Gisaka in the east and Kinyaga in the south-west, rejected the assimilation pursued by the royal court. Wishing to put in place a 'rational' organisation, like the Germans before them, the Belgians did not accept that parts of the country escaped royal authority and that indigenous borders were different from colonial ones. Traditionally the concepts of 'territories' and 'borders' were more fluid than Europeans could understand and accept. Neatly defined territories were only introduced under colonial rule.[54] In order to homogenise the entire territory's administration, the Belgians sought to end the (sometimes partial) autonomy of peripheral regions, a policy that was started by the Germans. It became more radical and systematic under the Belgian administration, which extended central royal rule across entire Rwanda (see Map 2.1). This entailed the gradual replacement of local Hutu authorities by Tutsi notables representing the court, even in regions where the latter had no historical legitimacy. Ethnic tensions were thus introduced where they did not exist before, and this profoundly modified command structures and ethnic relations.[55]

This policy of expansion and uniformisation was forcefully implemented in the 1920s in the north (Ndorwa, Mutara, Mulera), the north-west (Bushiru, Bugoyi) and the south-west (Bukunzi, Busozo). As these areas had never been permanently and effectively occupied and administered by the central court, it is remarkable that the Belgian administration justified these measures as the 'restauration' of the *mwami*'s authority.[56] The effects of this incorporation differed depending on the earlier history of the incorporated regions and their previous relations with the court. Three examples – Mulera, Bushiru, and Bukunzi and Busozo – show this.

When incorporating Mulera, the Belgian administrator himself appointed the chiefs, although they supposedly represented the king. Given the insufficient number of Tutsi with the necessary qualities, notables were 'imported' from the south, while lower functions were attributed to politically irrelevant or poor Tutsi from modest families. This recalls a similar situation in Uganda, where so-called Ganda

---

[54] Precolonial forms of spatial and political organisation and identity are addressed in Mathys, *Conflicts and Connections*.
[55] For a case study in the north, see Piton, *Dans les plis*.
[56] *Rapport 1925*, p. 64.

Map 2.1 Map of the historical regions of Rwanda. Absent or limited central court control ca. 1900 (borders are those of contemporary Rwanda). Map created by author.

agents from Buganda were sent to other regions to occupy 'customary' positions that were in reality newly created.[57] All resistance by influential Hutu lineages to the effective occupation of Mulera was vigorously repressed by the Tutsi notables and through the use of military force.

Unable to occupy Bushiru in the early 1920s and impressed by the effective resistance of the region's Hutu and their political organisation under one widely accepted monarch, the *umuhinza*, the Belgians initially accepted his rule.[58] However the obligations imposed by the administration on the population increased to the point that they no longer accepted Belgian authority, in turn leading to the *umuhinza* losing his legitimacy as

---

[57] H. F. Morris, J. S. Read, *Indirect Rule and the Search for Justice*, Oxford, Clarendon Press, 1972, pp. 27–29.
[58] Territoire de Kabaya, *Rapport politique 1921*, Derscheid Collection. On the political and social structure of Bushiru generally, see M. Pauwels, 'Le Bushiru et son Muhinza ou roitelet hutu', *Annali Lateranensi*, 1967, pp. 205–322.

he had to implement the administration's orders. Caught between the devil and the deep sea, he thus became unable to meet the expectations of his people or, more seriously, those of the administration. For the latter, this confirmed what it thought it knew for a long time, namely that the Hutu were incapable of correctly exercising political office (see Section 2.5.3 on the Hamitic Hypothesis). The residency proposed to Musinga to extend central and Tutsi rule to Bushiru, which he hastened to accept as the court had for long tried in vain to incorporate the region.[59] The chief sent to Bushiru in common agreement between the *mwami* and the resident divided the province between the notables appointed by him and destroyed the last vestiges of the *abahinza*'s political authority.[60]

The incorporation of Bukunzi and Busozo in Kinyaga was a very peculiar evolution as these regions enjoyed a great deal of autonomy due to the will of the royal court itself.[61] The special status of Bukunzi was due to the fact that its *mwami* supposedly controlled the system of rains for all of Rwanda. He paid a nominal tribute to the *mwami* of Rwanda but received the equivalent and even more from the court for the provision of rain at the right moment. The reasons for the protection of Busozo date back to mythico-history: King Ruganzu II Ndori, the founder of the Nyiginya dynasty (mentioned in the introduction), was royally received there upon returning from one of his expeditions. Other sources say Busozo produced the first honey, a product unknown in Rwanda before its discovery there. Until 1923, the Belgian administration did not intervene in the status of these small kingdoms. However, as this situation was considered contrary to the principles of a uniform administration, it first tried to occupy these regions peacefully by bureaucratic means, in vain and against Musinga's will. In 1925, it intervened militarily in Bukunzi: the local queen mother was killed and the young *mwami*, Ngoga, was jailed in Kigali, where he died. A year later, colonial troops occupied Busozo, and its command was given to a young Tutsi notable when the old *mwami* died in 1926.[62]

The occupation of Bukunzi and Busozo, 'insurrectionist regions',[63] shows that for the Belgian administration the efficacy of a uniform administrative system took precedence over the desire of the central court to

---

[59] Des Forges, *Defeat Is the Only Bad News*, pp. 199–201.
[60] Territoire de Kabaya, *Rapports politiques 1924 et 1925*, Derscheid Collection.
[61] See E. Ntezimana, 'Coutumes et traditions des royaumes hutu du Bukunzi et du Busozo', *Etudes Rwandaises*, No. 2, 1980, pp. 15–39; E. Ntezimana, 'L'arrivée des Européens au Kinyaga et la fin des royaumes hutu du Bukunzi et du Busozo', *Etudes Rwandaises*, No. 3, 1980, pp. 1–29.
[62] Ntezimana, 'L'arrivée', pp. 15–18.
[63] *Rapport 1925*, p. 64.

maintain, in certain cases, flexible arrangements that had shown their usefulness for generations. With the elimination, in Bushiru, Bukunzi, Busozo and elsewhere, of 'Hutu kinglets' and their replacement by imported Tutsi authorities, the ethnic aspect came more to the fore. In addition, even after a military occupation it proved difficult to absorb these regions into the mould of the central government: as late as in 1932, the Belgian local administrator drew the residency's attention to the situation in Busozo, which he considered in need of a 'more intensive administration'.[64]

The extension of central power under the form of a Belgian–Tutsi coalition ended in the north-east, where Ndorwa, Buberuka, Rukiga and Ruyaga resisted incorporation until the late 1920s.[65] After a period of passive resistance against the recently installed Tutsi authorities, the administration felt compelled to resort to repression when Hutu leader Semaroso, who sometimes claimed to be Ndungutse (see Chapter 1), mobilised the populations of Ndorwa and Rukiga against the Tutsi notables and the Belgian authorities. The revolt was quite easily defeated by the notables and Belgian troops, but a regime of military occupation was needed for more than three years to keep the region under Belgian and court control.[66] Other insurrections and acts of civil disobedience, in particular against compulsory crops, took place in Gisaka and Bugesera in 1926–1927 and in Bumbogo in 1930, but they were suppressed without major difficulties.

Therefore, only by the beginning of the 1930s, fifteen years after the Belgians took possession of the country, was the complete occupation of Rwanda achieved. The authority of the *mwami* was installed (rather than 'restored') everywhere, and the royal and colonial boundaries overall coincided. However, the position of the chiefs in the 'integrated' regions remained weak and did not conform to their traditional status, as the foundation of their rule was often the power and the authority of the coloniser. Particularly in the north, this hampered the acceptance of imported and imposed chiefs. As will be seen later, this northern peculiarity has remained a defining feature of Rwandan politics.

2.5.3 Tutsi Political Monopoly

For the European administrators and missionaries, the fact that the Tutsi were considered as 'Hamites' ideologically underpinned their right

---

[64] Territoire de Kamembe-Shangugu, *Rapport politique 1932*, Derscheid Collection.
[65] A survey shows that the installation of Tutsi chiefs with permanent residence was only achieved in Cyingogo in 1916, in Bushiru in 1919 and 1925, in Buhoma-Buhanga in 1924 and 1931, in Rwankeri in 1931, in Mulera in 1918, in Kibari in 1931 and in Bukonya in 1931 (Nahimana, *Le Rwanda*, pp. 291–314).
[66] Des Forges, *Defeat Is the Only Bad News*, pp. 229–231.

2.5 Early Political Measures

to rule 'Bantu' populations. Indeed the 'Hamitic Hypothesis', widely shared at the time of the European penetration in the Great Lakes region, held that 'everything of value found in Africa was brought there by the Hamites, allegedly a branch of the Caucasian race'.[67] For instance, when the British explorer Speke arrived in the kingdom of Buganda with its sophisticated political organisation, he attributed this civilisation to pastoralists related to 'Hamitic Galla'. As the 'Hamites' seemed to be cattle breeders, pastoralism and its attributes were given an aura of cultural superiority.[68] The attraction of this hypothesis was that, in this vision, physical characteristics could be linked to mental capacities: the 'Hamites' were born to rule, and in theory they were entitled to a past and future almost as noble as their European 'cousins'.[69] This feeling of kinship with Europeans is well rendered by Jamoulle's description of the Tutsi: '*Ils n'ont du nègre que la couleur*'.[70]

In order to reconcile the Tutsi political monopoly with the needs of a modern and rational bureaucracy, from early on schooling was proposed to the chiefs of the future. Already during the occupation, Major De Clerck attempted to convince the chiefs and the court to send their young men to the schools created by the missions. The *mwami* and the high nobility resisted this as they considered the European education system as poison (*uburozi*) intent on destroying traditional values, particularly due to their Christian nature. De Clerck and the White Fathers explained to Musinga that the administration intended to appoint educated young men to positions of authority and that if the court refused to allow Tutsi boys from influential lineages to acquire the necessary skills, these functions would be given to schooled Hutu or Tutsi of low standing.[71] Musinga understood the danger and explained that his only objection was to the religious nature of the existing schools.

In response, in 1919, the administration created its own 'School for sons of chiefs' in Nyanza.[72] Unlike a similar school in Muramvya

---

[67] E. R. Sanders, 'The Hamitic Hypothesis: Its Origin and Functions in Time Perspective', *Journal of African History*, 1969, p. 521. As late as in 1933, Pagès referred to Rwanda as a 'Hamitic kingdom' and adhered to the thesis of a 'Hamitic invasion' (A. Pagès, *Un royaume hamite au centre de l'Afrique*, Brussels, Institut Royal Colonial Belge, 1933, p. 72).
[68] Sanders, 'The Hamitic Hypothesis', pp. 528–530.
[69] Linden, *Church and Revolution*, p. 2.
[70] 'The only thing they have in common with the "negro" is their colour' (M. Jamoulle, 'Notre mandat sur le Ruanda-Urundi', *Congo*, 1927, p. 487). The same ideological view of the Tutsi was expressed by de Lacger: '*Avant d'être nigritisés, ces hommes étaient bronzés*' ('Before becoming black, these men were tanned') (*Ruanda*, p. 56).
[71] Des Forges, *Defeat Is the Only Bad News*, p. 162.
[72] *Rapport 1920–1921*, p. 11.

(Urundi), this was exclusively reserved for Tutsi pupils.[73] The administration's preferences were made abundantly clear: in 1925, the *mwami* 'had graciously acceded to the desire of the resident to appoint young literate Tutsi to positions of authority on hills where the chief died without leaving a male descendant'.[74] Following the school in Nyanza, four more were created elsewhere in the country, all 'strictly reserved for sons of chiefs and notables of the Tutsi race'.[75]

As will be seen in Chapter 3, the Tutsi political monopoly was threatened for a short time in the coming years, but it eventually remained intact until the late 1950s. In conjunction, the imposition of central power and the generalisation of this monopoly have considerably increased ethnic resentment. As seen earlier, Cathy Newbury noted that before the introduction of central rule in Kinyaga during the second half of the nineteenth century, ethnic identity was of little importance. However, the introduction of central administrative structures brought contact with political institutions and social distinctions to a new level, making ethnic distinctions salient and rigidifying the Hutu–Tutsi classification.[76]

2.6   Conclusion

Though Belgium ended up with Ruanda-Urundi as a League of Nations mandate territory without being initially interested in incorporating it in its colonial empire, once acquired it did closely administer the country. For reasons similar to Germany before it, a system of indirect rule imposed itself almost naturally: a well-organised, almost European political organisation was present, even more so in Rwanda than in Burundi, and the Belgians simply did not have the human resources required to apply a regime of direct rule. However, the problems and contradictions inherent in indirect rule Belgian style soon appeared. An example of such contradictions lay in the taking of 'civilising measures', which included reinforcing the position of the *mwami* while at the same time weakening and eventually destroying his symbolic power base. This led to a dramatic shift of authority, as did the imposition of central rule to the entire country and the introduction of a uniform and 'rational' administration, even in places where the Nyiginya kingdom had no historical presence or legitimacy.

[73] Enrolment figures for both schools can be found in Lemarchand, *Rwanda and Burundi*, p. 75.
[74] *Rapport 1925*, p. 65.
[75] *Rapport 1929*, p. 62.
[76] Newbury, *The Cohesion of Oppression*, p. 11.

2.6 Conclusion

Together with this extension of the central kingdom's reach, the spreading of the Tutsi political monopoly, while the Hutu had held political office in the past, has greatly contributed to Hutu resentment. While we have seen that ethnic consciousness existed in Rwanda even before the Europeans' arrival, the German and Belgian administrations have considerably exacerbated this reality by rigidifying and racialising it, as will be shown in more detail in the next chapter.

Like the German presence before, the first years of the Belgian administration introduced a crucial critical juncture to Rwanda's political development by fundamentally altering the kingdom's functioning and legitimacy. It took these colonising powers hardly twenty years to transform beyond recognition a political system that had taken centuries to become what it was at the end of the nineteenth century. The next forty years were to be path dependent, until a new critical juncture occurred at the end of the 1950s.

3 Consolidating Colonial Rule

This chapter addresses the concrete application of the regime of indirect rule in Rwanda. As seen in the previous chapter, Belgium started with a vague and general concept that from the outset contained the germs of its central contradiction: respecting indigenous political institutions and practices while at the same time adapting and using them in its 'sacred mission of civilisation'. The introduction of this policy was to induce profound modifications to the functioning of the indigenous authorities and their relations with the population.

3.1 Destitution and Relegation of Musinga, Accession of Rudahigwa

The initial enthusiasm of the Belgian administration for the monarchy, the foundation of its policy of indirect rule, rapidly waned. While in 1925 the administration reported that 'the agreement between the king and the residency has been total',[1] the 1926 report noted that Musinga, 'king without energy, tired and grown old before his time, pathologically susceptible, is of an unbelievable credulity in divination, sorcery and bad omens, and submits himself blindly to his sorcerers' injunctions'.[2] At the time, the administration began considering the possibility of deposing Musinga, and even of putting an end to the monarchical system.

From 1930, the influential apostolic vicar Monsignor Classe, who until then had taken Musinga's defence, began actively advocating his removal. At the end of 1930, he published an article with an unequivocal conclusion:

It must be recognised that practically speaking, rather than being an element of union for the chiefs, and later an auxiliary of little value for the government, he has become for all practical purposes an element of discord, suspicion, and

---

[1] *Rapport 1925*, p. 66.
[2] *Rapport 1926*, p. 66.

3.1 Destitution of Musinga, Accession of Rudahigwa

embarrassment for all, Tutsi and Hutu, without any usefulness for the country, as well as – this is my intimate conviction – a great inconvenience to the government.[3]

This negative assessment was largely shared from the bottom – the Nyanza territorial administrator – to the top – Governor Postiaux – of the Belgian administration.[4]

Musinga was well aware of the threat, and Kagame writes that, following the advice of the *abiru*, he considered enthroning one of his sons as co-ruler in order for him to deal with the Belgians. The *mwami* agreed with this suggestion, but the queen mother opposed it energetically, claiming that kings with Yuhi as the dynastic name never reigned with their sons. According to Kagame, the real motive for her resistance was that the *abiru* had affirmed that a queen mother was not allowed to see the reign of her grandson and that she would have to commit suicide if this happened.[5]

The history of the deposition of Musinga, on 12 November 1931, has been extensively documented elsewhere and will only be briefly discussed here.[6] As there was no written legal provision on this issue, customary constitutional law had to be applied. However, that law did not know nor recognise a procedure for the destitution of a reigning king, which is unsurprising given the divine nature of the royal function. The act of authority committed by the Belgian administration was therefore illegal and effectively a coup d'état. The administration did not even try to provide a legal basis but only insisted on Musinga's bad behaviour 'that each day compromised the authority of the dynasty, precious foundation of the indigenous political organisation'.[7] The measure was also justified based on Belgium's obligations under international law: Musinga's mentality and behaviour were seen as obstacles to the fulfilment of obligations imposed by the mandate of the League of Nations.[8]

Therefore, Musinga left as he had come, by a palace revolution, although in this case it was a 'coup d'état of the whites', while that of Rucunshu had been indigenous. The succession was no more legal. The *abiru* were not involved, and the rule that required that the *mwami*

---

[3] L. P. Classe, 'Un triste Sire!', *L'Essor colonial et maritime*, No. 494–495, 21–25 December 1930.
[4] Their statements can be found in Reyntjens, *Pouvoir et droit*, p. 88.
[5] Kagame, *Un abrégé de l'histoire*, pp. 180–181.
[6] See for example de Lacger, *Ruanda*, pp. 521–538; Des Forges, *Defeat Is the Only Bad News*, pp. 211–240.
[7] *Rapport 1931*, p. 58.
[8] Ibid.

himself designate one of his sons as successor was not respected, as Musinga had not made a choice. The European kingmakers had diverging views: the administration preferred a docile and well-formed functionary, while the White Fathers wanted a good Christian.[9] Rudahigwa, a practising Catholic and the chief of Marangara, where the seat of the apostolic vicariate was situated, was made the successor. Contrary to the rules, his name was not made public by the *abiru*, and the investiture formulation made clear where the source of authority lay. Governor Voisin declared: 'Rudahigwa, by the designation of the king of Belgians, I proclaim you king of Rwanda.' Monsignor Classe indicated Rudahigwa's dynastic name: 'The title of your reign is Mutara, as required by the dynastic rule.'[10] It is not surprising that Rudahigwa was considered the '*mwami* of the whites': the usual cry '*umwami alimye*' (the king produces) changed into the more modest '*Rudahigwa aragabanye*' (Rudahigwa is invested).[11] This change in popular mood expresses the change of 1931 more than a long commentary.

Under the new king, the royalty continued to shed its sacred elements. Immediately after Rudahigwa's accession, the resident limited the presence at the court of the great chiefs to a single two weeks' stay per year. At the end of 1933, the *mwami* traded his traditional hut for a modern residence built for him by the administration, and he drove his car himself. His being a practicing Catholic was an enormous boost for the Church as it registered a huge increase in conversions after Rudahigwa's accession. In Church circles, this period of the building of a Christian kingdom was known as *La Tornade*. The creation of Rudahigwa's 'Christian kingdom in the heart of Africa' was symbolically confirmed when he consecrated Rwanda to Christ the King in 1946.[12] This occurred a mere fifty years after the coup of Rucunshu.

3.2 Consolidation of Tutsi Political Monopoly

We have seen that the application of the Hamitic Hypothesis justified reserving political office for Tutsi. However, this policy was threatened when the streamlining of the indigenous bureaucracy, discussed in the next section, was met with resistance by conservative Tutsi chiefs and sub-chiefs. This led the administration to attempt a radical reform in

---

[9] W. Kagambirwa, *Les autorités rwandaises face aux pouvoirs européens à Nyanza (1900–1946)*, Butare, Université Nationale du Rwanda, mémoire de licence, 1979, p. 47.
[10] A. Van Overschelde, *Un audacieux pacifique: Monseigneur Léon Paul Classe, apôtre du Rwanda*, Namur, Grands Lacs, 1948, p. 156.
[11] Kagambirwa, *Les autorités rwandaises*, p. 55.
[12] de Lacger, *Ruanda*, pp. 672–674.

3.2 Consolidation of Tutsi Political Monopoly

1927–1928. Only the Tutsi notables that were just to their subjects and favourable to Belgian policy were to be retained, while the others were to be replaced by Hutu, considered more honest and less resistant to change.[13] These intentions challenged the political monopoly and the inherited privileges of the Tutsi aristocracy and therefore threatened the regime of indirect rule, which required that the Belgian authorities respect the existing institutions.

Classe feared what he saw as the potentially revolutionary implications of this change of policy and took the defence of the ruling class against 'the oscillations and hesitations of the colonial administration toward the traditional hegemony of the high-born Tutsi'.[14] In a letter sent to resident Mortehan on 21 September 1927, Classe was very clear:

> If we place ourselves on a practical level and aim at the real interest of the country, with the Tutsi youth we have an incomparable element of progress (...). If one asks the Hutu whether they want to be ruled by commoners or aristocrats, their answer leaves no doubt. They prefer the Tutsi, for good reason. Born chiefs, they have the sense of command ... This is the secret of their settlement in the country and their domination of it.[15]

In 1930, Classe warned the administration in an often-cited article:

> The worst disservice the government could do to itself and to the country would be to eliminate the Tutsi caste. *Such a revolution would lead the country straight into anarchy and a heinous anti-European communism.* (...) Generally speaking, we will not have chiefs that are better, more intelligent, more active, better capable of understanding progress, and even more accepted by the people, than the Tutsi.[16]

This passage is of course explicitly racist but only represents one part of Classe's reasoning. The other, less spectacular, part is not often quoted. The apostolic vicar continued by saying that 'however, from this I would not conclude *that all chiefs must come exclusively from the Tutsi, to the total exclusion of the Hutu*'.[17] His conclusion: 'Exclusivism is wrong and used with perseverance it becomes a real danger.'[18] Even with this nuance, the message was widely perceived as a vigorous plea in favour of a political monopoly for the Tutsi.

---

[13] G. Mbonimana, 'Christianisation indirecte et cristallisation des clivages ethniques au Rwanda (1925–31)', *Enquêtes et Documents d'Histoire africaine*, 1978, p. 152.
[14] de Lacger, *Ruanda*, p. 522.
[15] Ibid., p. 523.
[16] L. P. Classe, 'Pour moderniser le Ruanda', *L'Essor colonial et maritime*, No. 489, 4 December 1930 (italics in the original text).
[17] Ibid. (italics in the original text).
[18] Ibid.

Such an authoritative voice had a particularly important impact in 1930. It put an end to the 'oscillations and hesitations' of the administering power that unreservedly engaged on the road set out by Classe. All Hutu notables were removed from office and replaced by Tutsi while an active policy in favour of the protection and reinforcement of Tutsi hegemony was vigorously pursued. Classe supported it consequentially, as an example shows. Around 1935, because of his outstanding qualities, the local White Fathers and the territorial agent proposed a Hutu, Kidahiro, nephew of the last *umuhinza* of Bushiru, as the successor of an incompetent Tutsi sub-chief. This proposal was rejected by Classe, who 'feared creating a precedent'.[19] By thus barring the access of Hutu to even lower political functions, which they had sometimes occupied in the traditional system, the Belgian administration and the Church accentuated ethnic divisions. There was however a bonus: the threat of being replaced by Hutu convinced the Tutsi notables that it was in their interest to cooperate with the administration.

Belgium's ethnic policy was reinforced by this episode. Its consequences went beyond the consolidation of the Tutsi political monopoly. Quoting figures for 1958, Munyangaju showed that the monopoly was much more restricted. Among the forty-five chiefs (all Tutsi), only six of Rwanda's eighteen clans were represented. Tutsi lineages of only two clans, the Banyiginya and Bega, shared 80 per cent of all those functions; the reigning lineage of the Bahindiro alone occupied almost 30 per cent of them.[20] Supposing that, at the end of the nineteenth century, there were about 50,000 Tutsi adult males and around 2,500 political functions (chiefs, sub-chiefs, notables at court, diverse agents), this means that Rwandan society was ruled by merely 5 per cent of all Tutsi.[21] In other words, while political power was potentially a Tutsi monopoly, its effective exercise was in the hands of a handful of lineages.

3.3 Bureaucratisation of the Chiefly Function

The bureaucratisation of the customary authorities had been a gradual process, often conducted by the Belgian administration as a response to specific needs and challenges. The end result of this policy, deployed during the second half of the 1920s and the first half of the 1930s, was that yesterday's regional and local lords became indigenous civil servants of the European political and administrative apparatus. Like

---

[19] Mbonimana, 'Christianisation indirecte', p. 133.
[20] A. Munyangaju, *L'actualité politique au Rwanda*, s.l., s.ed., 1959, pp. 20–21.
[21] Linden, *Church and Revolution*, p. 18.

3.3 Bureaucratisation of the Chiefly Function

other reforms introduced by Belgium in the name of efficacy and financial viability, these changes contributed towards deepening the cleavages between ethnic groups and regions. In their efforts to radically transform the traditional order, the colonial authorities undermined the essential structure of norms, statuses and roles that once held Rwandan society together.[22] This fundamental contradiction of indirect rule as applied in Rwanda, and therefore of the position of customary authorities, is well summarised in the formulation of the political programme by Governor Ryckmans: 'Maintain public peace by leaning on the authority of the traditional chiefs: but *impose* on them, by *orders* and not merely by advice, the indispensable reforms.'[23]

3.3.1 Abolition of the Triple Chiefly Hierarchy

We have seen in the Introduction that three chiefs represented the *mwami* at the local/regional level: the *abatware b'ingabo*, the *abanyabutaka* and the *abanyamukenke*. From 1926, the administration set out to abolish this three-layered structure, which it considered 'irrational' and difficult to manage, but it did not realise that this reform was to have a profound impact on social relations, in particular on the Hutu's status of dependence. Unable to comprehend that three authorities could co-rule in the same geographic space, the administration aimed to achieve a situation more in line with European administrative concepts. The functions of the three chiefs were therefore merged into one. In most cases, the *umutware b'ingabo* became the sole chief, because the denomination *umutware* (chief) was seen as referring to the army chief.[24]

This reform had major consequences, well beyond those anticipated by the Belgian authorities, who merely saw this as a technical rationalisation. Social relations between ethnic groups were greatly impacted by a rapid evolution towards a more authoritarian system centred around a single provincial ruler.[25] Indeed, because before the reform the Tutsi authorities were permanently engaged in a struggle to protect or increase their power, they were attentive to complaints about competing chiefs, a situation that allowed Hutu to secure the support of one chief in their conflicts with another one. Therefore this system protected rather than threatened the Hutu. Thus, this reform not only increased

---

[22] R. Lemarchand, 'Rwanda', in R. Lemarchand (Ed.), *African Kingships in Perspective: Political Change and Modernization in Monarchical Settings*, London, Frank Cass, 1977, p. 79.
[23] Ryckmans, 'Le problème politique', p. 410. Italics in the original text.
[24] Kagame, *Un abrégé de l'histoire*, p. 188.
[25] Lemarchand, 'Rwanda', p. 78.

the possibility for Tutsi notables to rule in a more oppressive way but – more importantly in the longer term – it diminished the likelihood that the Hutu considered the Tutsi, or at least some of them, as their protectors or allies. The administration showed its inability to understand the normative concepts on which the relations between the chiefs and their subjects were based. The consequence was that the additional burdens imposed upon the masses made the perpetuation of traditional obligations all the more difficult to endure.[26]

3.3.2 Stabilisation of Political Functions

As seen in Chapter 2, the court was forbidden to appoint or dismiss chiefs without informing the administration. As the *mwami* often ignored this directive, in 1922 the administration announced that notables who accepted an appointment without the approval of the resident were liable to a jail sentence. A similar authorisation was required for the appointment and removal of subaltern authorities by the chiefs.[27] These measures meant that the administration effectively controlled appointments and removals at all levels of the indigenous system. The king's intervention was needed only to affix the seal of legitimacy.

The impact of these measures was considerable. They diminished the insecurity, instability and absenteeism of the chiefs who beforehand were practically obliged to spend much of their time at the *ibwami* (the royal court at Nyanza) in order to avoid rivals causing them to lose the *mwami*'s favours.[28] This state of affairs was not only harmful to the good administration of the chiefdom but it also had an effect the Belgians realised only later. As the important notables were so often at the court, they delegated their authority to lesser officials. Wishing to escape the obligations imposed by the administration, the latter in turn delegated the authority to even lesser subordinates. In the end, the Belgian territorial administrators ended up giving orders to obscure clients without power.[29] In 1923, the Gisenyi administrator noted: 'Certain office holders were the victims of the initial lie by seeing themselves replaced automatically by those they had deliberately put forward as a façade.'[30]

---

[26] Ibid.
[27] de Lacger, *Ruanda*, p. 490.
[28] *Rapport 1925*, p. 64.
[29] Former territorial administrator René Bourgeois offers a concrete example of this situation: Bushako, the titular chief of Bugoyi from 1898 to 1929, almost constantly resided in Nyanza; he had himself represented by Mulangira, Kiromba, Rwakadigi, Mbishibibishi and Gace, 'all straw men as incapable as parasitic' (R. Bourgeois, *Banyarwanda et Barundi, Vol. 2, La coutume*, Brussels, Institut royal colonial belge, 1954, p. 15).
[30] *Historique et chronologie*, pp. 23–24.

This difficulty of dealing with 'real' chiefs was by no means typical for Rwanda. Writing on the Tendana in Ghana, Margery Perham found that many chiefs 'feared for the effects of contact with these impatient revolutionary white men, and they sent unimportant agents to face the music. These became "chiefs".'[31]

In order to diminish the intrigues and to guarantee a more permanent and effective exercise of their function, the administration considered it necessary that the chiefs limited their stays at the court.[32] We have seen that after his accession King Mutara Rudahigwa implemented this instruction by a decision that contributed to his popularity but at the same time diminished the prestige of the royal function. In 1932, he drew up a list of courtiers and limited their stays at the *ibwami* to two weeks per year. By doing this he isolated himself from networks of influence that had attained a high level of cohesion. While becoming more accessible to the population, he abandoned several attributes of the ancestral royalty and became more vulnerable to European power, which became his principal partner.[33] This decision gravely affected the very conception of the royal function, of which the relations between the *mwami* and the great notables and the possibility for the king to play one notable against another were important elements. It also confirmed that effective power had shifted towards the Belgian authorities.

3.3.3 Territorial Reorganisation

The aim of the territorial reorganisation, which began in 1926, was the simplification, uniformisation and 'rationalisation' of the indigenous political structure. It was also linked to the extension of the reach of the central kingdom discussed earlier. The reorganisation started with the smallest political command unit, the *igikingi* (plural *ibikingi*). At the time of the reform, the *ibikingi* were small domains encompassing a hill or even just part of a hill inhabited by a few households. They were handed out in large numbers at the request of the *mwami* or at the initiative of chiefs or sub-chiefs, who thus created loyal followers or clients. The administration considered this excessive fragmentation of chiefdoms as politically unpractical but also found that it increased the obligations imposed on Hutu peasants.[34] In 1926, the *mwami* was forced to renounce the creation of new *ibikingi*, while existing ones becoming

---

[31] M. Perham, 'Some Problems of Indirect Rule in Africa', *Journal of the African Society*, 1934, Supplement to No. 2 of April 1934, p. 7.
[32] *Rapport 1930*, p. 58.
[33] Kagambirwa, *Les autorités rwandaises*, pp. 56–57.
[34] *Rapport 1926*, p. 67.

vacant due to the death of the holder were to be incorporated in the sub-chiefdom. All remaining *ibikingi* were abolished in 1930.

This was just the first step. In order to remedy the problems caused by the small size and often non-contiguous nature of the remaining political units, the administration started a policy of merging chiefdoms, with the aim of achieving a situation where chiefs were to become 'the pivots of a genuine administrative decentralisation'.[35] The reorganisation was achieved in 1932. There were then 65 provincial chiefs exercising authority over an average of 5,500 taxpayers and 1,043 sub-chiefs with an average of 343 taxpayers.[36] This simplification of the administrative structure, with just two layers between the *mwami* and the population, caused a hecatomb among the notables. Ten chiefs and 316 sub-chiefs were dismissed, and 968 political units (small sub-chiefdoms and *ibikingi*) were abolished. In total, 1,278 sub-chiefs and *banyabikingi* had disappeared, which is more than half those in function before the organisation.[37] Together with the abolition of the triple chiefly hierarchy and the regulation of customary performances (shown later), the effect of this reorganisation was to impoverish a considerable number of Tutsi and force them to work the land.[38]

3.3.4 Training of Customary Cadres

I have mentioned the training of cadres in passing in Chapter 2 when addressing the monopolisation of political office in the hands of Tutsi. The schooling of indigenous cadres was a constant concern in the administration's striving for bureaucratisation. As seen earlier, the 'School for sons of chiefs' (*Ecole pour fils de chefs*) created in 1919 immediately became successful after the resident explained to the *mwami* that the administration intended to increasingly appoint literate young cadres capable of assimilating European ideas to gradually replace the old notables. Musinga registered his three eldest sons in the school.[39]

The first class of thirty sons of chiefs came out in 1923, and they followed an internship of between six months and a year in a territorial administration post where they assisted the administrator in tasks that involved contacts with the population: census, tax collection and,

---

[35] *Rapport 1927*, p. 37.
[36] This regrouping continued in a more modest fashion during later years. By 1959 there were 45 chiefs and 559 sub-chiefs.
[37] Precise figures can be found in Reyntjens, *Pouvoir et droit*, pp. 122–123.
[38] M. d'Hertefelt, 'Stratification sociale et structure politique au Rwanda', *La Revue Nouvelle*, 1960, p. 451.
[39] Des Forges, *Defeat Is the Only Bad News*, p. 162.

above all, the settlement of disputes.[40] The aim of the administration was to gradually constitute 'a breeding ground for candidates imbued with civilising conceptions, among whom we will be able to select the ruling elements of the future'.[41] This policy soon bore fruits. At the end of 1935, 60 per cent of the chiefs and sub-chiefs were literate, which allowed the administrators to give instructions by circular letter rather than to convey them orally to each notable.[42] From 1929, the Nyanza school was progressively replaced by the *Groupe scolaire* of Astrida, where educational levels were higher and pupils developed a disdain for the conservative aristocracy at the centre of the royal court. We will see that this created divisions within the Tutsi elites when revolutionary dynamics unravelled in the late 1950s.

Literacy was not the only consideration. The administration also preferred to deal with Christian local authorities, a message that was well received: by 1928, nearly all pupils at the Nyanza school were catechist or Christian.[43] Alphabetisation went hand in hand with Christianisation, at first aimed at the local authorities: in 1936, when 78 per cent of the chiefs and 84 per cent of the sub-chiefs were Catholics, only 18 per cent of the ordinary population was converted.[44] This policy was in conformity with the directives of the White Fathers' founder Cardinal Lavigerie, who instructed to Christianise a country through its chiefs, a policy that Mbonimana called 'indirect Christianisation' in a parallel with indirect rule.[45]

3.3.5 The New Chiefs

The profound modifications that affected the functioning of the customary authorities were consolidated in the programme on indigenous policy made public in September 1930 by Ruanda-Urundi governor Charles Voisin. However, this formulation of what became known as the 'Programme Voisin' did not add anything new to policies that existed and had been outlined on several occasions. It however had the advantage of coherently presenting the steps made between the occupation in 1916 and the situation fifteen years later.

The customary authorities had increasingly become civil servants of an indigenous structure at the service of the Belgian administration.

---

[40] *Rapport 1925*, p. 65.
[41] *Rapport 1927*, p. 37.
[42] *Rapport 1935*, p. 73.
[43] Des Forges, *Defeat Is the Only Bad News*, p. 213.
[44] Linden, *Church and Revolution*, p. 195.
[45] Mbonimana, 'Christianisation indirecte', p. 136.

Other elements reinforced this tendency, chief among them the turning into wages of the chiefs' and sub-chiefs' revenues. New administrative functions imposed on them in addition to customary performances made the chiefs' authority heavier to carry for their subjects. In a comparative study of indirect rule across Africa, this bureaucratisation made Margery Perham conclude that 'it makes little difference whether the Chief was originally a natural authority, or is merely an appointed agent'.[46]

After a period of limited administrative ambitions that ended during the second half of the 1920s, the Belgians started to transform the traditional system into a bureaucratic European-style administration. What had been a hierarchy of hereditary rulers became one recruited on the basis of skills and competences, increasingly measured by the level of formal education. The chiefs' income derived from salaries rather than tribute,[47] and they were appointed, promoted, transferred and revoked in an administrative vein. It was the chief's and sub-chief's function that underwent the most profound change, as the administration imposed performances that were contrary to their traditional functions and duties. Lloyd Fallers observed in Busoga what was, mutatis mutandis, applicable to Rwanda:

Traditional Soga political institutions emphasised the value of particular rights and obligations, a pattern which Parsons has described by the terms *particularism* and *functional diffuseness*. (...) The value system associated with bureaucratic organisation is in most respects in opposition to this pattern. Here the guiding norm is (Weber) 'straightforward duty without regard to personal considerations'. Relations in such a system are to be, in Parsons' terms, *universalistic* and *functionally specific*.[48]

The roles played by office holders were indeed often contradictory, and traditional expectations clashed with bureaucratic ones, leaving them in a vulnerable position towards both their subjects and the colonial administration.

The last conflict was one of allegiance. Though under customary constitutional law the chiefs and sub-chiefs depended on the *mwami*, in reality they depended on the European administration. They had to constantly seek a balance between their two sources of authority, with

---

[46] Perham, 'Some Problems of Indirect Rule', p. 11.
[47] At least this was the theory. In reality, chiefs and their subordinates continued to demand tribute in the form of labour, cattle, firewood or various payments from their subjects (examples of such illegal or informal extractions can be found in Newbury, *The Cohesion of Oppression*, pp. 169–171).
[48] L. Fallers, 'The Predicament of the Modern African Chief: An Instance from Uganda', *American Anthropologist*, 1955, p. 290 (italics in original text).

the Belgian rulers continuously gaining importance for their survival. Attitude, functions, loyalty – the chiefs were constantly caught in conflicts caused by a mosaic of contradictory obligations and constraints. At the end of the road, while the Belgian administration and the Catholic Church had supported the position of the ruling class, at the same time they had made it totally dependent on that support. This was the inevitable consequence of the will to replace a traditional domination by a bureaucratic domination, in a Weberian sense, at all levels.

3.4 The Situation of the Hutu Masses

Next to the stabilisation and 'rationalisation' of the indigenous political institutions, the second aim of the Belgian administration was to improve the living conditions of the population, in particular of the Hutu, who were seen as *taillables et corvéables à merci* (unendingly cuttable and drudgery). The idea was to make support for the Tutsi elites conditional on the efficacious management of the country and on support for alleviating the Hutu's fate. The Belgians hoped that their social and economic situation could be bettered without jeopardising Tutsi political power.

Already in 1917, the resident had introduced the first measures in favour of the Hutu: if a Tutsi seized a Hutu's harvest, he had to reimburse him in double; a Tutsi having his cattle graze in a Hutu's field was to repay double the damage caused; notables were forbidden to claim performances not provided for by custom.[49] This text obviously raises two observations. Firstly, the formulation in strictly antagonistic ethnic terms is striking and reminiscent of the Hamitic Hypothesis: the administration reasoned in the framework of the simple stereotype that all Tutsi were lords and cattle breeders and all Hutu were subjects and peasants. Secondly, the respect for these rules must have been difficult to impose in the field, particularly if the territorial administrators, having to at the same time protect the weak and consolidate the power of the strong, generally opted for the easiest way, namely supporting the authority of the strong.[50] In July 1917, the *mwami* was forced to issue another important decision. The surface of land attributed to Hutu households was to be doubled, thanks in particular to recuperation of marshy soils used until then by cattle owners as the pasture for their herds during the dry season.[51]

---

[49] Letter No. 791/A/53, *Historique et chronologie*, pp. 22–23.
[50] Des Forges, *Defeat Is the Only Bad News*, p. 159.
[51] De Lacger, *Ruanda*, p. 466.

It was mainly in the area of customary performances that the administration attempted to improve the situation of the Hutu. This was a complex matter as at the beginning of the colonial occupation, there were many varied charges, duties, taxes and labour obligations, some of which were quite recent, and they all played a role in the social and political arsenal. The charges of *imponoke*,[52] *indabukirano*,[53] and *abatora*,[54] which all gave rise to abuse, were simply abolished in 1924.[55] It was also decided that the tribute owed to the *mwami*, *ikoro*, would no longer be recovered by his own traditional tax collectors sent directly by Musinga to every household but would be collected by the chiefs and sub-chiefs. This measure aimed at avoiding people paying more than what custom strictly imposed on them. Indeed the administration had realised that the *mwami*'s collectors sometimes claimed more than double the tax customarily due.[56] In 1931 a limited number of duties were recognised and organised, including the *ikoro*, which was replaced by the payment of one franc per year, and the *ibihunikwa*,[57] of which the tariff was clearly determined.[58] In 1934, all charges other than those consisting of labour were replaced by taxes collected together with the colonial head tax.

The administration was much more cautious in handling *corvée* labour owed by the Hutu to the chiefs and sub-chiefs. We have seen that *uburetwa* was introduced in the late nineteenth century under Rwabugiri and that it hardly existed in the peripheral parts of the kingdom. At the beginning of the Belgian occupation, every household (*urugo*) in the central kingdom had to perform labour two days out of every five (the Rwandan week), an equivalent of 146 days per year. *Uburetwa* was reduced by forty-two days in 1924 to reach two days out of seven (the European week).[59] In 1927, the residence decided a new reduction of labour duties, to one day out of seven per household, or a maximum of thirteen days per year for each male adult (*homme adulte valide* – HAV).[60] The administration claimed that this reduction

---

[52] Cattle claimed by a Tutsi from his clients when his herds were decimated by extraordinary mortality.
[53] Cattle and other exceptional demands imposed on subjects at the occasion of assuming command by a notable.
[54] Cutting of bananas in subjects' fields for the provisioning of a notable.
[55] *Ordre de service* No. 2213/Org. of 26 December 1924, *Historique et Chronologie*, p. 24.
[56] *Rapport 1924*, p. 7.
[57] Duties in the form of foodstuffs, objects and special duties in favour of chiefs and sub-chiefs.
[58] *Ordre de service* No. 2678/Org. of 24 December 1931, *Historique et Chronologie*, pp. 26–27.
[59] *Rapport 1924*, p. 7; *Rapport 1925*, p. 59.
[60] *Rapport 1927*, pp. 37–38; *Historique et chronologie*, p. 23.

was a considerable progress, but we will later see that, in actual fact, this reform also resulted in an additional burden for many Hutu men, because what was previously an obligation imposed on a group now became an individual one imposed on every male adult. In addition, the administration extended the application of *uburetwa* uniformly across the country, including where this practice did not previously exist. This caused considerable resistance, particularly in the north, where Hutu lineages refused to submit to *uburetwa*. Where this reluctance was coupled with the refusal to pay European taxes or to perform *akazi* (*corvée* labour for the administration), leaders of recalcitrant lineages were sometimes arrested and exiled. Often such measures were unable to break these groups' resistance.[61]

At the time, the administration was convinced that it was not possible to further extend the reduction of labour obligations. It was convinced that the authority of chiefs and sub-chiefs was based on their customary right to duties under the form of labour, without which the indigenous authorities would have 'neither prestige nor power'.[62] However, in politics things often move faster than anticipated or hoped. The 1938 report still underlined that 'while the suppression of these performances remains the ultimate goal, it will not be achieved for long'.[63] At the end of 1944 it was decided to allow the facultative replacement of labour by a monetary payment. Given the huge success of this measure, in 1949 the replacement by a tax was made general.[64]

The history of the suppression of *uburetwa* is interesting from several points of view. First, seeking uniformity, the administration attempted to generalise a recently created 'custom', even where it practically did not exist, while at the same time wanting to protect the population against excesses. Wishing to safeguard what the administration saw as the existing traditional order, including in northern, western and eastern areas where *uburetwa* was all but traditional, for a long time it resisted pressures for changes in the regime of labour performances. It was then forced in a brief period of time to accept the abolition of a custom earlier considered essential for the social and political order. Second, the evolution of *uburetwa* is also a good illustration of the bureaucratisation of the chiefly function discussed earlier, as a customary charge characterised by a personal relation between the ruler and the ruled was replaced by a tax, which is a means of bureaucratic management. At the close of this

---

[61] Des Forges, *Defeat Is the Only Bad News*, pp. 198–199.
[62] *Rapport 1927*, p. 37.
[63] *Rapport 1938*, p. 75.
[64] *Historique et chronologie*, p. 29.

evolution, many obligations owed to the king, the chiefs and the sub-chiefs had disappeared or were replaced by taxation. In the next chapter, we will see how the last formal link of personal dependence, *ubuhake*, disappeared.

Although the Belgian administration claimed to reduce the charges imposed on the rural masses, in reality the colonial period was one of heavy burdens, at least until the end of the 1940s. The first was taxation, used by all colonial powers to force the populations to integrate the monetary economy and produce goods and services. Following its introduction by Germany in 1914, a head tax of 3.5 francs per HAV was imposed in 1917, but the administration also burdened the population with other obligations. One of them was the already mentioned *akazi*, a Swahili word for non-remunerated work of public interest, mainly the building and maintaining of roads, work that could take up to sixty days per year. Other colonial obligations were defined as 'works undertaken in the interest of communities' and 'works imposed by the European authorities in the interest of the workers themselves'. These included labour on plantations, the culture of compulsory crops, reforestation, anti-erosion measures and campaigns aimed at the destruction of harmful animals.[65] These measures were all useful, but although taken in the general interest, they were introduced at a time of considerable mutations, more particularly from an economy of subsistence and exchange to a monetary economy.

Contrary to the official discourse, René Lemarchand concluded that the situation of the Hutu masses was worse under Belgian administration than at any time in the past.[66] For his part, Linden found that 'the quality of peasant life was little changed by the new *uburetwa* regulations, they merely freed the Hutu for more onerous *akazi* labour for the Belgians. The weak and unprotected would end up with both.'[67] The hardships that cumulated under colonial (and the court's and chiefs') policies were reflected in large-scale movements of permanent or temporary migration to Congo and Uganda. As will be seen in the next chapter, these frustrations contributed to creating the conditions for revolution. On the other hand, there is no denying that the introduction of monetary taxes and of cash crops, mainly coffee, had objectively contributed to the emancipation of some Hutu, who were progressively liberated from exclusive dependence on the economy of the cow.

---

[65] More details can be found in Reyntjens, *Pouvoir et droit*, pp. 138–139.
[66] R. Lemarchand, 'The Coup in Rwanda', in R. I. Rotberg, A. A. Mazrui (Eds.), *Protest and Power in Black Africa*, New York, Oxford University Press, 1970, p. 889.
[67] Linden, *Church and Revolution*, p. 187.

As will be seen in the next chapter, monetary revenue gave emerging Hutu elites the confidence and the economic base needed to envisage the rupture of personal clientship links.[68]

3.5 The Consolidation of the Indigenous Political Organisation

Until 1943, the indigenous political organisation was based on a single sentence contained in article 4 of law-ordinance No. 2/5 of 6 April 1917 discussed in Chapter 2.[69] Only by law-ordinance No. 347/A.I.M.O. of 4 October 1943 did Belgium define its indigenous policy in organic terms. A brief discussion of this text allows one to assess the political evolution during a quarter century of Belgian presence. What the text in reality did was to give a legal basis to a large number of powers the administering authority attributed to itself in a piecemeal fashion. It did not create anything new but recognised an existing structure and established powers by giving legal life to a de facto situation that resulted from operational measures of the local administration throughout the years.[70]

The 1943 law-ordinance first recognised the legal existence of indigenous political entities and authorities: the country (*pays*) headed by a supreme customary chief called *mwami*, the chiefdom (*chefferie*) led by a chief, and the sub-chiefdom (*sous-chefferie*) headed by a sub-chief. The country, chiefdom and sub-chiefdom were to be governed in conformity with custom, subject to two limitations, namely the provisions of the law-ordinance itself and the principle that 'custom shall not be contrary to provisions of public law, or legal or regulatory provisions aiming at replacing custom by other rules' (article 30). Although quoted as the first normative source, custom clearly was just complementary as it was to give way to contrary legal or regulatory instruments. In a similar vein, the customary authorities were designated by custom, however under the condition of the explicit agreement of the administering authority. The *mwami* and the chiefs had to be invested by the governor, the sub-chiefs by the resident.

The reduction of the indigenous authorities to the level of executing agents of the Belgian administration is also striking when considering

---

[68] A. L. Latham-Koenig, 'Ruanda-Urundi on the Threshold of Independence', *The World Today*, 1962, pp. 289–290.
[69] As a reminder: 'Under the direction of the resident, the Sultans exercise their political and judicial powers to the extent and in the way determined by indigenous custom and the instructions of the royal commissioner.'
[70] A more detailed discussion of this law-ordinance can be found in Reyntjens, *Pouvoir et droit*, pp. 143–148.

the duties imposed on them. Indeed, all their tasks were functions of support for or implementation of decisions of the administration, as was made clear by the provision in article 44 that these duties were executed 'following the requisitions and instructions of the competent territorial authority'. The funding needed for the fulfilment of these duties was closely scrutinised: the use of the *caisse du pays* (land budget) was ensured by the *mwami* under the resident's control, that of the chiefdom (*caisse de la chefferie*) by the chief under the control of the territorial administrator (article 65). As will be seen in the conclusion of this chapter, as they developed over the years the relations between the Belgian administration and the indigenous authorities can hardly be considered in tune with the policy of indirect rule as formulated when Belgium first occupied the country. Gahama's findings for Burundi apply mutatis mutandis also to Rwanda: 'The time of the "distributing" chiefs had gone, to be replaced by the "managing" chiefs. During the 1930s, the real chief was without doubt the territorial administrator'.[71]

3.6 The Dual Administration

After having looked at the indigenous political organisation and the impact of Belgian rule on its functioning, I briefly address the organisation of the colonial administration and its relations with the indigenous one. As seen earlier, the Act of 21 August 1925 provided for a governor of Ruanda-Urundi (also vice governor general of the Belgian Congo and Ruanda-Urundi), who was represented by a resident in Rwanda and one in Burundi. There was no text on the territorial organisation until 1932, when ten territories (*territoires*) were formally established under the command of territorial administrators (*administrateurs de territoire*). The functions of the Belgian administrative authorities were the same as the corresponding ones in the Belgian Congo.

The duties and powers of the territorial administrators were very wide and their means limited. Among other things they were judge, public prosecutor, bailiff, prison chief, notary, registrar, commander of the army detachment, agricultural extension agent, tax collector, census agent, territorial accountant, budget manager, geometer and cartographer, cemetery guard, social animator and much more.[72] In light of the limited number of personnel on the ground (an average of two or three

---

[71] Gahama, *Le Burundi*, p. 142.
[72] A survey of functions and duties can be found in Cl. Van Leeuw, *L'administration territoriale au Congo Belge et au Ruanda-Urundi: Fondements institutionnels et expérience vécue 1912–1960*, Dissertation *Licence en Philosophie et Lettres (Histoire)*, Louvain-la-Neuve, Université catholique de Louvain, 1981, pp. 87–106.

per territory in the 1930s) and the fact that the administrators had to spend on average two weeks per month of 'presence in rural areas' away from the territory's office (*jours de brousse*), the demands of the function were obvious. Former administrators described the territorial staff as

active, very itinerant – a particular characteristic of the Belgian territorial administration –, interested more in concrete realisations than in purely political or judicial action, very direct in his interventions, generally benevolent, a bit short-sighted. Overall it was an excellent personnel. His mobility and action proneness distinguished him from the imperial 'detachment' of our British neighbours in the North who sometimes chided at our ways of dealing with everything in indigenous matters, something they called a 'grand mum administration'.[73]

The active intervention by the territorial administration in indigenous matters was dual: positive, by imposing obligations and issuing prohibitions; negative, by vetoing decisions taken at the different levels of indigenous decision-making by the *mwami*, the chiefs or the sub-chiefs. We are far away from the formulation by the founder of the policy of indirect rule, Lord Lugard: 'There are not two sets or rulers, British and native, working either separately or in co-operation, but a single government in which the native chiefs have well defined duties and an acknowledged status equally with the British official. Their duties should never conflict and overlap as little as possible.'[74] Morris observed a similar departure from theory in Uganda: '[Governor] Mitchell was insistent that the right to give advice [to the king of Buganda] should be coupled with the right to ensure that such an advice was put into effect. Advice which must be followed is, however, scarcely distinguishable from a command.'[75]

3.7 Conclusion

The contradictions of a policy of indirect rule have never been resolved, and White has rightly observed that 'the classical concept of indirect rule might be said to contain the seeds of its own destruction'.[76] While at the time of the occupation, Belgium thought it necessary to

---

[73] Lebart, Mupangu, 'La "politique indigène" de la Belgique', p. 470.
[74] Lugard (Lord), *The Dual Mandate in British Tropical Africa*, 1st ed., Edinburgh–London, William Blackwood, 1922, 5th ed., London, Frank Cass, 1965, p. 203.
[75] H. F. Morris, 'Sir Philip Mitchell and "Protected Rule" in Buganda', *Journal of African History*, 1972, p. 309.
[76] C. M. N. White, 'Indirect Rule', in R. Apthorpe (Ed.), *From Tribal Rule to Modern Government*, Lusaka, Rhodes-Livingstone Institute for Social Research, 13th Conference Proceedings, 1959, p. 195.

recognise the existing hierarchy, it also wanted to modify, if 'with a cautious hand', its structure and functioning in order to make it into an instrument of 'civilisation'. When the Belgian administration used the term 'rationalisation' in the Weberian sense, this was opposed to the 'traditional' or 'magic-religious' ways characteristic of the old Rwanda kingdom.

Although it was never officially abandoned, by the end of the 1920s indirect rule had effectively ceased to exist, as can be clearly seen in the 1930 report of the Rwanda residency:

> This political activity *can no longer be called indirect rule*. Today the administration deals with every detail of implementation, is in constant contact with all sub-chiefs, controls their activities, and regularly intervenes to have replaced those whose incompetence, inertia or bad will impede the country's development. Without this *direct and efficient intervention*, our civilising mission would be constantly sabotaged by the dominant caste which is only interested in safeguarding a feudal system of which it profited and for the reform of which Musinga has never given the slightest help.[77]

Although these considerations are clearly in part inspired by the discontent prevailing at the time concerning *mwami* Musinga, this extract is very telling. It marked the end of the progressive burial of the policy of indirect rule. While the 1925 report described its virtues in almost lyrical terms inspired by Ryckmans (see Section 3.3), the 1926 one underlined that 'if left alone, the chiefs show nonchalant and arbitrary behaviour';[78] in 1927 one reads that 'this organisation needs reform and adaptation';[79] from 1930, although it is noted that no essential modification had been made to the policy previously applied,[80] all references to the merits of indirect rule disappeared. This evolution was confirmed and in a way made official by the law-ordinance of 1943. Giving a legal stamp to an existing situation, it left practically no autonomous power to the indigenous political authorities, from the *mwami* down to the chiefs and sub-chiefs, who had become agents of transmission and execution.

The contradiction inherent in a policy of indirect rule, on the one hand 'respecting' the indigenous organisation while on the other 'using' it in the 'civilising mission', was also found elsewhere. Thus in his authoritative *Native Administration in the British African Territories*, Lord Hailey noted that

---

[77] Résidence du Ruanda, *Rapport annuel 1930*, Africa Archive, RA/RU 2 (54), p. 121 (italics added).
[78] *Rapport 1926*, p. 66.
[79] *Rapport 1927*, p. 37.
[80] *Rapport 1930*, p. 57.

3.7 Conclusion

if originally there was some difference between [direct and indirect rule] in principle, there is today far less distinction in practice. (...) Those governments (...) which have relied in principle on the use of traditional institutions are seen to have so transformed them in the process that Africans of a past generation might find it difficult to recognise them. (...) Custom ceases (...) to be recognised as custom when it is stamped with the government seal.[81]

In Rwanda, another element played out that was to show its full impact in the 1950s, as will be seen in the next chapter. In a political organisation that was centralised and put to use by both the indigenous dominant group and the Belgian administration, indirect rule had a dual effect: it reinforced the 'dual consensus',[82] namely the traditional consensus linking the population to the Tutsi elites and the colonial consensus linking these elites to the European rulers, while at the same time extending the authority of the Tutsi elites to regions where it had not been recognised in the past.[83] The colonial deal struck between these two rulers ensured the continuation of power to traditional authorities and their support for, or at least non-resistance to, European overrule, which was shielded, in part thanks to this tacit pact, from the effects of African nationalism until the end of the 1950s.[84]

A characteristic Rwanda shared with all colonial territories was its executive nature. Administrative agents controlled and managed not only the bureaucratic organisation but also the legislative and judicial functions. The structure of the administrative hierarchy was the effective constitution.[85] Both the indigenous and colonial political organisations concentrated power, ignored the principle of separation of powers and the elective practice, and observed fundamental rights to a very limited extent. Both were paternalistic and authoritarian. As will be seen in Chapter 5, just like elsewhere in Africa, these characteristics continued to prevail after independence.

As it further built on the political and administrative principles followed by the Germans and continued during the regime of the military occupation, the phase of colonial consolidation was path dependent. That said, for both the political elites and the ordinary citizens, this period heralded more profound changes than the previous one. The era

---

[81] Lord Hailey, *Native Administration in the British African Territories*, London, H.M.S.O., 1950–1953, Vol. IV, p. 36.
[82] As argued earlier, these consensus were to a large extent apparent rather than real.
[83] R. Lemarchand, 'L'influence des systèmes traditionnels sur l'évolution politique du Rwanda et du Burundi', *Revue de l'Institut de Sociologie*, 1962, p. 343.
[84] F. Minani, 'Evolution des institutions rwandaises', in *Les constitutions et les institutions administratives des Etats nouveaux*, Compte-rendu de la 33ème session de l'Incidi, Brussels, 1965, p. 213.
[85] Morris, Read, *Indirect Rule*, 1972, p. 287.

of colonial consolidation deepened the destruction of the symbolic and political foundations of the autochthonous organisation and signalled the rapid abandonment of indirect rule, increasingly replaced by a paternalistic and interventionist mode of managing the country. Although path dependent, this profound modification of a centuries-old polity in merely a generation's time, from around 1900 to around 1930, is remarkable, as is the fact that this happened without noteworthy social or political upheavals. However, one of these path dependent evolutions specific to Rwanda (and neighbouring Burundi), namely the increasing role of ethnicity, eventually led to a critical juncture discussed in the next chapter.

4 Revolutionary Change

4.1 Conditions for Revolution

The 1950s were a period of profound change that culminated in the 1959–1961 revolution. As will be seen, this episode has determined Rwanda's future up to the present day. Revolutions bring change but are also the consequence of changes that the system is unable to accommodate. Although Chalmers Johnson does not mention the case of Rwanda, the conceptual scheme of revolutionary change he proposed offers an excellent explanation. Seeking to understand the causes of a revolution, he finds two clusters of intertwined underlying causes, namely power deflation (when the integration of a system depends increasingly on the deployment of force) and loss of authority (when the use of force by the elite is no longer considered legitimate). The immediate or precipitating causes are the ingredients, usually of a coincidental nature, that deprive the elites of their weapons for enforcing social behaviour. Johnson calls these causes accelerators.[1]

In the previous chapters I have addressed more remote causes of the weakening and even destruction of the protective mechanisms of the social and political order, such as the changes made to the *mwami*'s and indigenous authorities' functions, the imposed and often artificial extension of central Tutsi court power, the introduction of a monetary economy and the role played by the Belgian administration and the White Fathers in the emerging contradictions of indirect rule. In addition, in Rwanda, the centralised and hierarchical nature of the traditional political organisation made the system particularly resistant to reforms aimed at the dilution of power. Both this centralisation and the increasingly rigid ethnic structure, two elements obstructing orderly and peaceful change, contributed to disturbing existing equilibria.

Before addressing the premises of the revolution first and its accelerators later, a contingent evolution must be mentioned. Several changes in

---

[1] C. Johnson, *Revolutionary Change*, 2nd ed., Stanford, Stanford University Press, 1982, pp. 93–94. Specifically for Rwanda, these factors are addressed in Newbury, *The Cohesion of Oppression*, pp. 180–206.

European personnel played a prominent role. First there was *la relève*, the arrival in 1946 of a new generation of territorial administrators to replace the pre-war generation that had been blocked in Africa during the German occupation of Belgium. These new agents, who were often from more modest families than their predecessors, had lived under inhumane conditions during the occupation and they had no sympathy for the idea that a *Herrenvolk* was naturally destined to rule. The missionary also experienced a similar evolution. The social origins and nationalities of the newly arriving priests were more diversified than those of their predecessors.

Two leaders – one lay, the other ecclesiastical – whose influence was to prove considerable illustrate the importance of this changing of the guard. In February 1955, the conservative Catholic governor of Ruanda-Urundi was replaced by Jean-Paul Harroy, a moderate liberal.[2] A year later, Monsignor André Perraudin was appointed the apostolic vicar (bishop) of Kabgayi and thus head of the Rwandan Catholic Church. A Swiss from modest peasant origins, he was not subject to the 'Classe complex' towards the Tutsi. Perraudin put a strong accent on social justice, and his inauguration marked the beginning of a spectacular turnabout in the relations between the Church and the Tutsi aristocracy.[3] After the start of the revolution in 1959, another new arrival was to have a major impact: Colonel Guy Logiest, commander of *Force publique* troops sent from the Belgian Congo to restore order, in effect played a prominent political role in the success of the revolution.[4]

Of course, men alone do not make history. Several profound changes created the conditions for revolution. Although many elements of the social and political changes were linked, it would be difficult to establish causalities. Rather these factors seem to have mutually reinforced each other. I now turn to these premises.

4.2   Premises of the Revolution

4.2.1   Timid Steps towards Democratisation

The first premise was the introduction of the elective principle in 1952 for the first time in Rwandan history. The decree of 14 July 1952 on the indigenous political organisation of Ruanda-Urundi was part

---

[2] J.-P. Harroy, *Rwanda: De la féodalité à la démocratie 1955–1962*, Brussels, Hayez, 1984.
[3] A. Perraudin, *Un évêque au Rwanda: Témoignage*, Saint Maurice, Editions Saint Augustin, 2003.
[4] G. Logiest, *Mission au Rwanda: Un blanc dans la bagarre Tutsi-Hutu*, Brussels, Didier Hatier, 1988.

4.2 Premises of the Revolution

of a broader process. Missions of the United Nations Trusteeship Council had visited the country in 1948 and 1951, and their reports had expressed concerns about the slowness of political change (see Section 4.2.3). In 1951, the Belgian government published a ten-year plan for the economic and social development of Ruanda-Urundi. It considered political reform in the sense of democratisation essential: 'it will allow to resolve problems linked to economic and social development, it will answer the wish of the Trusteeship Council, and it will offer Belgium a new instrument to accomplish the eminent task it has assumed'.[5]

The 'democratisation' in the decree was very timid. Besides extending the powers given to the indigenous authorities, and to the *mwami* in particular, it put in place consultative councils at several levels: country, chiefdom, sub-chiefdom and territory, the latter being a colonial subdivision. The members of these councils were indirectly elected, without popular participation. For instance, the *Conseil supérieur du pays*, presided by the *mwami*, comprised the presidents of the territory councils, six chiefs elected by their peers, one representative of each territory council elected among its 'notables', and eight co-opted members. By operating the devolution to the *mwami* and the chiefs of certain powers hitherto exercised by the colonial administration, the decree could also be seen as a first step towards internal self-government. In light of later developments it must be pointed out that the system was strongly biased in favour of the Tutsi, whose share in the councils' membership increased towards the top layers: they held 52 per cent in sub-chiefdom councils, 88 per cent in chiefdom councils and 90 per cent in the *Conseil supérieur du pays*.[6] In other words, while the aim of the decree was to control the indigenous authorities by diluting their power, this control and this dilution operated inside the ruling group, whose position remained intact. Nevertheless, the *mwami* was less than happy with this reform, which he considered premature. He also feared, justifiably as it later turned out, that the instauration of councils, the *Conseil supérieur du pays* in particular, might give rise to the expression of opposition views. In addition, despite its timid nature, the 1952 decree allowed the Hutu access to political bodies, even in limited numbers, thus opening the perspective for the larger population of having a say.

---

[5] *Plan décennal pour le développement économique et social du Ruanda-Urundi*, Brussels, Editions De Visscher, 1951, p. xxxix.
[6] In 1956, the population was 82.74 per cent Hutu, 16.59 per cent Tutsi and 0.67 per cent Twa (Office de l'information et des relations publiques pour le Congo Belge et le Ruanda-Urundi, *Le Ruanda-Urundi*, Brussels, 1959, p. 35).

76   Revolutionary Change

   This perspective broadened with the popular consultation the Belgian administration organised in 1956, when the male adult population was involved in the composition of the sub-chiefdom councils. However, the sub-chiefs were not bound by the outcome of the vote – which is why it was called a consultation and not an election. Despite allowing a direct popular influence on the councils' composition, its impact was limited and decreased from the bottom to the top of the system. Although the Tutsi now held 45 per cent of the positions (down from 52 per cent) in sub-chiefdom councils, they secured 97 per cent (up from 90 per cent) in the *Conseil supérieur du pays*. While the 1956 experience showed the shortcomings of a multi-layered indirect system, the popular consultation drew attention to the numerical majority position of the Hutu. If they voted exclusively for members of their ethnic group, they would be in a position to eventually take power by the sheer force of numbers. The question then became whether further democratisation would not result in the overthrow of Tutsi rule.

4.2.2   Severing Individual Clientship Links: The Abolition of Ubuhake

The cattle-based clientship contract *ubuhake* has been widely researched and was briefly presented in the Introduction.[7] While it was a private contract between two individuals, *ubuhake* was also a political tool that protected the position of the ruling class. By according *abagaragu* (clients) a mere precarious usufruct, the Tutsi *shebuja* (patrons) maintained ultimate control of cattle, the symbol of political, social and economic power. The *ubuhake* relationship was therefore profoundly ambivalent, at the same time protecting clients and subjecting them to the owning class. In other words, *ubuhake* was at the micro level what the political structures were at the macro level.

   The introduction by the Europeans of a new element of wealth, namely money, and the means to acquire it, most notably through paid labour and the culture of coffee, caused profound changes. By allowing an accumulation of resources outside of traditional avenues, the introduction of money gradually disturbed existing relations of authority and dependence. As a result, already in the 1920s there were increasing signs that *ubuhake* ceased playing its original role, as parties to the contract started to end their clientship relation by mutual consent.[8] Indeed chiefs had

---

[7] Sources on *ubuhake* can be found in Reyntjens, *Pouvoir et droit*, p. 198, footnote 1.
[8] R. Bourgeois, *L'évolution du contrat de bail à cheptel au Ruanda-Urundi*, Brussels, Académie Royale des Sciences Coloniales, 1958, p. 11; Saucier, *The Patron-Client Relationship*, pp. 182–197.

gradually transformed *ubuhake* into a relationship of economic exploitation and extraction of labour. During the 1940s it became increasingly clear that the institution was losing its relevance as Rwandans more and more saw cattle as an economic rather than as a symbolic asset. In 1951, the ten-year plan found that, as it was contrary to private property, *ubuhake* was an obstacle to economic and social development.[9]

In 1954, on the advice of the *Conseil supérieur du pays*, the *mwami* decided to abolish *ubuhake*. Cattle was to be shared, with one third to the *shebuja* and two thirds to the *umugaragu*. Lemarchand remarked that the reactions of patrons and clients to this reform were not specifically linked to their ethnic affiliation. Some Tutsi patrons viewed it favourably, while some Hutu clients feared the loss of political and economic protection.[10] In some cases, both patron and client held on to the contract, and *ubuhake* continued clandestinely.[11]

Acting cumulatively with other developments during this period, the effects of this reform on the socio-political evolution were considerable. On the one hand, the liberation from clientship bonds led not only to individual social and economic emancipation for many Hutu but also to a process of political emancipation. On the other hand, the abolition of *ubuhake* was deficient in that it was not accompanied by a reform of land tenure. Indeed, former patrons retained the ownership of pasture land (*ibikingi*), and contrary to the principle that 'pastures belong to the cow' (*Igikingi ni icy'inka*), the sharing of cattle did not entail the sharing of pastures. This often meant that former *abagaragu* were forced into a new clientship relation to secure access to pasture land for the cows they had obtained. Major Tutsi owners of *ibikingi* resisted their distribution based on cattle ownership, and this problem had not been resolved by the time of the revolution. The incapacity to find a satisfactory solution made many Hutu aware of their continued dependence on the Tutsi aristocracy, and this frustration eventually contributed to the overthrow of the entire regime.

4.2.3 *The Role of the United Nations*

After the Second World War, Ruanda-Urundi became a trust territory. Contrary to the League of Nations, the United Nations, in its Charter adopted in 1945, adhered to activist principles in colonial matters: the primacy of the interests of the inhabitants of colonial

---

[9] *Plan décennal*, pp. 399–400.
[10] Lemarchand, *Rwanda and Burundi*, pp. 128–129.
[11] Bourgeois, *L'évolution*, p. 43.

territories over those of the metropoles, international control of the government of trust territories and progress towards self-government taking into account the political aspirations of the populations living in colonies and trust territories. The more active involvement of the United Nations must be seen in the context of a major reversal: while the colonial powers dominated global politics before 1940, after 1945 they became the accused, were forced into a defensive stance and were increasingly turned into a minority.

Two bodies within the United Nations exercised concrete monitoring of the administration of the trust territories, namely the Trusteeship Council and the Fourth Commission of the General Assembly. Starting in 1947, the trust authorities had to fill out an annual questionnaire on political, economic, social and cultural progress in the territories under their control. Since 1948, missions visited Rwanda every three years, and each time they became more pressing on the issue of political reform. While previously the voice of Rwandans was not heard, from 1957 both Rwandan indigenous institutions and emerging counter-elites voiced their complaints and aspirations. The 1957 visiting mission noted with satisfaction that political conscience expressed itself: in its view, the Hutu started questioning the bases of a 'feudal regime', while the Tutsi expressed concern about their rights and prerogatives. The mission clearly underestimated the potential for violent conflict between these two contradictory aspirations.

The trusteeship regime had an undeniable impact on the direction and speed of events. The growing insistence by visiting missions to set deadlines for internal autonomy first and independence later placed the country in a large movement of nationalism and decolonisation set in motion during the second half of the 1940s and amplified in Bandung in 1955. In this context, the United Nations has certainly played a role as a stimulator of reforms and propagator of political ideals. However, the Trusteeship Council's ambition to rapidly and simultaneously achieve internal democracy and national independence, while at the same time maintaining public order and security, encountered a situation in Rwanda not found in most other African trust territories. Both options were indeed difficult to achieve in a situation where an aristocratic minority led the country in an authoritarian way and where the ethnic situation was bipolar, with a large demographic majority of Hutu and a small minority of Tutsi, with the latter being the ruling elite.[12] Events on the ground were to impose themselves on both Belgium and the United Nations.

---

[12] The small (under 1 per cent) group of Twa are not included in the equation, because they played no political role.

4.2.4 The Emergence of Counter-Elites

Starting in the mid-1950s, two parallel developments were to have a major political impact. On the one hand, opposition came to the fore within the Tutsi hierarchy. On the other, Hutu elites emerged and became increasingly vocal.

Within the Tutsi hierarchy, by and large two groups came into conflict: on the one hand the *mwami*, the court at Nyanza and old school traditionalist chiefs and on the other the more progressive chiefs and notables who had benefited from a modern education. The latter group increasingly distanced itself from royal myths and showed its difference through European education and its rejection, at least in part, of ancestral traditions. Some of them were to later found the progressive Tutsi-dominated party RADER (Rassemblement démocratique rwandais) and had the favour of the Belgian administration, which hoped that with these progressive Tutsi it would be possible to modernise and democratise the country while maintaining Tutsi supremacy. Most had received their schooling in the *Groupe scolaire* of Astrida, hence their nickname 'Astridiens'. Hostilities between these two groups came out in the open in the *Conseil supérieur du pays*. This was an important development, as the antagonism moved from closed chambers to the public forum: council meetings were public and accessible to the press and the Hutu. The Tutsi opposition fully exploited this forum to weaken the *mwami*'s position and prestige. He understood this very well, and in 1955, after having been openly challenged by the progressive chief Bwanakweri, he declared that 'in the eyes of the Rwandans, attacking the *mwami* is a grave insult, which needs to be repressed in an exemplary fashion, the more so since the perpetrator is a chief'.[13] At the time the Hutu were mere spectators, but they were certainly emboldened by the spectacle that the 'bull of Rwanda' could be attacked with impunity by his own herd.

I have discussed the discriminatory recruitment of pupils in Chapter 3. Education that led to functions in the administration was largely limited to the children of Tutsi notables. Catholic seminaries long remained the only schools where the Hutu could access post-primary education. Indeed most leaders of what was to become the Hutu movement were formed at the Kabgayi and Nyakibanda seminaries. In that sense it could be said that 'the revolution came from the seminary'.[14] Those who did not become priest returned to lay life

---

[13] Letter of 10 May 1955, *mwami* to the Belgian resident, author's archives.
[14] Murego, *La révolution rwandaise*, pp. 678–679.

and faced a political and administrative system unable or unwilling to absorb them. It is not surprising under these circumstances that this group became a frustrated elite barred from putting its qualifications to good use. Sharing a similar anger towards customary authorities and being in daily contact with the ordinary, overwhelmingly Hutu, population, this group was ideally placed to act as an intermediary between those holding political power and the exploited rural masses. Particularly from the mid 1950s, this new elite started formulating the ethnic and social problems in political terms, thus giving form to a pressure movement challenging the status quo.

This polarisation led to heightened political activity on both sides of the divide. In 1955, the progressive Tutsi created the Mouvement démocratique progressiste, while in 1956, forty-three out of the forty-six chiefs expressed their loyalty to the *mwami*.[15] The year 1957 was particularly eventful, with the creation of the Mouvement social muhutu, the Aprosoma (Association pour la promotion sociale des masses – Hutu) and the Association des éleveurs du Ruanda-Urundi (conservative Tutsi), as well as the publication of the *Manifeste des Bahutu* on the Hutu side and the *Mise au point* of the *Conseil supérieur du pays* on the Tutsi side.[16] On 17 May 1958, twelve conservative Tutsi court notables, calling themselves *Bagaragu b'ibwami bakuru*, published a particularly provocative text stating that 'the relations between us (Batutsi) and them (Bahutu) have always been and remain based on serfdom; therefore between them and us there is not a single foundation of brotherhood', and that '[a]s our kings have conquered the land of the Bahutu by killing their kinglets and thus turning them into serfs, how can they now pretend that they are our brothers?'[17] In a declaration of 3 December 1958, Governor Harroy officially acknowledged the problem and through the apostolic vicar's *Mandement de carême*, the Catholic Church supported the Hutu claims. Rwanda entered a revolutionary era.

4.3 The Revolution

4.3.1 Accelerators

On 25 July 1959, *mwami* Mutara III Rudahigwa died in a Bujumbura hospital when consulting his Belgian doctor. Rumours ranging from

---

[15] Text in F. Nkundabagenzi, *Rwanda politique 1958–1960*, Brussels, CRISP, 1961, pp. 33–35.
[16] Documents published during this period can be found in ibid., pp. 13–43.
[17] Text in ibid., pp. 35–36. Interestingly, this provocative, even racist, statement is not mentioned in National Unity and Reconciliation Commission, *History of Rwanda*.

4.3 The Revolution

suicide to assassination immediately circulated, but the cause of death was probably a fatal vascular reaction to a megacillin injection. The *mwami* was indeed in poor health.[18] Three groups started to prepare for the succession: the Belgian administration, the Tutsi traditionalists at the royal court and the leaders of the Hutu movement. As the traditionalists wished to avoid a power vacuum and prevent solutions that would have been contrary to the traditional royal ritual, they rapidly agreed on Mutara Rudahigwa's half-brother Jean-Baptiste Ndahindurwa as the successor. In order to create a fait accompli, they staged what is known as the Mwima coup d'état. At the occasion of Mutara's burial, several speakers argued that the *mwami* could not be buried before the announcement of his successor, as the country could not be without a king. The representative of the *abiru*, the guardians of the esoteric code, then stated that Ndahindurwa was to be the new *mwami*, an announcement applauded by those present. Under the threatening circumstances around the grave, Governor Harroy could not but accept the choice after obtaining Ndahindurwa's promise that he would reign as a constitutional monarch.[19] Nevertheless, this round was won by the conservatives, who took the Belgian authorities by surprise and imposed their view, although strictly speaking the royal succession customs were not entirely respected. This taking of control by the conservatives at the court happened at a crucial moment, as the country entered into a period of intense political activities and of a steady deterioration of relations between the royal court and the Belgian administration, as well as between the latter and the United Nations. However the 'coup' was not only directed against the administration and the Hutu but it also affected intra-Tutsi relations. The traditionalist group that took control was not inclined to negotiate and compromise, and its intransigence was to contribute to the regime's collapse.

The second accelerator was the creation of political parties and 'the affair of the three chiefs'. The conservative, monarchist and Tutsi-dominated Union nationale ruandaise (UNAR) was created on 3 September.[20] The support of most chiefs gave the party important levers of action and pressure at the local level. The RADER, created on 14 September, was the political spin-off of the Mouvement démocratique progressiste (cf. Section 4.2.4), and it enjoyed the support of the administration and the Kabgayi diocese. The party wanted to bring

---

[18] Hypotheses on the death are examined in Reyntjens, *Pouvoir et droit*, pp. 239–241.
[19] More details on the Mwima coup can be found in Lemarchand, *Rwanda and Burundi*, pp. 156–158; Kagame, *Abrégé*, pp. 261–264.
[20] Although its president, François Rukeba, was a Hutu.

together progressive Tutsi and Hutu in a multi-ethnic setting. While its leaders were men of quality and its ideas moderate and democratic, RADER was too close to the Belgian administration and the urban elites to appeal to the general population. This last aspect was remarkably well achieved by the third party, the Parmehutu (Parti du mouvement de l'émancipation des Bahutu), founded on 9 October. As indicated by its name, the party's base was ethnic from the beginning. Its aim was to end the socio-economic and political hegemony of the Tutsi. For this to be achieved, democracy had to come first, independence only later. Initially not republican, the party accepted a constitutional monarchy, though with some reservations. Emanating from the same Mouvement social muhutu as Parmehutu, Aprosoma, which was created in 1957, had already become a political party in February 1959. Its leader Joseph Gitera virulently attacked the Tutsi and the existing social and political system. Other parties created at the time were small or local and were to play no significant role.[21]

While the creation of political parties was a general accelerator of the revolution, a concrete incident involving UNAR was a specific accelerator. At a meeting organised by the party on 13 September, three chiefs took the floor and criticised the Belgian administration. Arguing that while officials had the right to be party members they could not engage in party political action or propaganda, Governor Harroy transferred them to another chiefdom as a disciplinary measure. The chiefs refused their transfer and instead resigned, and for the first time the *mwami* sided with UNAR by publicly protesting the transfer. This was a decisive turning point that consecrated the rupture between the administration on the one hand and the *mwami* and UNAR on the other.

The third accelerator and indeed the final trigger occurred on 1 November, when one of only ten Hutu sub-chiefs, Dominique Mbonyumutwa, was attacked by young UNAR militants. The rumour circulated that he had been killed, and groups of Hutu demonstrated in Mbonyumutwa's chiefdom. A Tutsi sub-chief known for his arrogance and anti-Parmehutu behaviour was killed, along with two Tutsi notables who were with him. This was the beginning of a *jacquerie*,[22] which spread throughout the country, territory after territory, especially in Gitarama, Ruhengeri and Gisenyi. Only the territories of Cyangugu and Kibungo remained unaffected by the violence. Tutsi notables were attacked and

---

[21] A survey of parties created in the late 1950s can be found in National Unity and Reconciliation Commission, *History of Rwanda*, pp. 385–391.

[22] This term has been used frequently to refer to the insurrection of Hutu peasants in November 1959. It refers to the violent revolt of French peasants against the aristocracy that erupted in the Beauvaisis in 1358. This insurrection was repressed in blood.

4.3 The Revolution

chased away, some were killed, Tutsi homes were burnt down. Harroy noted that in some regions 'the Hutu seemed determined not to leave untouched a single Tutsi house and to discourage the Tutsi forever to remain in the area'.[23]

At the same time, the court and Tutsi notables attempted to 'restore order' as if the Belgian administration did not exist. Relying on its network of chiefs and sub-chiefs, already in October UNAR had mobilised 'traditional' armies (*ingabo*), each over a thousand men strong.[24] Several leaders of Parmehutu and of Aprosoma were killed. The royal court (*ibwami*) arrested other Hutu leaders, some of whom were tortured or executed. The traditional authorities' counter-insurrectionist effort largely targeted Hutu politicians and their sympathisers, at the local level, especially in Astrida, Nyanza and Gitarama, and more broadly across the country with the intention to decapitate the Hutu leadership. The arrest, interrogation and even assassination of Hutu political figures, especially at the court in Nyanza, ran in parallel with sweeping military operations against the Hutu.[25] Harroy recounted preparations by UNAR to raise a number of *ingabo* or army corps, thousands of men strong, which could be quickly mobilised to target Hutu politicians.[26] The outcome of the violence on both sides was a watershed: hundreds of people were killed,[27] thousands of houses were burnt, there were about 10,000 refugees and internally displaced persons (IDPs) and around 20 chiefs and 150 sub-chiefs were removed from office.[28]

On 7 November, resident Preud'homme placed Rwanda under the 'regime of military operation'. Two days later Belgian troops arrived from Congo under the command of Colonel Guy Logiest, who was appointed military resident. The military intervention allowed to halt both violence by Hutu mobs against Tutsi and an incipient 'full-scale Tutsi repression'.[29] After order was restored, Logiest was made 'special resident' and stayed on. As will be seen later, his role in subsequent events had been decisive. Military courts were made competent to deal with the judicial

---

[23] Harroy, *Rwanda*, p. 303.
[24] On military operations mounted by the court and UNAR, see J. R. Hubert, *La Toussaint rwandaise et sa répression*, Brussels, ARSOM, 1965, pp. 38–39.
[25] Desrosiers, *Trajectories*, p. 105.
[26] J. P. Harroy, *Rwanda*, p. 291.
[27] According to Hubert (*La Toussaint rwandaise*, p. 40), seventy-four persons were killed between 1 November 1959 and 31 May 1961, but several cases were not reported or judged, so the death toll was certainly higher.
[28] A more detailed treatment of the *jacquerie* and the Tutsi reaction can be found in Murego, *La révolution rwandaise*, pp. 915–922; Harroy, *Rwanda*, pp. 291–294.
[29] M. Mamdani, *When Victims Become Killers: Colonialism, Nativism, and the Genocide in Rwanda*, Princeton, Princeton University Press, 2001, p. 124.

treatment of the events. As this has been described in detail elsewhere,[30] suffice it here to summarise the outcome. In all, 1,240 suspects were prosecuted, of whom 94 were acquitted, with the others receiving prison sentences of between under a year and over ten years; two were sentenced to death, but they were not executed. In ethnic terms, 36 per cent of those prosecuted were Tutsi, 59 per cent were Hutu and 5 per cent were Twa, suggesting that justice was meted out even-handedly, at least from an ethnic perspective.

4.3.2 Reponses to the Political Situation and the Gradual Transfer of Power to the Hutu Elites

The first strictly political act of special resident Logiest, namely the installation of 'interim authorities', had a major impact on the course of events. At the end of November, after the *jacquerie*, a large number of chiefs and sub-chiefs, almost all of them Tutsi, no longer exercised their function as a result of arrest, flight, transfer, removal from office or physical elimination.[31] This gave Logiest, who saw his actions sabotaged by the Tutsi customary hierarchy, a unique opportunity to neutralise this force, at least partially. Considering support for the Hutu elites as an integral part of the maintenance of public order, he ordered the territorial administrators to propose the removal of as many Tutsi chiefs and sub-chiefs as possible, in addition to the positions that had become vacant as a result of the violence. This was strictly speaking illegal, but Logiest countered objections by referring to the need to pacify the country. At the end of the operation, by March 1960, half the chiefs and well over half the sub-chiefs were Hutu. In addition, most active members of UNAR had been replaced by officials sympathising with Aprosoma, Parmehutu and RADER. Compared to the situation just six months earlier, this was a landslide.[32]

The *mwami* reacted vigorously. In letters to the Belgian minister of the colonies and to the Belgian king, he called the measures illegal and demanded the 'rehabilitation of customary authorities arbitrarily deposed to satisfy political aims'. Legally the *mwami* was right. According to the 1952 decree, while the governor (for chiefs) and the resident (for sub-chiefs) had the right to demote, after hearing the king, the right to appoint them belonged exclusively to the *mwami*.

---

[30] Hubert, *La Toussaint rwandaise*.
[31] Twenty-three of the 45 chiefs and 158 of the 489 sub-chiefs were no longer effectively in charge.
[32] More details and sources on this crucial episode can be found in Reyntjens, *Pouvoir et droit*, pp. 267–272.

4.3 The Revolution

The special resident justified this violation of legal rules by invoking state necessity. Despite continued protest, the *mwami* was finally forced to accept the fait accompli, and the 'interim authorities' were there to stay.

This was a major and irreversible step in the promotion of Hutu political emancipation. The foundations for the success of the revolution were laid through the elimination of the operational base of the Tutsi hierarchical structure. Having lost the impact of chiefs and sub-chiefs on the population, the hands of the *mwami*, the court and UNAR were cut. From then on, Hutu and some progressive Tutsi increasingly occupied the field. Subsequent measures and legal actions consolidated the complete overhaul of the system.

The first legal step was the interim decree of 25 December 1959 on the political organisation of Ruanda-Urundi. Its aim was dual: to renew the different councils through universal suffrage, in order to increase their representativeness, and to put an end to the duality between the general (colonial) administration and the customary organisation. This second point meant that internal self-government was to replace the system of indirect rule. The sub-chiefdoms became 'provisional' municipalities (*communes*). Chiefdoms were maintained for the time being, but only as an administrative, not a political, unit. The newly created *Conseil du pays* became a parliament-like institution in which most members were indirectly elected by the heads and the members of the councils of the *communes provisoires*. The monarchy became constitutional: the *mwami* was politically irresponsible, and his acts were to be countersigned by the head of the government. In the meantime, the *Conseil supérieur du pays* could no longer function. Awaiting the election of the *Conseil du pays*, a *Conseil spécial provisoire* was put in place of which two representatives of each of the four main political parties were the members.

The next step was to be the municipal elections slated for June 1960, but the road leading to them was bumpy. Following the refusal of the *mwami* to accept recommendations made by the political parties in the *Conseil spécial provisoire*, on 30 April 1960 Aprosoma, RADER and Parmehutu sent a telegram to the Belgian king and the minister of the colonies, stating 'Mwami refuses collaboration with his Rwandan people. Declare break with Kigeri. Demand appointment of interim chief'. This kind of language would have been unimaginable just a year earlier. To make its point clear, on 8 May Parmehutu announced a telling change of name. It became the Mouvement démocratique républicain (MDR), thus confirming its break with the monarchy. As Parmehutu was well known among the population, the party's name was henceforth MDR-Parmehutu. At the end of June, the *mwami* left the country, never to return.[33]

Also, in May UNAR took the dramatic decision to withdraw from the *Conseil spécial provisoire* and to boycott the forthcoming municipal elections. The impact of this political suicide became clear only after the elections, but in the meantime this move allowed the other parties to occupy the field and take decisions without UNAR's involvement. The Belgian administration seized this opportunity to discredit UNAR and continued to promote other parties, the MDR-Parmehutu in particular. Logiest referred to the party as 'demanding a veritable democracy, the real union of all inhabitants of Rwanda and the abolition of the domination of a single race [sic]'.[34] However, UNAR was not just a victim. It organised a campaign of terror and launched an array of false rumours. During the elections, armed party members were stationed on roads leading to polling stations to prevent people from voting.

Between 26 June and 30 July 1960 Rwandans elected 229 mayors (*bourgmestres*) and 2,896 municipal councillors during the first large-scale democratic exercise in the country's history.[35] As UNAR had called for a boycott, it is interesting to first look at the participation rate at the polls: 21.8 per cent of registered voters did not turn out, but these figures were very different from region to region, and not all no-shows could be attributed to UNAR's call. The participation of 78.2 per cent of the voters was a success, all the more so because voting was not compulsory. The overwhelming winner was the MDR-Parmehutu, which obtained over 70 per cent of the vote nationwide. The predominantly Hutu parties, MDR-Parmehutu and Aprosoma, together secured an absolute majority in 211 out of the 229 *communes*. The political importance of this victory cannot be overstated. While Tutsi rule had been neutralised at the national level during the previous months, the municipal elections allowed the Hutu to take control of a crucial level, namely that of daily citizen governance, and to access levers of considerable means of pressure and control.

In the aftermath of the municipal polls, on 18 October a forty-eight-member provisional council (*Conseil provisoire*), replacing the *Conseil spécial provisoire*, and a provisional government were put in place. Based

---

[33] After a life in exile, Ndahindurwa died in the US in October 2016 and was buried in Rwanda without much ceremony in January 2017.
[34] Communiqué n° 7 du colonel G. Logiest, résident spécial, 8 February 1960, in *Rwanda Politique*, p. 219.
[35] However, for practical reasons only males were allowed to vote. This restriction was justified by the Belgian administration on the ground that the establishment of women voters list would have caused too long a delay in the organisation of the polls.

4.3 The Revolution

on the outcome of the municipal elections, the MDR-Parmehutu obtained thirty-one seats in the council, against nine for RADER, seven for Aprosoma and one for Aredetwa (a Twa party). UNAR was not represented. On 20 October, the provisional government was formed, with Grégoire Kayibanda as the prime minister. The eight cabinet positions were filled by a minister and a state secretary each, a Rwandan and a Belgian or vice versa. Parliamentary elections slated for January 1961 had to be postponed at the request of the United Nations, very much to the regret of the Hutu parties and the Belgian administration. Although this appeared as a defeat for them, they had the advantage of being on the ground, and they were to make full use of that position.

4.3.3 Material Consecration of the Revolution

As the administration and the Hutu parties wished to consolidate the revolution by legalising its achievements, they sidelined the United Nations by the operation known as the Gitarama coup d'etat. Following a plan set up by the Rwandan Hutu leaders and the resident, Logiest, the minister of the interior convened all mayors and municipal councillors to a national congress held in Gitarama, Kayibanda's fief, on 28 January 1961. The official order of business was labelled as 'Measures to be taken for the maintenance of order and the pacification of the country'. Nearly all *bourgmestres* and councillors were present, brought to Gitarama by vehicles of the residency and the territories. Thousands of ordinary citizens surrounded the market where the meeting took place. A platoon of Belgian paratroopers was discreetly deployed in the banana groves above the market, and Colonel Logiest was present in town.

Speakers announced that *mwami* Kigeri V Ndahindurwa was deposed and the monarchy definitively abolished, that the institutions of *Kalinga* and the *abiru* were removed, that henceforth the red, yellow and green flag was the symbol of the new Rwanda and that the country was now a republic. Dominique Mbonyumutwa, the former sub-chief the aggression against whom triggered the *jacquerie* in November 1959, was elected the president of the Republic. The congress then proceeded to the election of a legislative assembly, in which the MDR-Parmehutu and Aprosoma obtained forty and four seats respectively. The assembly in turn elected its president and vice president. Following Belgian constitutional practice, President Mbonyumutwa tasked Kayibanda with forming a government, which he immediately presented to the assembly. Its composition respected the spirit of internal self-government: the portfolios of defence and external relations, matters that remained in the hands of Belgium, were not attributed to ministers but to state secretaries. Mbonyumutwa also announced the creation of a supreme court and appointed its president.

Showing how well this event was prepared in advance, the assembly finally adopted the eighty-article 'Gitarama Constitution'.[36] Its sources of inspiration were the French constitution and those of the countries of the French Community in West Africa, as well as some provisions of Belgian texts on the political and administrative organisation of Ruanda-Urundi. However, this 'constitution' had no legal value, and it had not played the role expected of a constitutional document. It was not published in the *Official Gazette* and Belgium only recognised the authorities put in place in Gitarama de facto; in other words, it recognised the persons but not the institutions put in place on 28 January. This was made clear in a legislative ordinance of 6 February which held that the powers of internal self-government 'are exercised in Rwanda by the public authorities installed on 28 January 1961 by the general assembly that brought together in Gitarama the provisional government, the *conseil du Rwanda* and the burgomasters and municipal councillors'. In a *note verbale* addressed to the UN Commission for Ruanda-Urundi, the Belgian government insisted on the de facto nature of this recognition: 'These decisions are taken awaiting the definition of a de jure solution with the representatives of Rwanda and the United Nations.' The Belgian administration continued to legislate in constitutional matters and the Rwandan authorities abided by these rules. The colonial constitutional order remained the only effective one, and was not challenged by the revolutionaries. The Gitarama 'constitution' thus remained symbolic, as is shown again in the fact that the independence constitution of 1962 did not even refer to the Gitarama text (see next chapter).

However, this lack of legal validity does not diminish the crucial importance of the Gitarama congress. From the point of view of material legitimacy, its decisions consecrated the political success of the revolution that started in November 1959, and the Belgian residency recognised its achievements insofar as they were not explicitly contrary to the colonial legal order. The UN and Belgian circles hostile to democratisation were presented one fait accompli after the other,[37]

---

[36] Text in *Rwanda Politique*, pp. 391–397.

[37] These were predominantly those in place before *la relève*, who had excellent relations with the indigenous power structure that had helped them administer the country. Thus, Harroy wrote about Resident André Preud'homme that 'he personally knew all great Tutsi since the fraternisation before, during and after the war, and developed an almost reverential consideration for the *mwami*, the *mwami*'s brother, the old chief X'. He noted Preud'homme's 'all too personalised relations with those he would have to treat without mercy' (Harroy, *Rwanda*, p. 335).

and the conservative Tutsi leaders helplessly witnessed the disappearance of the monarchic and oligarchic regime. This was made possible only through the support of the Belgian administration, and of Colonel Logiest in particular. However, this support did not make this into a 'Belgian revolution'. While underlining that Belgian policies made a difference, the Newburys emphasise the role played by 'Hutu activists and Tutsi progressives' who 'called for changes in the exploitative practices of the central court authorities'.[38] Therefore, the revolution would not have taken place were it not for the desire of Hutu leaders, followed by the popular masses, to achieve political emancipation. It was not waged by the colonial administration but was protected and assisted by it in a rare reversal of roles, whereby those exercising power acted as revolutionary agents. This situation is well summarised by Lemarchand's notion of 'seizure of power from above'.[39]

4.3.4 *Legal Consecration: Parliamentary Elections and Referendum*

Even before the Gitarama coup, legislative ordinance 02/16 of 15 January 1961 had already given the country internal autonomy. The regime put in place was parliamentary, with a government, led by a *chef du pays* (an expression that left the monarchic and republican options open), needing parliament's confidence. The legislative assembly was to be directly elected.

The road leading to the parliamentary elections was replete with violence. The MDR-Parmehutu in particular engaged in a campaign of intimidation and abuse, so much so that the UN Commission for Ruanda-Urundi stated that a racist dictatorship of a party was being put in place and that one repressive regime was replacing another. Hundreds of deaths, thousands of burnt houses and tens of thousands of refugees were caused by the terror that rapidly spread throughout large parts of the country as the elections neared. UNAR also engaged in violent acts, but the difference between the two parties lay in the repression of crimes. UNAR members involved in killings and other violence and abuse were vigorously prosecuted and dozens of prominent party members were arrested by the Belgian authorities, while the criminal acts of MDR-Parmehutu propagandists remained largely unpunished and were even covered by the administration. The residency went out of its way to become a propaganda tool of the MDR-Parmehutu, with the obvious aim of turning it into a dominant or even

---

[38] Newbury, Newbury, 'Bringing the Peasants Back In', p. 869.
[39] Lemarchand, 'The Coup in Rwanda', p. 923.

the single party. For Logiest, this was the logical outcome of the support he gave to the party, as he was convinced that in a revolution there can be only one revolutionary party.[40] In addition, most burgomasters were party members, and they played a crucial role during the campaign. This fact underscored the crucial error committed by UNAR when it boycotted the 1960 municipal elections. Deprived of power structures at the bottom, the party was unable to prevent the MDR-Parmehutu's rise to power.

The elections were held on 25 September 1961 and confirmed the landslide victory of the MDR-Parmehutu at the municipal elections. The party captured almost 78 per cent of the votes, against almost 17 per cent for UNAR and 3.5 per cent for Aprosoma. The referendum on the monarchy held at the same time confirmed the resolutions of the Gitarama congress: 80 per cent of the voters opposed the monarchic form of government. Thus, 25 September came to be referred to as *Kamarampaka*, 'a final end to differences'. Implementing the outcome of the referendum, a legislative ordinance of 1 October on the 'head of the country' stipulated that 'the institution of the *mwami* is abolished in Rwanda', thus putting an end to a centuries-old institution, and that the legislative assembly was to elect the *chef du pays*. On 2 October, the assembly was installed. After electing its speaker, on 26 October the assembly elected Kayibanda as the president of the Republic by thirty-six votes (MDR-Parmehutu and Aprosoma), with the seven UNAR members abstaining. Kayibanda immediately presented his government, which obtained the confidence of the assembly. After the elections, the referendum, the presidential election and putting in place of the government, the revolution was finally legally complete. In less than two years, from a 'feudal' Tutsi monarchy, Rwanda had become a 'democratic' Hutu republic.

4.4 From Absolute Tutsi Monarchy to 'Democratic' Hutu Republic

The support given by Belgium to the dominant Tutsi class in the context of its policy of indirect rule objectively reinforced the position of this group. As seen in the previous chapters, this support was simultaneously accompanied by measures that imposed profound

---

[40] Logiest did not hide his preferences, even in public statements, as one example shows. He referred to the MDR-Parmehutu as 'demanding a veritable democracy, the real union of all inhabitants of Rwanda and the abolition of the dominance of one race' (Communiqué n° 7 du colonel G. Logiest, résident spécial, 8 February 1960, *Rwanda Politique*, p. 219).

4.4 From Tutsi Monarchy to Hutu Republic

modifications on the system. Although some Belgian interventions in fact increased the exploitative capacities of the indigenous authorities, particularly of the chiefs and sub-chiefs, the mechanisms of protection and allegiance that in the past had made this supremacy tolerable were gravely undermined in the process. I have earlier described this as an inherent contradiction of the system of indirect rule.

From the early 1950s, modest steps were taken towards the democratisation of a system that could not accommodate it and towards the emancipation of large sections of the population by the abolition of personal links of dependence. This heightened a conscience of ethnic antagonism. Many in the population, or at least its national and foreign spokespersons, increasingly became aware of their numerical force.

Two movements with different inspirations and distinct geographical bases became the vectors of what was to be the revolution. In the north, the movement was essentially restorative. We have seen that Tutsi political supremacy there was relatively recent and not deeply implanted. The latent agitation in these regions was revivalist, and the disintegration of Tutsi structures allowed, at least partially, the restauration of old institutions, such as the land-based clientship system *ubukonde*, which, as will be seen in the next chapter, remained resilient. By contrast, in the south and centre, the movement contained the classic ingredients of a *jacquerie*, notably the invocation of the monarchy's legitimacy, which was not contested at the beginning, during the actions against the exactions and following the loss of legitimacy of chiefs and sub-chiefs.

Indigenous authorities reacted in an intransigent fashion to these challenges, while their European partners (the administration and the Catholic Church) hesitated about which side to choose. They eventually decided that historically the majority could not lose and set out to support – cautiously at first, firmly later – the Hutu cause. For the local territorial administration, this choice was in part inspired by the realisation that independence was coming: after ceding power as demanded by the Tutsi leaders, the minority would inherit the state without restrictions, and political change would be impossible to achieve. It is paradoxically the *jacquerie* that resulted from the Tutsi elites' intransigent attitude and repression that brought Colonel Logiest to the scene, initially in a military operation aimed at restoring order. He stayed on and assumed political authority, decided that the numerical majority was entitled to hold the reins of power and acted in accordance in an extremely rectilinear fashion.

Several stages have led to the revolution's success. First, the Belgian military deployment ended the royal court's and UNAR's capacity to use their repressive force. It is very likely that without this protection the Hutu insurrectional movement would have been decapitated by the Tutsi reaction. After this phase of neutralisation of Tutsi paramilitary actions came the gradual transfer of authority to the Hutu through both political and legal means: the eviction of a large number of Tutsi chiefs and sub-chiefs; the illegal installation of interim authorities, most of them Hutu; the replacement of the *Conseil supérieur du pays* by a *Conseil spécial provisoire*; the municipal elections and finally the institutional transfer of power at the central level of the state. At each of these stages the role of the Belgian administration was crucial and always in favour of the Hutu.

While the revolution might well have failed and ended in major bloodshed without Belgian support and protection, Rwandan social and political forces were its main actors. The Belgian administration, Logiest in particular, assisted and facilitated, but politically and on the ground, the revolution was achieved by Hutu leaders. Harroy pointed at the exceptional historical event of an 'insurrectional phenomenon under tutelage' followed by an 'assisted revolution'.[41] As underlined by the Newburys,

> Belgian policies (…) did not act in a vacuum; they were often responses to internal peasant grievances. (…) Hutu activists and Tutsi progressives – those who sought alliances across ethnic lines – called for changes in the exploitative practices of the central court authorities. They advocated measures to address problems of poverty, inequality, insecure access to land, inadequate opportunities for education, and issues facing youth.[42]

Starting with the Mwima 'coup', the conservative Tutsi leaders decisively contributed to their own demise. After the *jacquerie* began, they accumulated errors that made revolutionary change inevitable: the attempts to 'restore order' by the mobilisation of traditional armies; the rejection of the *Conseil spécial provisoire*; the boycott of the municipal elections and finally the recourse to terrorism. Intransigence was the defining mark of traditionalists' actions, and it allowed a limited revolt to become a full-fledged revolution. It also explains why, after the death of *mwami* Mutara III, the consensual couple Belgium–Tutsi, which was the base of the regime of indirect rule, was replaced by a brief moment of internal self-government with the consensual couple Belgium–Hutu at the helm. As the revolutionaries have shown intransigence too, they share part of the blame. Had they privileged the social issues, as some advocated, they probably would have attracted the support of many

---

[41] Harroy, *Rwanda*, p. 292.
[42] Newbury, Newbury, 'Bringing the Peasants Back In', p. 869.

Tutsi, but they chose to stress the ethnic aspect, thus alienating them. These dramatic choices on both sides occurred at a crucial moment, namely that of the handover of the state apparatus to national leaders on the eve of independence.

4.5 Conclusion

The 1959–1961 revolution was a crucial critical juncture. It toppled a centuries-old political system and was at the same time a consequence of the previous critical juncture – the colonial intrusion – and the cause of the next one – the 1990–1994 civil war, the genocide against the Tutsi and the seizure of power by the RPF. Indeed colonisation, while maintaining the outer trappings of the precolonial order, changed the Rwandan polity beyond recognition by destroying its symbolic foundations, replacing its source of authority and creating the conditions for the emergence of counter-elites, both Tutsi and Hutu. Although pre-1895 Rwanda was a violent society, a revolution inspired by social, economic and ethnic frustrations would in all likelihood not have taken place. When it occurred, it would have been decapitated under the old regime, but it was protected and allowed to succeed by the colonial administration. But the revolution also paved the way for the next critical juncture. The departure into exile of hundreds of thousands of Tutsi, among them most members of the traditional elite, who settled mainly in neighbouring countries, and the frustrations caused among many Tutsi by the takeover by Hutu elites created the conditions for the armed return of the Tutsi exiles. As will be seen in the next chapter, covering the brief interlude between 1959 and 1990, the Hutu regime and the so-called international community – including the donors, the media and the academic world – had been practising business as usual without being aware of this grave danger.

5   The 'Hutu Republics'

While colonial rule was based on highly centralised, bureaucratic and quasi-military structures, the constitutional systems introduced upon independence everywhere in Africa were founded on the principles of West European constitutionalism, with its characteristics of diffusion of power, checks and balances, the elective principle, limited government and the protection of individual rights. The attitude of African leaders after independence was therefore not so much a break with a constitutional past they rejected but rather its continuation under another label. Lavroff has stressed that one of the reasons for the emergence of authoritarian regimes after independence was the fact that the colonial powers not only developed an administrative system which required a strong central executive branch but also exercised power in a manner that could only bear very few institutional checks.[1] The elites that inherited the African states underwent a latent acceptance of the authoritarian values of the colonial state while at the same time proclaiming democratic values: 'This resulted from the dual inheritance or legacy of the colonial power – an authoritarian one (colonial practice), and one stressing participation and equity (the metropolitan values of the colonial power). The former was implanted during seventy-five years of imperial domination; the other was a last-minute hypocritical legacy.'[2]

Rwanda was no exception. I will now first address the constitution-making process (law in the books) and then look at political practice and how it developed (law in action).

5.1   An Autochthonous Constitution

As the Gitarama constitution had no legal validity (cf. Chapter 4), the constitutional text that remained in force until independence day on 1 July 1962 was legislative ordinance 02/16 of 15 January 1961

---

[1] D. G. Lavroff, *Les partis politiques en Afrique noire*, Paris, P.U.F., 1970.
[2] T. M. Callaghy, *The State–Society Struggle: Zaire in Comparative Perspective*, New York, Columbia University Press, 1984, p. 411.

5.1 An Autochthonous Constitution

(as amended by legislative ordinance 02/234 of 15 July 1961), which had given the country internal autonomy. Although it had no constitution-making powers, on 4 October 1961 the legislative assembly started debating a constitutional draft presented by the thirty-seven MDR-Parmehutu and Aprosoma members of parliament (MPs). The next day, the UNAR MPs decided to boycott the proceedings, stating that 'the opposition rejects the idea of a coup d'état, and will never accept a constitution born out of a coup d'état',[3] an obvious reference to the Gitarama constitution. UNAR leaving the process meant that not a single Tutsi politician was involved in the constitutional process. However, the four UNAR MPs remaining in the country resumed their participation in April 1962.

The first reading ended on 23 May 1962, slightly over one month before independence. There was no vote on the entire text, but each article obtained a majority, although a narrow one in a number of cases (six articles only obtained a positive vote from the MPs present but not of all members).[4] In the absence of a vote approving the full draft, Rwanda thus became independent without a constitution. A second reading took place from 30 July to 2 August 1962, when amendments were discussed and even new articles added. A vote on the entire text returned thirty-two votes in favour, none against, and two abstentions (one from UNAR, one from the MDR-Parmehutu). Eight MPs were absent or excused (four UNAR and four MDR-Parmehutu). So the full draft was adopted by 73 per cent of the MPs.

As both the draft and the debates had been in French,[5] a commission was appointed to translate the text into Kinyarwanda. When the translation came before the assembly on 2 October, some MPs insisted that further amendments be discussed, and one was indeed adopted. This was therefore a third reading, but not the last. The text was put to a final vote on 14 November, when another twenty-five articles were amended – that is almost a quarter, quite a considerable number for a fourth reading. The global and final vote took place on 23 November, when the text was adopted by twenty-eight votes in favour, none against, and four abstentions (three UNAR, one Aprosoma). Nine MPs were absent (five MDR-Parmehutu, four UNAR). The next day, the authentic text was signed by

---

[3] Assemblée législative, Doc. No. 3 (1961–62), meeting of 5 October 1961, p. 2.
[4] A breakdown, article by article, can be found in Reyntjens, *Pouvoir et droit*, pp. 327–328.
[5] As several MPs hardly knew French, they were in practice excluded from the debates. Some MPs justified their abstentions at some votes by saying they were unable to understand the text or to follow the debates (see for instance the abstentions of MPs Banzi and Nsengiyumva, Assemblée législative, Doc. No. 6 (1961–62), Meeting of 10 October 1961, p. 3).

forty MPs in the presence of the president of the Republic, who in turn signed and promulgated the constitution of 24 November 1962.

Two characteristics of this constitution-making process are peculiar. The first is the absence of rules, in particular on the number of readings and the required majorities. Four readings took place, and it seems nothing would have prevented MPs from adding more, as long as the text was not promulgated by the president. While the finally adopted text, as well as the first draft, required a three quarters majority for constitutional amendments, the two global readings obtained thirty-two and twenty-eight positive votes respectively out of forty-four members of the assembly, which each time was less than three quarters. Some individual articles were adopted by a simple majority of the MPs present. This absence of rules does not appear to have been raised during the proceedings.

The second peculiarity is the autochthonous nature of the constitution. Rwanda was an exception in Africa, where almost all countries attained independence with a constitution inherited from the coloniser. Apart from Guinea, which opted for immediate independence, France's colonies accepted to live under the French constitution of 4 October 1958 and to remain in the French *Communauté* until independence. The former British colonies 'received' a constitution, negotiated at Lancaster House, promulgated by the Queen before independence and inspired by the 'Westminster Model'. In Belgian Africa, Congo became independent with a 'Fundamental Law' adopted by the Belgian parliament just before independence on 30 June 1960, but Rwanda and Burundi had no constitution upon independence.[6] Constitutional autochthony is merely a procedural notion, referring to the characteristic of a constitution that in its elaboration is free from subordination or a legal link to foreign legislative power, even if its source of inspiration may be foreign.[7]

Just like Burundi and Guinea, Rwanda thus became independent without a constitution inherited from the trustee and without formal rules for elaborating a fundamental law. Beyond the constitutional vacuum a more general legal vacuum could arise. In order to avoid this, a legal ordinance of 12 September 1962, with retroactive effect to independence day, prolonged the validity of all legislative and executive

---

[6] Burundi had a 'provisional' constitution adopted by its legislative assembly on 26 October 1961, promulgated by the *mwami* on 28 November 1961 and recognised by (Belgian) legislative ordinance of 30 January 1962. However this was abrogated by a legislative ordinance on 30 June 1962, the day before independence.

[7] On constitutional autochthony, see for example K. C. Wheare, *The Constitutional Structure of the Commonwealth*, Oxford, Clarendon Press, 1960, pp. 89–113, and K. Roberts-Wray, *Commonwealth and Colonial Law*, London, Stevens, 1966, pp. 289–301.

5.1 An Autochthonous Constitution

instruments in force on 30 June. The need to ensure juridical continuity was definitively covered by article 108 of the constitution, which provided for the maintaining in force of all legislation existing on 24 November, the date of the entering into force of the constitution, provided it was not contrary to the constitution or abrogated or replaced by new legislative or executive instruments. In practice this meant that virtually all colonial legislation, except the one organising the political system, remained in force.

Space allows only a brief look at the constitution's main characteristics.[8] As the regime was the fruit of a revolution, the text understandably marked a clear separation from the *ancien régime*. Article 2 abolished the monarchy 'that cannot be restored'; *mwami* Kigeri and his dynasty lost royal prerogatives. In addition to the prohibition of discrimination in articles 3 and 16, article 17 reaffirmed that 'caste privileges are abolished and cannot be restored'. Likewise, remembering unequal access to schools in the past, article 33 abolished privileges in the field of education and prohibited their restoration. The constitution also put an end to precolonial and colonial practices such as slavery (article 25) and extrajudicial forced labour (article 40). Religion took an important place, and the text did not hide its Christian ideological inspiration,[9] an unsurprising feature in light of the close links between the revolutionaries and the Catholic Church. By prohibiting 'all communist activities and propaganda', article 39 was unique among African constitutions. The Rwandan state has been aptly described as 'religious, anti-Communist and social'.[10]

The political regime put in place was hybrid, combining elements of a parliamentary and a presidential system. It was parliamentary in that the president and, through him, the government could be forced to resign by a vote of no confidence in the National Assembly. This was combined with a feature usually found in presidential systems, namely the election of the president by direct universal suffrage. This created a contradiction in that both the president and parliament were a direct emanation of popular sovereignty, but this potential conflict has never been tested.

Finally, the constitution contained quite a full inventory of civil and political rights. However, article 13 stipulated: 'The fundamental freedoms, as defined by the Universal Declaration of Human Rights, are

---

[8] An extensive analysis of the 1962 constitution and its genesis can be found in Reyntjens, *Pouvoir et droit*, pp. 325–364.
[9] Up to the last reading, the successive drafts prohibited divorce, which was eventually allowed.
[10] J. Vanderlinden, *La République rwandaise*, Paris, Berger-Levrault, 1970, p. 29.

guaranteed for all citizens. Their exercise can be regulated by laws and executive orders (*règlements*).' In other words, not only the legislative but also the executive branch was competent to limit the exercise of fundamental rights and freedoms.

5.2 From De Jure Multi-party to De Facto Single-Party Rule

As seen in Chapter 4, several political parties were created prior to independence, four of which (MDR-Parmehutu, Aprosoma, UNAR and RADER) could be seen as national. By the first post-independence parliamentary elections in 1965, the MDR-Parmehutu was the only party not just to obtain seats but even to field candidates. This evolution had started before independence and was even actively pursued by Colonel Logiest, who believed that, in a revolution, there can only be one revolutionary party (cf. Chapter 4). Successive elections showed the speed of this phenomenon: the MDR-Parmehutu obtained 70.4 per cent of the vote at the 1960 municipal elections, 77.7 per cent at the 1961 parliamentary elections, 97.9 per cent at the 1963 municipal elections and 100 per cent at the 1965 parliamentary polls. In an evolution seen all over the African continent, from being dominant in 1960 the MDR-Parmehutu had become the de facto single party five years later.

The causes of their disappearance had been different for the other three main parties. Aprosoma was in large part the victim of the personality of its founder, Joseph Gitera Habyarimana, a poor organiser who had no precise and coherent political ideas, was engaged in constant sterile conflict with his associates and mainly relied on his charismatic self-styled legitimacy of '*mwami* of the Hutu'. In addition to its own divisions, Aprosoma was also the victim of an effective policy of absorption of its members by the MDR-Parmehutu.

As for RADER, we have seen that the party was a rather artificial creature mostly of progressive Tutsi elites with the support of certain circles in the Belgian administration and the Catholic Church. Although it had excellent leaders and its options and methods were moderate and democratic, RADER was uncomfortably squeezed between the MDR-Parmehutu and UNAR. In addition, as its most visible leaders were Tutsi, its power of popular mobilisation was limited, and it failed to position itself as a progressive and anti-racist alternative. RADER did not fulfil the promises it seemed to have in 1959, and its impact on political life had been negligible.

That was not the case of UNAR. Representing the views of the great Tutsi chiefs and *mwami* Mutara Rudahigwa's and, briefly, Kigeri

Ndahindurwa's court, the party's aim was to defend and restore the pre-revolutionary political and social order. Although it enjoyed international communist support because of its nationalist and anti-colonialist discourse,[11] its programme was reactionary. As its base was mainly among the minority ethnic group, UNAR could not hope to conquer political power through the ballot box after the revolution. The party was also handicapped by its division in an internal or legal and an external wing. Certainly until independence, the latter's influence was considerable and negative, for instance in the suicidal decision to boycott the 1960 municipal elections. While leaders of the internal wing appeared to choose to play the democratic game, the external wing radically rejected the political dispensation that followed the revolution. The dramatic events of December 1963 (discussed later) were to deal a fatal blow to the party, which had disappeared by the 1965 parliamentary elections.

Meanwhile, the MDR-Parmehutu actively pursued a policy of weakening and eventually destroying the other parties. It did not hide that intention, as had already become clear in President Kayibanda's speech at the occasion of the first anniversary of independence. He wanted 'a majoritarian party, with an overwhelming majority, flanked by a minority opposition', adding that 'a proliferation of parties distracts the population, renders national progress incoherent, and causes divisions prejudicial to the nation'.[12] At the time, arguments like these in favour of the single-party state were put forward all over the continent.[13] The elimination of Aprosoma was mainly achieved by political means, which in practice meant 'convincing' local party leaders to join the MDR-Parmehutu.[14] By the end of 1963, Aprosoma had effectively disappeared, although the party was never formally dissolved.

The destruction of UNAR was much more violent and illegal. The party was a constant victim of intimidations, arbitrary arrests and physical abuse. Its meetings were forbidden 'for security reasons', and its members were forced to adhere to the MDR-Parmehutu. The run-up to the 1963 municipal elections was made into a calvary, as all sorts of administrative

---

[11] In this logic, UNAR received support from the Lumumbist Mouvement National Congolais (MNC), which offered financial and military assistance (Rusagara, *Resilience of a Nation*, p. 143).

[12] This speech can be found in *Le président Kayibanda vous parle*, Kigali, 1964, pp. 83–84, and in 'Décolonisation et indépendance du Rwanda et du Burundi', *Chronique de politique étrangère*, 1963, p. 482.

[13] See for example L. Sylla, *Tribalisme et parti unique en Afrique noire*, Abidjan–Paris, Université nationale de Côte d'Ivoire-Presses de la Fondation nationale des sciences politiques, 1977.

[14] Even Aprosoma founder Joseph Gitera became member of the MDR-Parmehutu in 1967 and was elected as an MP for the party in 1969.

obstacles made it impossible to deposit lists of candidates and to register voters. After the polls, ballots in favour of UNAR candidates disappeared or were destroyed. The aim was clearly to achieve a de facto single-party situation, and it was achieved in the context of what Ibingira has called 'Winner-Take-All Politics': 'the belief and practice where those politicians who inherited power on independence (...) proceeded by all means, available or contrived, fair or foul, to concentrate all (or a disproportionate share of) power, resources, jobs, and patronage in their hands and for their supporters for all time, to the detriment of groups of different political, religious, ethnic or regional background.'[15]

The annihilation of UNAR also had a clear ethnic revanchist overtone, as was admitted ten years later by the regime at the occasion of the tenth independence anniversary: '[The municipal elections of 1963] have for ever convinced the Tutsi that they should no longer hope to govern. The Hutu won, and the entire world recognised this victory; these elections covered UNAR and its supporters with shame. On that day the MDR-Parmehutu eliminated all the other parties.'[16]

The final blow to UNAR and more generally to the Tutsi political leadership followed at the end of 1963. I now turn to this dramatic episode.

5.3 *Inyenzi* Attacks and Massacres of Tutsi

Apart from some internal displacements, in particular of Tutsi from Ruhengeri to the Bugesera region, the events of late 1959 did not cause large refugee movements. However, from mid 1960, mainly during and after the campaign for the June–July municipal elections, a considerable exodus of Tutsi got underway. The largest contingent fled to neighbouring countries after the parliamentary elections and the referendum of September 1961. By the end of the year, some 300,000 refugees had left the country, most of them Tutsi but also some Hutu and Twa relatives and clients. This departure of many of its local cadres created a serious problem for UNAR. With independence looming, the Tutsi leaders were facing three tactical possibilities: (i) loyally play the republican game; (ii) undermine the regime from the interior by participating in the institutions or (iii) overthrow the regime by force from abroad. These divergent views were reflected in the deep opposition between the interior UNAR and the UNAR in exile.[17]

---

[15] G. S. Ibingira, *African Upheavals since Independence*, Boulder, Westview Press, 1980, p. 63.
[16] Prezidansi ya Repubulika, *Ingingo z'ingenzi mu mateka y'u Rwanda: Imyaka cumi y'isabukuru y'ubwingenge 1.7.1962–1.7.1972*, Kigali, Ibiro by'amakuru muli Prezidansi ya Repubulika, 1972, p. 80. The translation is not the author's.
[17] On this, see Lemarchand, *Rwanda and Burundi*, p. 200.

5.3 *Inyenzi* Attacks and Massacres of Tutsi

Most refugees were UNAR members or sympathisers, and they refused to accept as inevitable a permanent exile and definitive settlement in neighbouring countries. UNAR believed that it, and only it, retained the core of true Rwandan culture. In a later context, the refugee movement was said to be 'able to (...) mediate the various conflicts that characterised the deconstruction of pre-genocide Rwanda'.[18] The military ethos that accompanied this conviction will be addressed in Chapter 7. The refugees interpreted the 1959–1961 events as the result of political manoeuvres by the Hutu elites and of a direct attack of the Belgian administration and the Catholic Church against their traditional national culture. As the revolution had been achieved through well-known mechanisms of power seizure, they were convinced that the situation could be reversed by similar means.[19] However, although UNAR in exile found an arena favourable to its ideas of return by force among the refugees, it was deeply divided. 'Traditionalists' or 'monarchists'; 'moderates', 'progressives' or 'socialists'; 'activists' or 'militarists': all these fractions and more were found in most refugee groups.[20] A recurrent cause of friction between and even inside factions was the use of funds received, before and after independence, from countries like China, Cuba and the Soviet Union in support of what they considered the only nationalist and anti-colonialist Rwandan party.

Armed combatants among the refugees, called *inyenzi*,[21] conducted raids from neighbouring countries since before independence.[22] Most attacks did not go far militarily, but the random killing of local civilian officials created an atmosphere of terror and caused a threatening environment for those Tutsi who remained in the country.[23] At the end of

---

[18] Rusagara, *Resilience of a Nation*, p. 195.
[19] R. Yeld, 'Implications of Experience with Refugee Settlement', E.A.I.S.R. Conference paper, Kampala, Makerere University, 1962, p. 4.
[20] An attempt at mapping out these factions and their shifts between 1961 and 1966 can be found in Reyntjens, *Pouvoir et droit*, pp. 456–460.
[21] *Inyenzi* means 'cockroach'. The term's origin is unclear. Some say it was coined by the refugee-combatants themselves to stress their flexibility and invisibility and their capacity to infiltrate and operate at night. Other sources claim the term was used by the republican authorities in a pejorative sense. A third meaning, which however seems to have been proposed only after 1994, says *inyenzi* was an acronym for 'INgangurarugo zi YEmeje kuba ingeNZI', a reference to an army under Kigeri Rwabugiri. Whatever the origin, the meaning of the word changed over time. As will be seen later, during the 1994 genocide it was eventually used to designate all Tutsi.
[22] A survey of attacks between March 1961 and May 1962 can be found in Ministère des Affaires étrangères, *Toute la vérité sur le terrorisme 'Inyenzi' au Rwanda*, Kigali, 1964, pp. 10–12. This government publication describes thirty-six terrorist incidents, most of which involving the use of firearms. For another survey, see National Unity and Reconciliation Commission, *History of Rwanda*, pp. 417–421.
[23] An inside view of the *inyenzi* can be found in Rusagara, *Resilience of a Nation*, pp. 142–155.

1963, a major attack had dramatic consequences. On 21 December, a group of a few hundred *inyenzi* under the command of former UNAR president François Rukeba attacked from Burundi and captured the Gako military camp in the southern Bugesera region. As the camp was under construction, it was only lightly guarded, and the assailants seized some weapons and vehicles. They were well received in the Nyamata *paysannat*, home to many Tutsi displaced from the north in 1959–1960, some of whom joined them. While they were celebrating their first victory, the Rwandan army, assisted by Belgian officers, took positions at Kanzenze bridge about twenty kilometres south of Kigali, and the *inyenzi* were defeated after a brief but violent battle. Several were killed, but most succeeded in withdrawing back to Burundi.[24] The consequences of this incursion that came so close to Kigali were twofold.

The first was the elimination of the Tutsi political leadership. At the moment of the Bugesera invasion, most leaders of UNAR and RADER happened to be in Kigali. On the day of the attack, the national police conducted raids all over town. Several hundred influential Tutsi, as well as some Hutu, were arrested and detained in the Kigali military camp. During the night of 21 to 22 December a triage was operated, and around fifteen prisoners were transferred to Ruhengeri, where they were extrajudicially executed. The victims included UNAR leaders Afrika, Burabyo, Rutsindintwarane, Rwagasana, Gisimba, Ndahiro and Mpirikanyi, as well as RADER leaders Ndazaro and Karinda. A dozen others, mostly notables from Bugesera who had sympathised or collaborated with the *inyenzi*, were sentenced to death or long prison terms by a court martial. At the insistence of the diplomatic community and particularly the apostolic nuncio, the executions were not carried out. A third group, composed mainly of those who had been arrested in Kigali during the attack, were transferred to the Kigali central prison, where they were held without valid legal title. About six months later, they were released against payment of a symbolic fine (often less than 1,000 Rwandan francs). The physical elimination of UNAR's and RADER's main leaders of course led to the disappearance of these parties, although two UNAR MPs returned to the National Assembly and continued to sit until the 1965 elections.

The second consequence was the massacre of a large number of ordinary Tutsi. The *inyenzi* attack created considerable fear and uncertainty across the country. The national army (*Garde nationale*) was small, and threats came from all neighbouring countries with borders that were

---

[24] More details on this invasion can be found in Lemarchand, *Rwanda and Burundi*, pp. 220–223.

difficult to defend. The fear of activities of a 'fifth column' composed of hundreds of thousands of Tutsi who had remained in the country was reinforced by the fact that part of the Tutsi population in Nyamata had joined the attackers, who had clearly played on ethnic solidarity. Communications between the central and local (municipal and prefectoral) authorities were weak, thus enhancing the impact of rumours. In an atmosphere of destabilisation, President Kayibanda despatched his ministers to their home *préfectures* with the task of setting up 'civilian self-defence committees' (*comités civils d'auto-défense*) against terrorism and internal agitation.

An orgy of violence started in Gikongoro *préfecture* at the instigation of *préfet* André Nkeramugaba. Rumours played a prominent role in inciting the killings. Just days before the attack, some local Tutsi were said to have announced that they were to recapture power and restore the monarchy, while during the attack it was rumoured that Kigali had fallen into the *inyenzi*'s hands and that former *mwami* Kigeri was returning from exile.[25] The Gikongoro population, which had lived close to the royal court and suffered directly from its excesses, was receptive to panic and ready to heed calls for violence. An estimated 5,000 to 8,000 Tutsi, representing between 10 and 20 per cent of the Tutsi population in the *préfecture*, were killed in Gikongoro. As always under such circumstances, scores were settled and personal interests pursued. The *préfet* was even said to have eliminated certain Hutu to appropriate their land; at any rate he had become a large landowner after the events. Apart from Gikongoro, the regions most touched by the violence were Rusumo and Bugesera. Although the rest of the country was less affected, many Tutsi felt sufficiently threatened to leave the country.

A precise countrywide casualty figure is unknown. The figure of 870 put forward by the Rwandan government was clearly far lower than the reality.[26] By contrast, some spectacular press reports and propaganda from UNAR and the Burundian government proposed vast exaggerations.[27] Independent and impartial observers arrived at estimates of between 10,000 and 14,000 victims, half of them in Gikongoro alone.[28] As to the legal qualification of the massacres, the special representative of the UN General Secretary, Max Dorsinville, found no evidence of genocide. His 3 March 1964 report reads in part:

---

[25] A. Segal, *Massacre in Rwanda*, London, Fabian Research Series Pamphlet 240, 1964, p. 15.
[26] Ministère des Affaires étrangères, *Toute la vérité*, p. 19.
[27] A brief survey can be found in Reyntjens, *Pouvoir et droit*, pp. 466–467.
[28] Lemarchand, *Rwanda and Burundi*, p. 225.

It now seems clear that these brutal acts were in no sense dictated by the Government in Kigali, but rather took place in areas over which the Government had little control due to lack of troops. In such areas a 'popular militia' took reprisals on some of the Batutsi population as a result of the raids of 20–21 December and the fear and panic which they inspired in the Bahutu population. (...) It is noteworthy that some 45 per cent of the Rwandese administrative services are still staffed by Batutsi, and the teachers of secondary schools and above are in the majority Batutsi. It would seem, therefore, that, despite the violent reprisals of late December, there is no question of a systematic elimination or extermination of the Batutsi, or of what some sources have hastened to call genocide.[29]

This is also Segal's view: 'There was no government policy decision to engage in genocide against the Tutsi',[30] for which he finds confirmation in the fact that the authorities have not prevented thousands of Tutsi from leaving the country.[31] That said, when President Kayibanda sent his ministers across the country to fight the 'fifth column' and left the responsibility to restore order to local authorities, he opened the gates to ethnically inspired massacres. Desrosiers observes that failures to act, muted responses or even support at the national level appear to have created the space for local *préfets* and *bourgmestres* to support or condone the local violence.[32] Therefore, even if a genocidal intent had not existed at the central level, facts show that it was present among some *préfets* and mayors, as was clearly the case in Gikongoro.

However, the leaders of the external UNAR and of the *inyenzi* also bear part of the blame. Indeed they knew that the lives of civilian Tutsi would be lost in case of an attack.[33] The initiators may have felt that the sacrifice of some lives was acceptable and that those Tutsi who had remained inside the country were traitors anyway.[34] In addition, Desrosiers notes that the focus on reprisals and authorities' involvement should not overshadow how overwhelmed national authorities felt as the events unfolded, another aspect Dorsinville's assessment of the situation highlighted. The attack must be set in the broader context of similar border threats throughout the first republic, of which the 1963 attack was one of the more serious manifestations.[35] In line with the general

---

[29] This document titled 'The situation in Rwanda and Burundi' can be found in 'Décolonisation et indépendance', pp. 704–707.
[30] A. Segal, 'Rwanda: The Underlying Causes', *Africa Report*, April 1964, p. 5.
[31] Segal, *Massacre in Rwanda*, p. 16.
[32] Desrosiers, *Trajectories*, p. 220.
[33] Because he feared these consequences and doubted the chances of success of a military operation, *mwami* Kigeri had formally forbidden it in writing (author's interviews with Kigeri Ndahindurwa, Nairobi, 2 July 1981, and François Rukeba, Nairobi, 4 July 1981).
[34] As will be seen later, in this and other respects there are similarities with the 1994 genocide.
[35] Desrosiers, *Trajectories*, pp. 221–222.

tendency to read Rwanda through ethnic lenses, the focus has indeed been less on the raids themselves than on their consequences, namely reprisals against Tutsi. Yet these raids were very threatening, causing considerable destabilisation and affecting the regime's sense of grounding and control.[36]

Although sporadic raids occurred until 1967, the Bugesera attack was the last genuine threat of the republican regime by UNAR. Both inside and outside the country the party disappeared, but we will see later that Tutsi refugees continued organising themselves and that in the end they would prevail.

5.4 Internal Conflicts

Despite the appearance of monolithic power exercised by the de facto single party, the regime's contradictions soon came out in the open. As its objective of securing power for the Hutu was achieved, the MDR-Parmehutu found itself without much of a political programme. After the elimination of the opposition and the disappearance, or so it seemed, of the *inyenzi*'s military threat, the party soon lost the cohesion imposed by common enemies. Personal oppositions and opportunism emerged rapidly, and this had become clear by mid 1966. Realising that the party was dying a slow death, the leadership called an important national congress on 23 October 1966. The resolutions that were adopted offer a good survey of the ills it was suffering: poor vitality, regionalism, subversion, rumour mongering, corruption, embezzlement, opportunism.[37] A close and sympathetic observer of the first republic added that the party also suffered from an old Rwandan political disease, 'this subtle and indirect way of communicating, generally very common in Rwandan political circles, that imposed on all participants an untiring prudence and patience'.[38]

The discontent in party ranks reached unprecedented levels two years later. Distrust in the government was so widespread that the National Assembly put in place a commission of inquiry with a very broad mandate, that of studying 'everything the country suffers from'. Its mission was 'to inform us of the state of the nation and its economic and social development'.[39] The mission order issued by the Assembly's speaker

---

[36] Ibid., pp. 211–212.
[37] The resolutions can be found in MDR-Parmehutu, *Manifeste-Programme, Statuts, Résolutions*, Gitarama, Secrétariat exécutif national, s.d., pp. 74–91.
[38] B. Paternostre de la Mairieu, *Le Rwanda: Son effort de développement*, Brussels–Kigali, A. De Boeck-Editions rwandaises, 1972, p. 292.
[39] Assemblée nationale, Doc. No. 342 (1967–68), meeting of 9 April 1968, pp. 6–7.

indicated that the commission was to report on the following issues: administration and politics, justice, prison management, state of the intermunicipal treasuries and the implementation of the development budget.[40] Although some institutions, most prominently the prison service, the supreme court and the general prosecutor's office, refused to cooperate, the commission produced a very critical report of 107 pages and dozens of pages of annexes.

In addition to many detailed observations too long to address here, the commission's general findings were very severe. It 'is in a position to affirm that the ideals of the Hutu regime increasingly weaken'. While the Hutu victory during the revolution satisfied the population, now 'discord reigns among the people, and this is provoked or encouraged by the authorities themselves. Mayors, *préfets*, ministers and certain MPs do not enjoy the confidence of the population (...), they are the first to generate hatred, fend for themselves, ignore the law, and neglect the work of common interest.'[41] As for the MDR-Parmehutu, the party 'gives rise to many complaints in all corners of the country': 'The popular masses complain that their leaders have cheated them when saying that their revolution of 1959 would free them from injustice. They now realise that this was a way for them to capture functions; once they were secured, injustice is worse than before.'[42]

The commission's observations were very grave and spared no one.[43] Unsurprisingly its publication caused great controversy. When the report came up for debate in the Assembly on 4 December, MP Mulindahabi tabled a motion, signed by twenty lawmakers, that proposed to reject the report without debate. He explained that 'the wish of the (motion's) signatories is to publicly disavow this report and its disgusting content of insults to the most respected values of our country, and to ban it from all documents and proceedings of the National Assembly'.[44] The debate on the motion to reject the report lasted five days, during which the substance of the commission's findings was not discussed. Harsh words were used: the report was called subversive,[45] and its drafters had

---

[40] *Raporo ya komisiyo y'ubugenzuzi y'inteko nkuru y'amategeko muwa 1968* (*Report of the Parliamentary Commission of Inquiry 1968*), Kigali, 29 October 1968, annex 1 to the introduction. The text is in Kinyarwanda; the translation is not the author's.

[41] Ibid., p. 97.

[42] Ibid., p. 101.

[43] In an annex on Gitarama *préfecture*, President Kayibanda himself was accused of having used municipal wood for the brick ovens he operated for the construction of the local prison.

[44] Assemblée nationale, Doc. No. 372 (1968–69), meeting of 4 December 1968, p. 1.

[45] This opinion was well expressed by MP Munyarugerero when he told the commission's members 'If I had some power, I'd put you all in jail right away' (Ibid., p. 3).

5.4 Internal Conflicts

de facto become an opposition party by 'deviating from the party line'. Under a great deal of pressure, more MPs joined those who signed the motion to reject, which was finally adopted on 11 December.[46]

Occurring less than ten years after the revolution, this episode showed how fragile the MDR-Parmehutu's ideology was. Fourteen MPs were victims of a real political massacre: they were either excluded from the party or excluded from the candidates lists for the 1969 parliamentary elections. All of them were among Kayibanda's first allies who waged the revolution with him. The list included a former president of the republic (Mbonyumutwa), four former ministers, the sitting and a former speaker of the Assembly and two signatories of the 'Bahutu Manifesto'. The consequences of this episode were crucial for the country's immediate post-independence political history. Kayibanda became increasingly isolated and put under the control of a small coterie of Gitarama politicians led first by Calliope Mulindahabi and from 1971 by Athanase Mbarubukeye. As will be seen later, these incidents were to herald the end of the first republic.[47]

There were also signals of divides within the security sector. In late 1968, in the middle of the political turmoil discussed earlier, a rumoured attempted coup targeted not civilian powers but Lt Col Juvénal Habyarimana, the minister of the *Garde nationale* and police. Captain Joachim Muramutsa and the platoon he commanded apparently attempted to kidnap or depose Habyarimana. Hence, the attempt came to be known as the *coup de Muramutsa*. Muramutsa was eventually convicted of conspiracy against Habyarimana and sentenced to twenty years in jail. The *coup de Muramutsa* resurfaced a few years later, in 1971, when participation in the plot was offered as the rationale for the arrest of another officer suspected of planning a coup, Commandant Pierre Nyatanyi, who was eventually also court-martialled and sentenced to twenty years in jail.[48]

Like in precolonial days, rumours were used for political purposes, in this case to weaken Kayibanda's position. In 1970, rumours on the president's health persisted for months. Another rumour suggested that the president faked health problems to test his ministers' loyalty, wanting to see how they would act if his hold on power appeared to be weakening.[49]

---

[46] Thirty voted in favour, none against, while eleven abstained in order to defend the report as mentioned in the justification of their abstention (Assemblée nationale, Doc. No. 376 (1968–69), meeting of 11 December 1968, p. 14).
[47] More details on the 1968 commission of enquiry and its consequences can be found in Reyntjens, *Pouvoir et droit*, pp. 387–395.
[48] Desrosiers, *Trajectories*, pp. 243–244.
[49] Ibid., pp. 1–2.

For lack of space, other conflicts that weakened the regime can only be mentioned here.[50] Some were personal, for example old guard versus new generation; Catholics versus Adventists; Singa versus Sindi clans in the North; politicians from Butare versus those from Gitarama; and Mulindahabi versus Rwasibo. Other conflicts had distinctly regional overtones: north versus centre–south on the status of the *ubukonde* clientship system and, within the north, Gisenyi versus Ruhengeri. These regional conflicts must be briefly discussed.

5.5   Regional Conflicts

We have seen in the previous chapter that the revolutionary motivation in the centre and south of the country was different from that in the north. Its restorative nature in the north is well illustrated by the issue of *ubukonde*. Unlike the cattle-based *ubuhake*, this was a clientship system based on land. Briefly summarised, this institution was based on the fact that a lineage that cleared the forest and transformed it into agricultural land became its owner (*umukonde*) on account of the fact that the clearing of virgin forest involves heavy work and that under all traditional systems of tenure the expenditure of labour creates rights.[51] When all land was cleared or at least owned by a lineage, newcomers could no longer become *umukonde* and had to engage in an *ubugererwa* clientship relation with an existing owner. In exchange for an initial fee and regular gifts of sorghum beer, the *umugererwa* became a client and obtained the right to use the land, which remained the property of the *umukonde*. The client owed fidelity and allegiance to his patron, who in turn owed protection to his client.[52]

Given the similarities with *ubuhake* and after the revolution, maintaining the institution of *ubukonde* became a delicate issue, even if it was 'hutu'. However, mainly because the revolution was restorative in the north and *ubukonde* was not a 'tutsi' institution, the *abakonde* were not ready to abandon it without a fight. Unsurprisingly, the '*ubukonde* problem' resurfaced regularly after independence, pitting politicians from Gisenyi and Ruhengeri against the rest of the country. The National

---

[50] For more details see Reyntjens, *Pouvoir et droit*, pp. 479–495. Internal conflicts are also addressed in F.-X. Munyarugerero, *Réseaux, pouvoirs, oppositions: La compétition politique au Rwanda*, Paris, L'Harmattan, 2003, pp. 99–109; 119–130.

[51] C. K. Meek, *Land Law and Custom in the Colonies*, London, Oxford University Press, 1949, p. 23.

[52] On *ubukonde*, see J. J. Maquet, S. Naigiziki, 'Les droits fonciers dans le Ruanda ancien', *Zaïre*, 1957, pp. 340–359.

Assembly attempted to settle the problem in 1964, 1965 and 1966, but the northern politicians, more particularly the *abakonde* among them, succeeded in sliding it on the long track. After the conflictual episode of the 1968 parliamentary report and the 1969 elections, it quietly disappeared from the political agenda. After the 1973 coup d'etat (discussed later), which brought northerners to power, the issue remained in the drawer. For them, the survival of *ubukonde* relations was not an economic necessity in the first place but a political one, as they ensured a large clientship base and were therefore a substantial political asset. Although the issue was never formally settled, the problem solved itself. After a sufficiently long use, *abakonde* voluntarily ceded the land for free. If relations between former patron and client continued, it was generally on a friendly basis.[53]

Throughout the years, the basis for regional competition narrowed considerably. Geographically, the revolutionary movement developed along the axis Butare–Gitarama–Ruhengeri. This base became smaller over the years: already in 1963, Butare was eliminated as a relevant political player, followed by the north in 1968 as a result of the conflict surrounding the parliamentary commission of enquiry. By 1972 the power grab by a small circle of 'Gitaramists' was complete: Mbarubukeye was the party's national executive secretary, one third of the government was composed of ministers from Gitarama and the National Assembly had lost all power since the 1969 elections. This concentration of power created a strong sense of isolation, and it was to lead to the end of the first republic.

5.6 The End of the First Republic

The Rwandan army was created only in 1960 when special resident Logiest decided to recruit a 650-man '*Garde territoriale*' (called *Garde nationale* after independence), 85 per cent of which was to be Hutu and 15 per cent Tutsi. From the outset, the north was the preferred recruiting ground, as the men there were supposed to be 'stronger' (*des farouches montagnards*) than those of the south and centre. An author considered the north as the 'gorilla' of the national authority.[54] This reminded paradoxically of the monarchical past, as *mwami* Kigeri Rwabugiri incorporated in his personal guard the famous company of

---

[53] Author's conversations with former *abakonde* Wellars Banzi (Gisenyi, 20 May 1981), Otto Rusingizandekwe (Ruhengeri, 20 May 1981) and Thaddée Bagaragaza (Kigali, 21 May 1981).
[54] Rutabuzwa Buranga, *Rwanda et Burundi: les nouveaux sorciers*, Paris, author's edition, 1979, p. 10.

Abarashi (arrow shooters) who came from the north, more precisely from Gahunga, at the foot of Muhabura volcano.[55]

After Juvénal Habyarimana from Gisenyi became the defence minister in 1965, this 'nordist' accent became irreversible. Although the army showed professionalism and remained politically neutral, by 1967 rumours about a coup d'état were circulating, so much so that President Kayibanda felt the need to issue a warning in a speech on the occasion of a graduation ceremony at the Officers School in March 1967. Claiming that 'subversive persons use subtle propaganda to attribute ideas of a *coup d'état* to certain officers', he told them 'they waste time given the fidelity and wisdom that characterise our officers'.[56] Apart from an enigmatic coup attempt that led nowhere in September 1968 (cf. Section 5.4), the army stayed out of politics until 1973.

In February 1973 serious tensions erupted, successively in schools, the civil service and private companies, and the broader public, in that order.[57] Initially, the resentment was in part ethnic, due to the fact that about half the pupils and teachers in many institutions of secondary and higher education were Tutsi.[58] President Kayibanda, who wished to 're-establish' 'normal proportions', was prevented from doing so by the legislation that provided for national exams to determine access to a higher level of education. By 1972, Kayibanda's patience had reached its limits. The December issue of the MDR-Parmehutu's journal *Le Mois* announced that '[t]his year (…) we have seen children of the people reach normal proportions in the country's schools, despite subtle manoeuvres by the combined reactionary and neo-colonial forces.'[59] Clearly this was not enough, and the destabilisation of schools during the following months was organised by Kayibanda himself, together with the party's executive secretary Mbarubukeye and minister Makuza. Lists signed 'Students' movement' or 'Committee of public salvation' were posted in all institutions of secondary and higher education.[60] The pupils and students on these lists, almost all of them Tutsi, were told to leave, which most of them did, failing which 'commandos' forced them out. In some cases, these expulsions were violent.

The movement rapidly extended in two ways: on the one hand to the civil service and private businesses following the same lists system and

---

[55] A. Kagame, *Les milices du Rwanda précolonial*, Brussels, ARSOM, 1963, pp. 165–166.
[56] This speech is reproduced in *Rwanda Carrefour d'Afrique*, No. 64, March 1967, pp. 4–5, 9.
[57] For a more detailed treatment, see Reyntjens, *Pouvoir et droit*, pp. 501–504.
[58] 'Le sort des Tutsi au Rwanda', *Remarques Africaines*, No. 418, 16–31 March 1973, p. 19.
[59] *Le Mois*, No. 22, December 1972, p. 1.
[60] Spicy detail: Pasteur Bizimungu, an RPF leader who was the president from 1994 to 2000, was a member of these committees.

on the other to rural hills, in particular in the *préfectures* of Gitarama and Kibuye, where Tutsi were told to leave and some of their houses or huts were set on fire. The violence caused the death of several hundred persons, and the processes were reminiscent of the November 1959 *jacquerie*. However, the movement soon spun out of control. Ministers appeared on lists in Kigali; Hutu from the centre and south were chased away near Ruhengeri; houses and shops of well-off Hutu were ransacked. What had started as ethnically inspired strife became a class struggle and a regional conflict, overtly opposing the north (Bakiga) and the centre–south (Banyenduga). After a long period of complicit silence, the government finally tried to address the situation. On 22 March Kayibanda pronounced a message of pacification, and from 14 April a ministerial commission toured the secondary schools and institutions of higher education. The bishops appealed for calm. Order seemed to have returned by the end of April.

Several elements converged to bring about these events that heralded the end of the first republic. The genocide against the Hutu in Burundi a year earlier and the arrival of tens of thousands of Hutu refugees caused emotional reactions in Rwanda. Many Hutu felt that despite the revolution Tutsi were overrepresented in schools and private businesses. Perhaps most importantly, the Kayibanda regime was collapsing, and it opted to draw attention away from the deep contradictions that had become so visible in 1968. Chrétien has remarked that putting the ethnic issue forward had an obvious use for the ruling circles: an 'objective' (in this case ethnic) criterion allows to monopolise functions of command in a poor society where places are scarce, 'whereby the real conflicts and stakes are constantly deviated toward alienating reflexes of racial solidarity'.[61] However, the Gitarama politicians who stirred these troubles lost sight of the unforeseen dynamics such events often create in a situation of incomplete control. As a result people started attacking the wealthy rather than the Tutsi as such; northern Hutu chased those of the centre and south; pupils targeted the children of certain Hutu politicians; politicians from the north extended the movement to ministries and businesses where they felt marginalised. As a response, Kayibanda reinforced his isolationist policy, for instance by transferring high-ranking officers from the north to civilian positions far away from Kigali. Most ministries' permanent secretaries and nine out of ten *préfets* were replaced.

In March and April, there were coup rumours, and probably even an attempted coup in April. Other steps brought the regime's end nearer.

---

[61] J.-P. Chrétien, 'Les fratricides légitimés', *Esprit*, 1976, p. 833.

On 18 May, the constitution was amended to allow Kayibanda to continue in office after the elections slated later in 1973: besides increasing the president's tenure from four to five years, the limit on the number of terms disappeared, as did the maximum age for candidates. This theoretically opened the way for a life presidency. Another measure caused great concern. On 18 June, Kayibanda promulgated a law creating the *Office national du commerce*, in an attempt to organise state control of private commerce. In the eyes of many, this confirmed that the president had fallen into the hands of a small 'socialist' entourage.

The 1 July celebrations of the eleventh anniversary of independence took place in a real pre-coup atmosphere. During the ceremony the sound technicians boycotted the presidential speech; northern civil servant Alphonse Ribanje grabbed the microphone and told the president '*vaho twakurambiwe!*' ('go away, we don't want you any more'); Lt Col Alexis Kanyarengwe, a native from Ruhengeri and the second highest ranking officer, left the event, openly showing his contempt for Kayibanda. In this atmosphere, the president uttered his famous challenge: 'If someone feels more capable than me to lead the country, let him come and take my place.'[62] This happened less than a week later. During the night of 4 to 5 July, the National Guard, under the command of Maj. Gen. Juvénal Habyarimana took power in a bloodless coup d'état.[63]

5.7   The Birth of the Second Republic

The proclamation of the National Guard's high command was remarkably understanding for Kayibanda.[64] It stated that 'Grégoire Kayibanda, elected by the people and for whom the High Command of the National Guard maintains its respect, has unfortunately allowed himself to be carried away by individuals who refused to understand that all Rwandans are brothers, whatever their region of birth', a clear reference to the concentration of power in Gitarama and the conflicts between the north and centre. Kayibanda was nevertheless deposed and replaced by the defence minister and the chief of army staff, Habyarimana. The government was 'temporarily' replaced by a Committee for Peace and National Unity (Comité pour la paix et l'unité nationale – CPUN) composed of eleven

---

[62] The events of 1 July are summarised in Rutabuzwa Buranga, *Rwanda et Burundi*, pp. 101–102.
[63] More details on the events during the spring of 1973 and the lead up to the coup can be found in Munyarugerero, *Réseaux, pouvoirs, oppositions*, pp. 130–144; Desrosiers, *Trajectories*, pp. 121–148.
[64] Published in the Official Gazette (*Journal officiel*), special issue, 5 July 1973.

officers. The National Assembly was dissolved. Political activities were forbidden across the country, and the organs of the MDR-Parmehutu were dissolved. Thirty-one articles of the constitution were in whole or in part 'provisionally suspended'.

A year later, the appeasing language of the 5 July 1973 proclamation had given way to recrimination:

> The party that we have abolished had become the instrument of obscure manoeuvres. It is through it that measures of pressure, exaction and unfortunate combinations transited. (...) Around the former head of state the administrative apparatus had transformed itself into a 'court' populated by intriguing courtiers, avid for promotions and privileges justified neither by their intellectual capacity nor by their personal merit.[65]

A judicial sequel of the coup followed a year later, when a law-decree of 9 June 1974 created a court martial that was deemed competent to judge offences against the security of the state, with the aim of trying the political leaders of the first republic. The court, which sat in Ruhengeri, condemned Kayibanda and seven leading figures of his regime to death and other former politicians to prison sentences. The death sentences were commuted to life in prison, though Kayibanda spent most of his term under house arrest at his home near Gitarama, where he died in December 1976. The other Ruhengeri convicts received clemency in January 1979, but dozens of them had by then died in the political section of Ruhengeri prison as a result of bad treatment.[66]

5.8 Civilianisation

The return to constitutional government after a period of military rule can take place in two ways. Either the army effectively withdraws from politics by transferring power to civilians under a new or the pre-coup constitution (demilitarisation) or the military withdraws in its de facto capacity but maintains power through a new constitutional arrangement that legitimises its regime (civilianisation). Initially, the return to constitutional rule in Rwanda was of this second modality.

The first step came before the constitution. A new single party, the Mouvement révolutionnaire national pour le développement

---

[65] 'Message du chef de l'Etat à l'occasion de la fête de la paix et de l'unité nationale', Kigali, La Relève, 1974, p. 52.

[66] After having fallen in disgrace (as shown later), Théoneste Lizinde and eleven others were convicted for their role in these killings in 1985. A summary of the judgment can be found in S. J. Barahinyura, *1973–1988: Le Général-Major Habyarimana – Quinze ans de tyrannie et de tartuferie au Rwanda*, Frankfurt am Main, Editions Izuba, 1988, pp. 123–132.

(MRND), was created on 5 July 1975, two years after the coup. Its manifesto contained rather vague intentions, such as 'the definitive eradication of sequels of hatred and division created by our country's history between the three ethnic groups and the regions' and 'the creation of a coalition of all the Nation's live forces against underdevelopment in the mental and socio-economic domains'. The initial composition of the central committee caused resentment because of the overrepresentation of Habyarimana's home *préfecture*: out of the sixteen members appointed in July 1976, seven hailed from Gisenyi. In particular the political leaders of the neighbouring *préfecture* of Ruhengeri, which had been closely associated with the military takeover, expressed discontent. This imbalance was later reduced, though the north as a whole remained predominant. The functions of the CPUN were transferred to the central committee, in which some leading CPUN members were appointed.

An initial draft constitution made by an MRND commission was almost a copy of the 1974 Zairean constitution and generated critical comments and observations. As a result, in early 1978 three lawyers were tasked with proposing a new draft based on general guidelines formulated by the president and the central committee. A report and a draft constitution were submitted in July.[67] Things then moved quickly. On 10 October, a joint meeting of the government and the central committee adopted the draft with some amendments. On 17 December, the constitutional referendum returned 89.09 per cent of positive votes, and a week later Habyarimana obtained 98.99 per cent of the votes at the presidential election.

Space forbids a detailed analysis of the constitution.[68] Suffice it to say that the text was inspired by the French constitution for the organisation of the branches of government and their relations, by the Belgian one for the protection of human rights and by the Tanzanian one for the status and role of the single party. The MRND was institutionalised as the single party: of Zairean inspiration, article 7 stated that the Rwandan people were politically organised within the MRND, 'single political formation outside of which no political activity can be exercised'. Every Rwandan was a birth-right member of the movement whose mission it was 'to unite, stimulate and intensify the efforts of the Rwandan people with a view to achieving its development in peace and national unity'.

---

[67] R. De Wolf, A. Ntashamaje, F. Reyntjens, *Projet de constitution de la République Rwandaise: Rapport présenté à Monsieur le Président de la République*, July 1978.

[68] An analysis can be found in F. Reyntjens, 'La nouvelle constitution rwandaise du 20 décembre 1978', *Penant*, 1980, pp. 117–134.

5.9 Elections

Since the return to constitutional rule, six elections were organised at the national level: presidential polls in 1978, 1983 and 1988 and parliamentary polls in 1981, 1983 and 1988. Not much needs to be said about the presidential elections. As the chair of the MRND was the only candidate allowed to 'run', like elsewhere in Africa the polls were an illustration of what Rouquié has called 'the dynamics of risk-free elections'.[69] Habyarimana was credited with 98.99 per cent of the vote in 1978, 99.85 in 1983 and 99.98 in 1988, thus leaving little scope for progress in his popularity score. Even if the president had honestly wished free and fair elections, that was impossible to achieve, as officials at every level (polling station, municipality, *préfecture*) wanted the 'right' result and used pressure and fraud to achieve it if necessary.[70]

Apart from some isolated cases of fraud, parliamentary elections were more competitive and overall relatively honestly conducted, and they showed that polls can have a meaning even in a single-party context. The electoral process allowed the party, which at other times was coterminous with the state, to profile itself and establish links with the population. Elections also allowed the expression of competition, which routinely was prohibited or at least viewed negatively, in an orderly and controlled fashion. In that sense, elections were 'a mode of periodic revitalisation of the party'.[71] This was in part made possible by the fact that the MRND proposed a number of candidates double that of MPs to be elected in each constituency, namely the *préfecture*. Although the lists were approved at the central level, this requirement allowed the voters to modify the order and send less well placed candidates to parliament. For instance, in 1988 thirteen candidates were thus elected.[72] This did not change the fact that parliamentary polls remained a marginal exercise in the periphery far from the centre of political power. This is shown by the fact that violent purges took place in case the centre was threatened.

---

[69] A. Rouquié, 'La dynamique des élections sans risque ou la voie africaine de l'Etat', in Centre d'étude de l'Afrique noire, *Aux urnes l'Afrique! Elections et pouvoir en Afrique noire*, Paris, Pedone, 1978.
[70] Examples of fraud can be found in F. Reyntjens, 'La deuxième république rwandaise: évolution, bilan et perspectives', *Afrika Focus*, No. 3–4, 1986, p. 284.
[71] J. F. Bayart, F. Constantin, C. Coulon, D. Martin, 'Par le canal du scrutin: Comment dépouiller les élections africaines?', in Centre d'étude de l'Afrique noire, *Aux urnes l'Afrique!*, p. 17.
[72] F. Reyntjens, 'Cooptation politique à l'envers: les législatives de 1988 au Rwanda', *Politique Africaine*, No. 34, 1989, pp. 121–126.

5.10 Internal Conflicts, Again

We have seen that politics in Rwanda at the core of power have been highly conflictual from precolonial days on. Since independence, a considerable reduction of the base of these conflicts could be observed. The one opposing the main ethnic groups that ended with the elimination of Tutsi as a political force during the years around independence was followed by one between Hutu from the north and those from the centre and south. While the first republic had increasingly concentrated power in a small elite from Gitarama, the 1973 coup ended this conflict in favour of those from the north. However, the north was not homogenous, and a latent conflict between the *préfectures* of Gisenyi and Ruhengeri came to the fore. Habyarimana's Gisenyi became predominant, but as soon as the supremacy was achieved, Gisenyi in turn divided between Habyarimana's Bushiru and neighbouring Bugoyi. This marked the resurgence of an old antagonism between these regions, which had remained staunchly autonomous in precolonial and early colonial days (see Sections 1.1 and 2.5.2).

While the regime appeared monolithic, fissures soon appeared. Already in March 1974, six officers were arrested amidst rumours of a coup planned for the previous month.[73] Trouble was brewing in and around the CPUN in 1974 and 1975, amidst frustrations among lower- and middle-ranking personnel regarding salaries and agitation in the university. Coup rumours intensified in late 1978. The fractionalisation played out around the original core of the regime: those behind the coup, the original *Camarades du 5 juillet*, more particularly high-ranking officers such as Alexis Kanyarengwe, Aloys Nsekalije and Théoneste Lizinde.[74]

In the meantime, the northern divide increasingly impacted central governance, as was well illustrated by the so-called Lizinde affair. In November 1979, the powerful chief of the Central Intelligence Service (Service central des renseignements – SCR) Major Théoneste Lizinde was sacked. Due to his function, this influential figure from Bugoyi was one of the regime's strongmen, and his sidelining suggested tensions at the core of the system. This was confirmed a few months later, in March 1980. The hostilities were publicly opened when the respected governor of the central bank, the mugoyi Jean Birara, sent an open letter to President Habyarimana, in which he defended himself against attacks by three high-ranking military officers close to the head of state.

---

[73] Desrosiers, *Trajectories*, p. 246.
[74] Ibid., pp. 247–251.

5.10 Internal Conflicts, Again

He wrote that 'if I were attacked because I wasn't born in a chosen region (a reference to Bushiru), I would light-heartedly accept this if it were clearly said'. In the letter and the minutes of a meeting held on 7 March in the central bank, Birara settled scores with influential Colonels Buregeya and Serubuga and Major Rwagafilita. The finance minister supported the governor in a letter of 12 March, where he called these officers 'ignorant, rapacious thieves' and invited Birara 'not to take into account the considerations voiced by the scum on issues of which it totally ignores the alphabet'. In a country where discretion and reserve are held in high esteem, this was unheard language, particularly since the position of those attacked in these terms made the attacks seen as aimed indirectly at Habyarimana himself.

Birara's initiative attracted followers. Anonymous tracts and pamphlets started to circulate.[75] For instance, the Artisans of change (Artisans du changement – Parmehutu rénové) launched a text under the title 'In order to redress the situation before it is too late'. Vox Populi Vox Dei published a 'Position in face of the scandals of the powerful'. A document addressed to the president, signed by 'Those who love the land of Gahutu, Gatutsi and Gatwa', contained a direct attack against Habyarimana personally, wherein he was accused of misappropriation of funds, abuse of power, anti-democratic behaviour and nepotism. Apart from other claims, most of the tracts drew attention to the problem of regionalism in general and more particularly to the privileges the Bushiru region was said to be accumulating. In a speech made on 31 March 1980, while admitting that some situations needed improvements, Habyarimana insisted on stopping addressing complaints 'to the street' by way of tracts, and he denounced the 'long drinking sessions', particularly in certain Kigali milieus, as the main cause of the agitation.[76]

Based on the names mentioned and the ideas developed in the tracts, clearly a coalition between Bugoyi region and Ruhengeri *préfecture* against Bushiru was in the making. On 23 April, Théoneste Lizinde was arrested, suspected of plotting a coup d'etat. During the following days and weeks dozens of other personalities were jailed. In December, Colonel Kanyarengwe, fearing arrest, fled to Tanzania.[77] After a second

---

[75] The texts of some of these documents are reproduced in Barahinyura, *1973–1988*, pp. 83–114. Others are in this author's archives.
[76] 'Mise au point du Président de la République à propos des rumeurs et tracts circulant dans le pays', Agence Rwandaise de Presse, *Bulletin quotidien*, No. 1455, 1 April 1980, pp. 1–5.
[77] Earlier that month, he was not re-appointed to the MRND central committee, which he could only interpret as a threatening fall from grace. Kanyarengwe and Lizinde were to join the RPF in 1990 and 1991 respectively.

wave of arrests and a long judicial investigation, forty-seven persons were tried before the court of state security (*cour de sûreté de l'Etat*), which sat in Ruhengeri from 17 September to 25 November 1981.[78] Twenty-four of the accused were acquitted and twenty-one were condemned to prison sentences of between two and twenty-five years. Lizinde and Alphonse Kagenza, a businessman, were sentenced to death.[79]

While the affair of the 'plotters of March 1980' was a telling illustration of conflicts among northern elites, antagonism between the north, Gisenyi in particular, and the rest of the country continued. This problem was particularly resented in the area of education, where the percentage of pupils from Gisenyi admitted to secondary schools was double that of other *préfectures*. Statistics for the mid 1980s of major positions in the state political, administrative and military apparatus showed an average of five to eight posts for the other *préfectures*, a slight bias for Ruhengeri with eleven, and a strong overrepresentation for Gisenyi with twenty-four. In addition, the defence and security apparatus was almost completely controlled by Habyarimana's *préfecture*.[80] According to data from the early 1990s, thirty-three public entities out of a total of sixty-eight were led by directors from Gisenyi and Ruhengeri (nineteen and fourteen positions respectively).[81] The 'disparity index' of scholarships abroad for the period 1979–1986 was 1.83 for Gisenyi and 1.44 for Ruhengeri (the least well served *préfecture*, Kibungo, had an index of 0.67).[82]

Before the final, and lethal as it turned out, assault, the last threatening moment for the regime was the assassination of Colonel Stanislas Mayuya in April 1988. Very close to Habyarimana, he was considered as a possible presidential successor. The sergeant who killed him was caught and died under suspicious circumstances. Several rumours and hypotheses about those behind Mayuya's death circulated,[83] but the results of an official investigation were never published. The Mayuya Affair again suggested regime fragmentation, especially in high military circles. Unknown at the time, the security sector was to face a fatal challenge two and a half years later.

---

[78] Ruhengeri is associated with political repression, as we have seen earlier in the cases of the fate of Tutsi politicians in late 1963 and that of leaders of the first republic after the 1973 coup.

[79] A more detailed treatment of the Lizinde–Kanyarengwe affair can be found in J. Gasana, *Rwanda: du parti-Etat à l'Etat-garnison*, Paris, L'Harmattan, 2002, pp. 27–32; Munyarugerero, *Réseaux, pouvoirs, oppositions*, pp. 188–194; Desrosiers, *Trajectories*, pp. 253–61.

[80] More data can be found in Reyntjens, 'La deuxième république rwandaise', pp. 288–289.

[81] *Kinyamateka*, No. 1344, April 1991, p. 10.

[82] *Dialogue*, No. 143, November–December 1990, p. 92.

[83] Desrosiers, *Trajectories*, pp. 262–263.

By the late 1980s, the political malaise was profound. The situation was well summarised by the Belgian ambassador who noted in January 1989 that 'while there is no credible alternative to Habyarimana, his wait-and-see attitude has nevertheless favoured the emergence of a certain malaise, where new resentments and rivalries (north-south, city-country, barons of the regime-rising elites) have come to dangerously overlap with the traditional centrifugal forces of Rwandan society'.[84] This pessimism was picked up by the Belgian press (also see Section 5.13).[85]

5.11 The Situation of the Tutsi: A Festering Wound

As seen in the previous chapter, the 1959 revolution marked the beginning of the departure into exile of Tutsi, most of them in 1959–1961, 1963–1964 and 1973. These refugees numbered about 600,000 at the end of the 1980s, and most of them lived in neighbouring countries.[86] This was a factor of structural insecurity, as these refugee communities never accepted that their exile was permanent. To the contrary, they always claimed their 'Rwandaness' and hence their right to return home. We have seen that, already before independence, groups of refugees attempted to force this ambition through armed attacks and terrorist operations. The violent attempts of the *inyenzi* ended in 1967.

The attitude of governments towards this problem evolved. While the regime of the first republic repeatedly invited the refugees to return and promised to integrate them, the conflicts that led to their exile persisted: in light of continued ethnic antagonism and discrimination against the Tutsi, the refugees did not see a wholesale return as a viable option. While the policy of ethnic pacification under the second republic from 1973 alleviated this problem, without however leading to its solution, another constraint was put forward by the regime. Rwanda was said to be 'full', a position that was made official by a declaration of the MRND's central committee on 26 July 1986. Mentioning demographic constraints, the document affirmed that 'in this conjuncture, Rwanda is absolutely unable to ensure even the food security of an increased population as a result of a massive return of refugees'. However, 'Rwanda will continue (…) to examine with benevolence demands for individual, free and voluntary repatriation.' Return was possible in principle, but it was made subject to conditions that allowed

---

[84] Quoted in ibid., p. 293.
[85] Marie-France Cros in *La Libre Belgique* observed 'Une atmosphère de fin de règne' (31 October 1989).
[86] A. Guichaoua, *Le problème des réfugiés rwandais et des populations banyarwanda dans la région des Grands Lacs africains*, Geneva, UNHCR, May 1992, pp. 16–19.

a discretionary interpretation. It was, for instance, provided that a candidate for repatriation had to 'prove his ability to ensure his needs of subsistence and fulfilment, once returned to the country'.[87] Hundreds rather than thousands returned under these conditions. It is probably faced with this seemingly 'definitive' position that, in August 1988, for the first time in their history the refugees organised an international conference in Washington.[88] They rejected the government's position and reaffirmed their integral right to return.[89]

The second consequence of the unravelling of the revolution was the virtual exclusion of Tutsi from political life. This occurred in two ways. On the one hand, the Tutsi parties underwent the same fate as the other parties in the early 1960 (cf. Section 5.2); on the other, Tutsi as such were victims of physical abuse described earlier in this chapter. Nevertheless, the 1973 coup brought ethnic appeasement. Thus Chrétien noted that 'a certain effort at reconciliation was made under the 2nd republic of President Habyarimana (…), even causing him to get in trouble with (Hutu) extremists'.[90] After their dramatic experiences under the previous regime, many Tutsi inside the country welcomed the transfer of power, and the country did not experience ethnically inspired violence between 1973 and 1990. While they remained politically marginalised, and only some token Tutsi (referred to as *Tutsi de service*) served in the government, the parliament and the army, Tutsi elites secured influential positions in the private sector and were engaged in juicy business relations with members of the Hutu elite.[91] Tutsi nevertheless continued to suffer from an informal (and illegal, as it was not provided by any legal text) quota system that admitted only 10 per cent of Tutsi in public and private employment, as well as in post-primary education, even though this was not strictly enforced.[92] Although the quota

---

[87] République rwandaise, MRND, *Position du comité central du MRND face au problème des réfugiés rwandais*, 26 July 1986. On this declaration, see F. Ndagijimana, *L'Afrique face à ses défis: Le problème des réfugiés rwandais*, Geneva, Arunga, 1990, pp. 23–68.

[88] This venue can be explained by the fact that the meeting was facilitated by Roger Winter of the US Committee for Refugees. A long standing RPF advocate, he was decorated by Kagame in 2012.

[89] For the conference proceedings and resolutions, see *Impuruza*, Special issue No. 12, November 1988.

[90] J.-P. Chrétien, 'Pluralisme démocratique, ethnismes et stratégies politiques: La situation du Rwanda et du Burundi', in G. Conac (Ed.), *L'Afrique en transition vers le pluralisme politique*, Paris, Economica, 1993, p. 143.

[91] Apart from Hutu, Tutsi and Twa, Claudine Vidal mentioned a 'fourth ethnicity', that of the westernised high, middle and petty bourgeoisie (C. Vidal, *Sociologie des passions (Côte d'Ivoire Rwanda)*, Paris, Karthala, 1991, pp. 28–35).

[92] On ethnic (and regional) 'balance' (*équilibre*) in education and employment (with precise figures), see E. Munyantwali, 'La politique d'équilibre dans l'enseignement', in

system was criticised, Mamdani noted that the regulation of Tutsi participation was based on the fact that Tutsi were a historically privileged group and that some redistribution through affirmative state action was needed within previously Tutsi-dominated institutions, particularly the Catholic Church, education and employment. Mamdani also remarked that the quota system was not rigorously enforced and that the proportion of Tutsi in public, parastatal and private sector employment exceeded the quota.[93] While the system obviously limited Tutsi access, it simultaneously secured minimal access that would possibly not be ensured in an exclusively ethnocratic political regime. In addition, the quota system could be, and often was, bypassed, especially by those who had money and connections. Desrosiers notes that the privilege and ability of some over others to bypass quota may have been a greater source of frustration than the quota system itself.[94]

5.12 The Two Republics Compared

The second republic differed from the first in several respects. First, the country engaged in a modernisation drive, expressed by an opening to the outside world, the improvement of infrastructures, the acceleration of urbanisation and increasing 'affairism'.[95] While the regime of the first republic was solitary and seemingly afraid of the exterior, the second republic embarked on a policy of opening up. The number of Rwandan diplomatic missions abroad increased considerably, as did the number of foreign embassies in Kigali. Contrary to Kayibanda, Habyarimana frequently travelled abroad and received guests. Kigali hosted the summit of the now defunct Organisation commune africaine et malgache (OCAM) in 1975 and the Franco-African conference in 1979. Rwanda co-founded the Communauté économique des pays des grands lacs (CEPGL) in 1976 and the Organisation pour l'aménagement et le développement du bassin de la rivière Akagera (OBK) in 1977. Infrastructure, in particular roads, electric power and telecommunications, was developed. Kigali, which had a population of 15,000 in the mid 1960s, was home

---

Les relations interethniques au Rwanda à la lumière de l'agression d'octobre 1990: Genèse, soubassements et perspectives, Ruhengeri, Editions universitaires du Rwanda, 1991, pp. 300–307; L. Uwizeyimana, 'La politique d'équilibre ethnique et régional dans l'emploi', in *Les relations interethniques*, pp. 308–322.
[93] Mamdani, *When Victims Become Killers*, pp. 138–140. The 10 per cent mark was based on the assumed proportion of Tutsi in the population, a figure more or less confirmed in censuses from 1978 onwards.
[94] Desrosiers, *Trajectories*, p. 82.
[95] On 'affairism', see ibid., p. 249.

to 300,000 inhabitants by the end of the 1980s. The resulting increased mobility was often contrary to attempts at strong social control, the maintenance of order and 'morality' and the fight against rural exodus.

A new ethic replaced a certain 'republican' austerity,[96] as around the mid 1980s a political–military–business class of 'haves' became increasingly visible and the close links between urban and rural Rwanda gradually loosened. Bézy showed how the myth of the 'egalitarian republic' disappeared as a fourfold (military, political/administrative, business and technocratic) bourgeoisie diverted an important part of national income.[97] Former minister James Gasana's final judgement on the second republic is severe. He observed a rapid emergence of clientelism, accumulation, regionalism and socio-economic disparities, characteristics that resulted in a systemic social, economic and political crisis.[98]

The loosening link between city and countryside, which in the past was an important element of cohesion, was well rendered by one of Hanssen's interviewees: while the leaders of the day were still very 'peasant' in their hearts, 'the children of these cadres have urban models, and when they will be in power, they will have lost contact with reality. This leads to a zairisation of Rwanda with elites neglecting social infrastructures in order to serve their personal well-being.'[99] The process of rupture between the small urban minority and the overwhelming rural majority was fully engaged in the 1980s.[100] Cathy Newbury observed that one of the consequences of these changes was the broadening of the gap between rich and poor, as well as a clearer affirmation of class interests by those in power.[101] With the benefit of an extended field experience, de Lame noted that the elites 'maintained close ties with their rural setting but were also eager to distance themselves from it culturally'.[102] 'The most striking feature of the second republic was in fact the rapid enrichment, in monetary terms, of a

---

[96] Symbolised by President Kayibanda shuttling nearly every day between his home in Gitarama and his office in Kigali, driving himself an old VW beetle.
[97] Bézy, *Rwanda 1962–1989*.
[98] Gasana, *Rwanda*, pp. 52–60.
[99] Hanssen, *Le désenchantement de la coopération*, p. 128.
[100] With the rurals representing about 95 per cent of the population in the late 1980s, Rwanda was among the least urbanised countries in Africa. On the gap between the ordinary rural citizens (*abaturage*) and the urban elites, see Desrosiers, *Trajectories*, pp. 324–328.
[101] C. Newbury, 'Rwanda: Recent Debates over Governance and Rural Development', in G. Hyden, M. Bratton (Eds.), *Governance and Politics in Africa*, Boulder–London, Lynne Rienner, 1992, p. 203.
[102] de Lame, *A Hill among a Thousand*, p. 4.

middle class composed of civil servants cum businesspeople who still maintained ties with their rural origins.'[103] For a regime born out of a 'popular revolution' this trend was particularly grave and reminds of the warning by one of the fathers of the revolution: in 1959, Aloys Munyangaju wrote that the problem of inequality would not be solved 'by according to the Hutu the caste privileges currently reserved to the Tutsi high aristocracy'.[104]

Akazu ('the little house') was the term coined to describe the political–commercial network of the president, or more accurately that of his wife and in-laws. Their control of important functions in both the state and the private sector allowed to ensure the political and financial reproduction of this group. Nick Gordon offered plausible indications of the implication of members of the presidential family-in-law in mafia-like activities such as traffic in gorillas, gold and even drugs, as well as the murder of the gorilla conservationist Diane Fossey.[105] The resistance of the *akazu* against the democratisation process after 1990 will be addressed in the next chapter.

5.13 A Looming Political Crisis

Although Rwanda was a decent performer, at least compared to the average African country, and was even for long considered a model of development ('The Switzerland of Africa', as it was often called), the regime showed signs of exhaustion by the end of the 1980s. Regional conflicts increasingly invaded the political scene, a predatory class tried to consolidate itself, the rural world regressed, 'affairs' rocked Kigali, and the economy and public finances ran into trouble. Civil society seized the opportunities offered by the regime's growing weakness and uncertainty. The second half of 1989 was marked by attempts to secure some freedom of expression, witnessed by the birth of new media outlets (among the first were *Kanguka*, *Kangura* and *Umuranga*). Together with other journals that already existed before, in particular *Kinyamateka* and *Dialogue*, these increasingly dared to publicly criticise certain regime policies and actions.

---

[103] Ibid., pp. 62–63.
[104] Munyangaju, *L'actualité politique*, p. 43.
[105] N. Gordon, *Murders in the Mist*, London, Hodder and Stoughton, 1993. On the *akazu* also see Gasana, *Rwanda*, pp. 33–42; Munyarugerero, *Réseaux, pouvoirs, oppositions*, pp. 175–179, as well as, from opposing perspectives, B. Collins, *Rwanda 1994: The Myth of the* Akazu *Genocide Conspiracy and Its Consequences*, New York, Palgrave Macmillan, 2014; A. Wallis, *Stepp'd in Blood: Akazu and the Architects of the Rwandan Genocide against the Tutsi*, Winchester–Washington, Zero Books, 2019.

Beyond political vulnerability, from the mid 1980s the country was also facing increasingly grave economic and social difficulties. Rwanda's terms of trade deteriorated dramatically, and the crash of international coffee and tea prices affected both household incomes and government revenue.[106] The International Monetary Fund's Structural Adjustment Programme caused a devaluation of the Rwandan franc and increased inflation and the cost of health, education and transport. Ecological challenges, land shortage and droughts in particular, increased the hardship of many ordinary Rwandans.[107] All this contributed to increasing tensions, which were fatally exacerbated by the war that started in 1990 (see Chapter 6). Social and economic stress were to be deeply intertwined with military and political issues to come. Desrosiers finds an organic link between the political situation of the country and its economic problems.[108]

When Habyarimana admitted the need for political renewal for the first time in early 1989, he still placed it in a familiar framework, that of the single party. In a speech on 15 January 1989, he wanted 'a real political *aggiornamento* to inspire our political movement (…), so that it can respond, in every period, to new challenges. This major effort of modernising our main political institution, namely the MRND, will need to mobilise everyone.'[109] The winds of change were not yet blowing over Africa, and Habyarimana could not yet imagine that hardly two and a half years later integral multi-partyism would be introduced. To him, the issue was not to abolish single-party rule but to improve it, a position shared at the time by both his African peers and western partners.

The end of the Cold War opened up political systems all over the continent, and the Habyarimana regime initially hesitated on the course of action it was to take. However, in January 1990 the boss of the intelligence service SCR issued a warning to printers, editors and journalists against 'subversive articles (…) susceptible of irritating the country's highest authorities'. He specifically mentioned subjects like ethnic and regional problems, the opposition between rich and poor and those 'contrary to the imperatives of development and social peace'.[110]

---

[106] When peasant farmers started to uproot their coffee plants, the source of their main monetary income, this was both an economic and political statement.
[107] Bézy, *Rwanda 1962–1989*; S. Marysse, T. de Herdt, E. Ndayambaje, *Rwanda: Appauvrissement et ajustement structurel*, Brussels–Paris, Institut Africain-CEDAF-L'Harmattan, 1994, Cahiers Africains, No. 12; Desrosiers, *Trajectories*, pp. 294–311.
[108] Desrosiers, *Trajectories*, p. 294.
[109] *Discours-programme*, Kigali, 15 January 1989.
[110] *Dialogue*, No. 141, July–August 1990, pp. 189–190.

5.13 A Looming Political Crisis

The press did not seem very impressed and to the contrary claimed the right to express itself, but the regime reacted by attempts at repression. From early 1990 onwards, half a dozen journalists were arrested or prosecuted for sedition. While some were condemned to light or suspended sentences, others received long prison terms.[111] An increasingly outspoken civil society engaged in an episode of arms-wrestling with the regime. This became clear when on 18 September 1990 the editor-in-chief of *Kinyamateka*, *abbé* André Sibomana, along with three of his journalists, was tried. Sibomana used his court appearance to demonstrate the veracity of the incriminated articles published between June and December 1989. His plea became a real indictment of the regime, as he denounced the power's loss of popular confidence, inequalities in access to resources, concentration of land holdings and intimidation of the press.[112] On 26 September, the four accused were acquitted.

Habyarimana finally recognised the winds of change sweeping through Africa after François Mitterrand's speech at La Baule in June 1990. In an address made on 5 July at the occasion of the seventeenth anniversary of the second republic, he repeated the need for a 'political aggiornamento': while stressing achievements of his regime, he also acknowledged that a number of issues needed to be redressed. He announced the need to separate the organs of the MRND from those of the state and cautiously opened the possible perspective of multi-partyism. A new 'political charter' was to be elaborated after large consultations, and the process was to be crowned by a constitutional revision at the latest on 1 July 1992, at the occasion of the thirtieth independence anniversary. On 1 September, thirty-three intellectuals considerably increased the pressure by publishing a note titled 'For multipartyism and democracy'. On 24 September, Habyarimana appointed the National Synthesis Commission (*Commission nationale de synthèse*), charged among other things with 'identifying what the concept of democracy means for the majority of the Rwandan population', defining a National Political Charter (*Charte politique nationale*) and elaborating a draft constitution. The perspective of multi-partyism was no longer excluded as the charter 'will specify the principles to which the creation of political formations that wish to constitute themselves will have to abide'.[113]

---

[111] Amnesty International, *The Republic of Rwanda: A Spate of Detentions and Trials in 1990 to Suppress Fundamental Rights*, October 1990.
[112] A summary of his demonstration can be found in *Dialogue*, No. 143, November–December 1990, pp. 90–96.
[113] For a survey of the political 'opening' in 1989–1990 see Munyarugerero, *Réseaux, pouvoirs, oppositions*, pp. 224–231, 238–244.

126   The 'Hutu Republics'

A week later, the RPF invaded the country. The civil war, the political transition and the genocide are discussed in the next chapter.

5.14   Conclusion

As is the case for most authoritarian regimes, Rwanda under the two 'Hutu Republics' was never a strong authoritarian state. Desrosiers describes the regimes' trajectory as one of elusive control, rather than its establishment,[114] and called its authoritarianism 'unexceptional'.[115] Internal power struggles and fractionalisation suggest that they were weaker and less effective than often claimed, and certainly less monolithic. They were under constant threat or so they feared. Therefore, the idea of a strong authoritarian state ruling over an obedient and complying population did not correspond to reality. As a Rwandan friend told Desrosiers, 'people support the president, but they will support the next one when the opportunity arises'.[116] Gasana described the Habyarimana regime as an 'enlightened despotism' but not as a repressive dictatorship.[117] Desrosiers also finds that, contrary to what is widely assumed, outside of their worst crises both the first and second republics tended to opt for a moderate, positive public face and rhetoric, more than for an ethnocentric discourse.[118] Publicly targeting the Tutsi as a group in Kayibanda's speeches was the exception rather than the rule,[119] and his regime promoted positive conciliatory themes rather than ethnic division.[120] Mamdani calls the political agenda of the second republic 'less ideological' than that of the first one.[121]

There is strong continuity or path dependency from the revolution to 1990. This period is very brief, hardly covering one generation. Both the first and the second republic invoked the revolutionary legitimacy, as can be seen in the preambles of the constitutions of 1962 and 1978: 'With a view to consolidating the liberation of the Rwandan people of the feudal-colonialist yoke' (1962) and 'Considering the task of liberation undertaken by the Revolution of 1959' (1978). This narrow base inevitably entailed a focus on the past and a strongly felt need to preserve the fragile foundations of a new political order. The *inyenzi*

---

[114] Desrosiers, *Trajectories*, p. 15.
[115] Ibid., p. 17.
[116] Ibid., p. 362. Although he was talking about the current regime, it could as well have applied to Habyarimana.
[117] Gasana, *Rwanda*, pp. 61–62.
[118] Desrosiers, *Trajectories*, p. 181.
[119] Ibid., p. 75.
[120] Ibid., p. 181.
[121] Mamdani, *When Victims Become Killers*, pp. 142–143.

5.14 Conclusion

attacks until the late 1960s reminded the threat of a return to the pre-revolutionary regime. As this regime was linked to ethnocratic rule by the elite of the Tutsi minority, it constantly kept the ethnic issue alive, even after Habyarimana's takeover heralded a relaxation. Inside the country, however, Tutsi were politically marginalised, and the external threat posed by a large refugee community remained present under the surface. The abscess finally burst on 1 October 1990.

6 The Abyss
Political Transition, Civil War and Genocide

6.1 Political Transition and Civil War

Starting in 1990, the lethal combination of three factors led to genocide: political transition, civil war and bipolar ethnicity. The first two will be addressed in a moment, but it is necessary to start by drawing attention to the inherent difficulties in managing bipolar identities.[1] Rwanda and Burundi are exceptional in Africa, where situations are commonly multi-ethnic. No ethnic group is generally a majority elsewhere, and there is not one ethnic group facing another. 'The other' does not exist; there are several 'others'. Elsewhere in the world bipolar situations are also difficult to manage and easy to instrumentalise. This is made clear by examples such as Greeks and Turks in Cyprus, Catholics and Protestants in Northern Ireland, Dutch- and French-speakers in Belgium, Tamil and Sinhalese in Sri Lanka, Shiites and Sunnis in the Middle East, to quote just a few. In situations of crisis and violence, entrepreneurs of ethnicity succeed in mobilising these identities and in presenting the 'other' as an enemy, even an existential threat. In Rwanda, this mobilisation had been actively pursued in the 1990s – in 1994 in particular.

6.1.1 'Democratisation'[2]

After the fall of the Berlin Wall and the 1990 speech at La Baule where President François Mitterrand made French aid conditional on democratisation and respect for human rights, like his African peers President Habyarimana was forced to adapt to the constraints imposed by the new international political landscape. Like elsewhere in Africa,

---

[1] As explained earlier, the Twa are not taken into consideration here, because they played no role in the political equation.
[2] I put this term between inverted commas because, like in most African countries, the democratisation process has been essentially formal, articulated around phenomena such as multi-partyism, elections and press freedom. Political life is limited to a competition between urban elites that only marginally integrates the rural world and even most people living in towns and cities.

6.1 Political Transition and Civil War

this development was not just externally induced. As seen in the previous chapter, domestic pressures forced Habyarimana to reluctantly start opening up the political system. Hardly a week after the National Synthesis Commission was put in place, the civil war broke out on 1 October 1990 (discussed later). This rather accelerated the work of the commission, which published the pre-draft National Political Charter at the end of December. After wide debates the draft charter was published at the end of March 1991. At the same time, the commission proposed drafts of a new constitution and of a law on political parties.

While article 7 of the 1978 constitution, which provided for a single-party system, was still in force, initiators of opposition parties started organising semi-clandestinely from February 1991 onwards. The first to come out in the open was the Mouvement démocratique républicain (MDR). In March, the newspaper *Le Démocrate* published an 'Appeal for the relaunching and renovation of the MDR' (*Appel à la relance et à la renovation du MDR*) signed by 237 persons. The text clearly linked up with the line of the MDR-Parmehutu, which was abolished by the 1973 coup. However, the 'renovated' MDR did not keep the name 'Parmehutu', and one of its objectives was 'the reconciliation of consciences and the peaceful coexistence of the Rwandan ethnic groups in equality and mutual respect'. During the following weeks and months, other parties were created, the most important being the Social Democrat Party (Parti social-démocrate – PSD), the Liberal Party (Parti libéral – PL) and the Democratic Christian Party (Parti démocrate-chrétien – PDC).[3]

On 10 June 1991, a new constitution was promulgated, followed a week later by a law on political parties. During the following months, a dozen opposition parties developed an intense activity with the main aim of putting in place a broad-based transitional government. At the end of July, the MDR, the PSD, the PL and the PDC put in place a Concertation committee of democratic political parties (*Comité de concertation des partis politiques démocratiques*), which was to become a formidable political actor that forced an initially reticent government into more and more concessions. Faced with these pressures and rapidly expanding public demonstrations, the regime was eventually forced to accept putting in place a coalition government. On 13 March 1992, the MRND, the MDR, the PSD, the PL and the PDC signed a memorandum of understanding (*Protocole d'entente*) comprising a minimum programme of seven points, among which were peace negotiations with

---

[3] A list of parties created between June 1991 and July 1993 can be found in Munyarugerero, *Réseaux, pouvoirs, oppositions*, p. 249.

the RPF rebels (see Section 6.1.2), the settlement of the refugee problem and the organisation of elections.

The coalition government took office on 16 April with a prime minister from the MDR, Dismas Nsengiyaremye. The MRND retained nine portfolios, while the opposition obtained ten ministerial positions, in addition to that of the prime minister. The government's trajectory was replete with incidents and blockages. Several violent incidents caused hundreds of victims in an atmosphere of widespread insecurity characterised by threats, assassinations and attacks with the use of mines and grenades. Discipline inside the army deteriorated, and several politically inspired mutinies took place. The government was paralysed by constant conflicts between the MRND and the former opposition parties. Even within the MRND and the other parties, particularly in the MDR, scissions impeded the proper running of the state. As will be seen later, from mid 1993 these contradictions increasingly took on an ethnic connotation in the contexts of, on the one hand, the race for power and privileges and, on the other, the negotiations with the RPF.[4]

Conflicts like these are not uncommon during periods of profound political change. Other countries in Africa and elsewhere had experienced them in the early 1990s, and Rwanda could have gone through similar processes. The difference was that the country was the scene of a civil war at that time, and this injected an additional measure of extreme violence.

6.1.2 *The Attack of the RPF and the Civil War*

On 1 October 1990, less than a week after the installation of the National Synthesis Commission, the country was attacked from Uganda by an armed group of Tutsi refugees. The assailants called themselves *inkotanyi* (Those who fight bravely) and presented themselves as the military wing (Rwandan Patriotic Army – RPA) of the RPF. Mostly part of the Ugandan army (National Resistance Army – NRA), they were several thousand well-trained and well-equipped men. The attack occurred at a time when progress seemed to be made towards the resolution of the refugee issue. Set up in February 1989, the Special Commission on the Problems of Rwandan *émigrés* (*Commission spéciale sur le problème des*

---

[4] More details on the domestic side of the political transition can be found in Gasana, *Rwanda*; Munyarugerero, *Réseaux, pouvoirs, oppositions*; A. Guichaoua (Ed.), *Les crises politiques au Burundi et au Rwanda (1993–1994)*, Paris, Karthala, 1995; G. Prunier, *The Rwanda Crisis: History of a Genocide*, New York, Columbia University Press, 1995; F. Reyntjens, *L'Afrique des Grands Lacs en crise: Rwanda, Burundi – 1988–1994*, Paris, Karthala, 1994.

émigrés rwandais) had produced a first report in May 1990,[5] and a joint Rwandan–Ugandan ministerial committee on the problem of Rwandan refugees living in Uganda had proposed some concrete measures at the end of July. In this context, a delegation of refugees was due to visit Rwanda at the end of September under the auspices of the United Nations High Commission for Refugees (UNHCR). The convergence of the perspective of progress in the areas of democratisation and refugees on the one hand and the timing of the RPF's attack on the other was probably not a coincidence. Indeed, a positive evolution in these two areas, which became the RPF's spearheads, would have strongly diminished, and possibly destroyed, the legitimacy of the war, including in the eyes of international opinion.[6]

On 3 October, the attackers reached Gabiro, around seventy kilometres from Kigali, where their progression was halted by the Rwandan army (Forces armées rwandaises – FAR) with the support of elements of the Zairean Division spéciale présidentielle (DSP). While most Rwandans considered the invasion as an attempted return by force of Tutsi refugees, the RPF claimed it was pursuing a project going beyond that aim. It presented itself as an alternative to the regime in power in Kigali, which it accused of corruption, nepotism and massive human rights abuse. It also claimed to be multi-ethnic, regrouping Hutu and Tutsi indistinctly. In reality, the eight points of the political programme that the RPF published at the beginning of the war were already the subject of large debates inside the country, including within the single party.[7]

At the beginning, the attack objectively benefited Habyarimana, whose position had been weakening, as we have seen. Most Hutu restored unity around him in the face of an enemy presented and perceived as an existential threat. The predominantly Tutsi composition of the RPF and the apparent continuity between the October invasion and the *inyenzi* attacks of the 1960s reinforced this representation. Although the coexistence between the two main ethnic groups was relatively peaceful since 1973, the ethnic reflex re-emerged immediately, and the Tutsi again paid the price. They were suspected of being the

---

[5] République rwandaise, Commission spéciale sur les problèmes des émigrés rwandais, *Le Rwanda et le problème de ses réfugiés*, Kigali, May 1990.
[6] G. Prunier, 'Eléments pour une histoire du Front patriotique rwandais', *Politique africaine*, No. 51, October 1993, p. 130.
[7] (1) Consolidation of national unity; (2) Reinforcement of democratic institutions; (3) Building of a dynamic economy; (4) Elimination of corruption and embezzlement; (5) Solution to the refugee problem; (6) Putting into place social services; (7) Security of goods and services; (8) International cooperation.

RPF's fifth column, and the vast majority of those arrested during the first days of the war were Tutsi.[8] During this period, hundreds of Tutsi were killed in several places in the country.

At the end of October 1990, after its initial defeat the RPF withdrew to Uganda, from where it embarked on guerrilla operations, which proved more efficient than the conventional war waged at the beginning. In May 1992, the RPF launched an attack that allowed it to occupy a couple of municipalities (*communes*) in the extreme north of the country. Hundreds of thousands fled towards the centre, where they ended up in large IDP camps. In February 1993, a more important offensive allowed the RPF to occupy a contiguous zone in Ruhengeri and Byumba *préfectures*, an area that however covered under 10 per cent of the national territory. The number of IDPs grew to nearly one million, a mass of people living in very poor conditions and who considered the RPF responsible for their fate. Many of these deeply frustrated and angry people were to become a recruiting base for killers during the genocide.

Elsewhere in the country, massacres engineered by extremist Hutu leaders resulted in over a thousand Tutsi victims, particularly in the Bugesera region in March 1992, in Kibuye *préfecture* in August of the same year and in the north-west in late 1992 and early 1993. The dynamics were each time the same, whereby MRND extremists launched provocations followed by 'spontaneous' violence. The role of 'death squads' and the *akazu* (see Section 5.12) in this destabilisation project is well documented.[9] In the zone it controlled, the RPF also committed large-scale massacres, which at the time were less publicly known (see later).

6.1.3 The Arusha Peace Accord and Its Collapse

Two factors were at the origin of the talks that were to lead to the Arusha peace accord: the military impasse on the ground and the political evolution in Kigali. While cease fire deals had been agreed upon earlier, real political negotiations started in Brussels in May 1992, when the three main opposition parties (MDR, PL and PSD) met the RPF. A few days later, a meeting took place in Paris between the Rwandan government and the RPF. Issues discussed included the democratisation process, the merger of the two warring armies and putting in place a broad-based

---

[8] Nearly all of those detained were however released during the first months of 1991. This was in large part due to the intervention of Sylvestre Nsanzimana, who was appointed Justice Minister in February.
[9] See Reyntjens, *L'Afrique des Grands Lacs*, pp. 188–192.

transitional government. Though an armed movement, the RPF was now drawn into a political process to which it needed to adapt. After several rounds of talks, during which the governmental side made considerable concessions, a political accord progressively emerged: a cease fire in July 1992, a protocol on the rule of law (*État de droit*) in August and protocols on power sharing in October 1992 and January 1993.

The process was in constant jeopardy. On the one hand, the MRND adopted an ambiguous position, arguing that there was no consensus in the governmental delegation on the strategy to be followed during the talks. The government indeed was in an awkward position during the negotiations, with its delegation comprising members of the opposition, among them the minister of foreign affairs, who on many issues held positions close to those of the RPF. Both were objective allies, as the internal opposition benefited from the war waged by the RPF to obtain concessions from the MRND that were inconceivable in the absence of a military threat, while the RPF benefited from the undermining tactics of the opposition. Divided in the face of the RPF, which was united and followed a coherent line, the government thus negotiated from a weak position. The ambiguity among those who feared losing power also expressed itself in the violence committed at the MRND's instigation (partly pushed by the small extremist Hutu party Coalition pour la défense de la République – CDR) against its opponents and the Tutsi, particularly in 1992 and the beginning of 1993.

On the other hand, in February 1993 the RPF launched a major offensive, which was halted only about thirty kilometres from Kigali with the support of the French army, present in the country since October 1990. By showing the RPF's military capabilities, this operation created a great deal of alarm among civil society and opposition parties, which up to then had maintained rather good relations with the rebel movement. Doubts immediately arose: did the RPF genuinely want a negotiated transition to democracy or did it aim at a military victory in order to replace one dictatorial regime by another? The condemnation of the RPF's aggressive act was unanimous. The RPF also lost part of the credit it had garnered in international opinion.

The Arusha talks were nevertheless resumed. In May 1993, an accord provided for the return and reinstallation of displaced persons and for the administration of a demilitarised zone. In June the parties signed a protocol on the repatriation of refugees, in principle putting an end to an old problem that was at the origin of the civil war. It was finally after the very difficult negotiation of an accord on the merger of the two armies signed on 3 August that the global accord was signed in Arusha on 4 August 1993.

The accord heralded a fundamental reshuffling of political cards. The president lost the substance of power and became a ceremonial head of state. The broad-based transitional government (*gouvernement de transition à base élargie* – GTBE) was made the centre of the transitional ordering, appointed not by the president but by the parties that were to compose it (MRND, RPF, MDR, PSD, PL and PDC). Combining the attributes of a head of state and of a government, its powers were wide. The registered political parties and the RPF were to fill the seats of a transitional national assembly (*Assemblée nationale de transition* – ANT). Typically consociational techniques were to manage political decision-making.[10] Decisions in the government were to be taken by consensus in the first stage and by a two thirds majority in the second stage. In the ANT a minimum of four parties were needed to reach a simple majority and five were required for matters needing a two-thirds majority. The new national army was to be composed of 60 per cent FAR and 40 per cent RPA, except in command functions from the army staff to the battalion level, where positions were to be allocated on a fifty-fifty basis. The transitional institutions were to be put in place within thirty-seven days following the signing of the accord, an obviously unrealistic timeframe. In the second stage, the transitional period was to last twenty-two months after the GTBE taking office. An international force, the United Nations Assistance Mission for Rwanda (UNAMIR), was to oversee the implementation of the accord.[11]

The concessions made by the former regime were formidable and deprived it from the essential pillars of its power. The presidential function lost most of its substance, the MRND became a party like the others and the military monopoly was shared with the RPF. This explains the reticence of the elites in power whose privileges stood to be jeopardised and who had reason to fear that they might even be called to account for their past governance. Beyond personal interests, many Hutu (and not merely the 'extremists') considered that the RPF obtained much more than it deserved and were worried about the Trojan horse that entered Rwanda, particularly in the army.

Two main factors were to impede the implementation of the Arusha accord. First, while during the negotiations the political structuring was

---

[10] Consociational techniques attempt to combine majoritarian rule and the protection of minorities. This objective is pursued by classic instruments such as minority overrepresentation, quota and minority veto (on consociationalism see A. Lijphart, *Democracies: Patterns of Majoritarian and Consensus Government in Twenty-One Countries*, London–New Haven, Yale University Press, 1984).

[11] More details on the Arusha accord and the negotiations can be found in Reyntjens, *L'Afrique des Grands Lacs*, pp. 248–256.

6.1 Political Transition and Civil War

tripolar (MRND, internal opposition, RPF), it gradually became bipolar. In mid 1993, most opposition parties split into two wings, one moving towards the MRND in an 'anti-Arusha' tendency, the other towards the RPF in a 'pro-Arusha' tendency. These repositionings were partly political,[12] but ethnicity also played a role, in particular within the PL, the party that had attracted many Tutsi, when the Hutu and Tutsi separated. Centrist politicians were in reality 'eaten up' by the MRND and the RPF, while they could have had a considerable political influence had they remained a third force able to arbitrate between the two extremes and tilt the balance.

Second, on 21 October 1993, a brief democratic experience was violently destroyed in neighbouring Burundi, when the Tutsi-dominated army staged a coup and killed the first democratically elected president, Melchior Ndadaye, a Hutu. Many Hutu in Kigali immediately came to the conclusion that the Tutsi, and thus the RPF, would never accept democracy. As it could not hope to conquer power by the ballot, the RPF would do so by the bullet.[13] This analysis may well have been shared by the RPF itself after a concrete experience. At local elections organised in September 1993 in the demilitarised zone in the north of the country, which was not physically controlled by the FAR or the MRND and where the RPF had campaigned and fielded candidates, the MRND won all positions except one, which went to the CDR. This is probably the moment the RPF became definitively aware that it would not capture power through democratic means. Guichaoua noted that this experience 'marked a turning point, anchoring the deep contempt of the RPF's military leadership for "democracies," as well as its rejection of the electoral process set out in the Arusha peace accord'.[14]

6.1.4 Strategies of Tension

Clearly the leaders of the two principal politico-military forces – the MRND and the RPF – no longer believed in a political solution. While giving the impression of first negotiating and later applying the Arusha accord, they developed increasingly violent strategies of tension. Although these forces were at the opposite sides of the political landscape, they shared the rejection of the accord, as the MRND radicals wanted to stay in power and the RPF military wanted to seize it.

---

[12] The February 1993 offensive of the RPF played un undeniable role in this splitting of the political landscape.
[13] It is no coincidence that at a rally held in Kigali 'in support of the Burundian people' two days after the putsch in Bujumbura, the slogan 'Hutu Pawa' (kinyarwandisation of 'power') was launched by Froduald Karamira, a leader of the MDR's anti-Arusha wing.
[14] A. Guichaoua, *Rwanda, de la guerre au génocide: Les politiques criminelles au Rwanda (1990–1994)*, Paris, La Découverte, 2010, p. 135.

On the one hand, the MRND – itself facing internal splits – attempted to divide the domestic opposition, in particular the MDR, which it considered a serious threat and feared the most. It also resorted to violence, such as the engineered massacres mentioned earlier in the Bugesera region, in Kibuye and in the north-west in 1992 and at the beginning of 1993. The use of incitement to hate was well illustrated by a now famous speech, pronounced at the end of November 1992 by Léon Mugesera, the MRND vice chair in Gisenyi *préfecture*. He incited the massacre of their opponents ('Their punishment is death, nothing less') and of the Tutsi ('Ethiopia is your country, and we will expedite you there via the Nyabarongo river in express voyage. I therefore repeat that we must rapidly start working').[15] In mid 1993, elements of the MRND's youth wing, the *interahamwe* ('Those who fight together'), began receiving paramilitary training and weapons. These activities were hardly hidden: militiamen were transported by buses of the public transport company ONATRACOM and by army trucks. Recruits were selected by the MRND national secretariat and by army officers, mostly of the presidential guard. All this was facilitated from July 1993 by the replacement of the moderate defence minister James Gasana by a radical, Augustin Bizimana.[16]

On the other hand, beginning in mid 1991, the RPF carried out several attacks in public spaces with the obvious intention of causing many civilian casualties. For a long time, it succeeded in having MRND extremists carry the blame for this terror, but the reality gradually emerged. After its electoral defeat in the north, the RPF massacred dozens of people in November 1993. Several of these victims were local MRND and CDR leaders elected at these polls, but some were also members of their families.[17] Through the targeted assassination of extremist Hutu politicians, and also of moderates, the RPF succeeded in destabilising the domestic political sphere at the beginning of 1994, thus contributing to the creation of a context undermining all hopes of a political solution.[18] It is noteworthy that the RPF put in place cells across the country led by political cadres trained in the RPF-controlled zone. In early April 1994, around 600 such cells were in place, of which 147 were in Kigali alone.[19]

---

[15] After being extradited from Canada where he had fled, Mugesera was condemned to life in prison by a Rwandan court in April 2016.
[16] More details on these destabilising activities can be found in Guichaoua, *Rwanda, de la guerre au génocide*, pp. 234–239.
[17] Ibid., p. 135.
[18] Ibid., pp. 188–196.
[19] Ibid., p. 409, footnote 1.

By early 1994 it had become increasingly clear that the Arusha accord would not be implemented. While UNAMIR had been in place since early November 1993 and an RPF battalion had been present in Kigali since the end of December,[20] incessant blockages by both sides prevented putting the transitional institutions in place. The logic of these blockages can be understood in light of the consociational arithmetic mentioned earlier: the RPF camp wanted by all means to achieve a majority of more than two thirds, whereas the MRND wanted to avoid that by ensuring a blocking minority of one third plus one. As each bloc was close to its objective, the stakes were finally reduced to one ministerial portfolio and one or two seats in parliament. One here again measures the historical error and responsibility of the democratic centre when it allowed to be split in mid 1993. Against the background of this political impasse, both military players prepared for the resumption of the war, including by reinforcing themselves in ways clearly contrary to the peace accord. The spark was lit on 6 April 1994.

6.2 The Genocide

6.2.1 Preparations

At 8.22 PM on 6 April 1994, president Habyarimana's Falcon 50 plane crashed near Kigali airport on its final approach after being hit by one or two surface-to-air missiles. Habyarimana was returning from a regional summit on Burundi and Rwanda that took place in Dar es Salaam. There were no survivors among the nine persons aboard, including Habyarimana, Burundian president Cyprien Ntaryamira and the French crew of three. Until 1998, no serious enquiry was conducted on this attack, although it marked the resumption of the civil war, the genocide and, in later years, immense regional conflicts. After the family of the French pilot lodged a formal complaint, a judicial investigation was opened in Paris. The initial investigating judge (*juge d'instruction*), Jean-Louis Bruguière, concluded that the attack had been committed by the RPF and in November 2006 issued international arrest warrants against nine Rwandan officials. After he retired in 2008, Bruguière's successors continued the inquiry; they did not find sufficient evidence and decided in July 2020 not to prosecute. This decision did not clear the RPF and designated no other suspects and thus left

---

[20] It was installed in the parliament premises, the Conseil national de développement. The encampment of the RPF battalion in this symbol of national sovereignty had created strong hostility from certain Hutu quarters, and not only the most extremist.

the crime unpunished. Although several indications point at the RPF as the perpetrator,[21] there will probably never be a judicial determination of criminal responsibility.

During the night of 6–7 April, two parallel tracks were followed in Kigali – one visible, the other clandestine. The army top met at the high command (*état-major*), where the chief of army staff who perished in the crash was replaced. The meeting examined the way in which the institutional void left by the president's death needed to be filled. It apparently agreed with UN special representative Jacques-Roger Booh-Booh's recommendation to respect the Arusha peace accord, to ask the MRND to propose an interim president and to let the government expedite current affairs. The permanent secretary of the Defence Ministry, Col Théoneste Bagosora – who, in the absence of the minister who was on a mission abroad, emerged as the strong man – agreed with the first two recommendations but refused to involve the prime minister, Agathe Uwilingiyimana, who was considered part of the 'pro-Arusha' wing of the MDR. Bagosora belonged to the radical 'anti-Arusha' or 'anti-RPF' bloc.

The second track was invisible, and short-circuited what the visible structure had decided. Bagosora left the high command around 2 AM on 7 April and re-emerged at the Defence Ministry at 7 AM. It is during these five hours that the killing machine was put in motion, which started functioning at around 5.30 AM. Bagosora had a radio network parallel to that of the army which linked him to the presidential guard, the para-commando battalion and the reconnaissance battalion. These were the units, more specifically the presidential guard, that early in the morning started the massacres.

The targeted killings that happened on the morning of 7 April were politically rather than ethnically motivated. Elements of the presidential guard went from house to house, setting out to kill personalities needed to safeguard the Arusha process: prime minister Uwilingiyimana in charge of current business, the two candidates for the position of speaker of the Transitional National Assembly, Félicien Ngango and Landoald Ndasingwa, and the president of the constitutional court, Joseph Kavaruganda, who was to administer the oaths of office. Ndasingwa was the only Tutsi, but all were considered part of the pro-RPF bloc. The human and institutional void thus created allowed Bagosora's group to put in place an interim government that organised the genocide.[22]

---

[21] F. Reyntjens, 'The RPF Did It: A Fresh Look at the 1994 Plane Attack That Ignited Genocide in Rwanda', Antwerp, IOB Working Paper 2020.05, 2020.

[22] The circumstances surrounding the start of the genocide are described in more detail in Guichaoua, *Rwanda, de la guerre au génocide*, pp. 241–353, and F. Reyntjens, *Rwanda: Trois jours qui ont fait basculer l'histoire*, Paris, L'Harmattan, 'Cahiers Africains' No. 16, 1995.

Dozens of real or supposed opponents were killed in a similarly targeted fashion. Among them were not only politicians but also civil servants, judges and prosecutors, journalists and civil society leaders. The fate imposed on the opposition and other dissenting voices allowed for the elimination of potential obstacles to the genocidal project or, by terror, dissuaded those who might have been tempted to oppose it.

While the massacres started, the RPF launched a military offensive early in the morning of 7 April from the zone it controlled in the north. In the late afternoon, its battalion stationed in the parliament compound engaged in battle with elements of the presidential guard and other FAR units. This was the start of hostilities that allowed the RPF to gradually extend its control in Kigali, and eventually to win the war in July.

6.2.2 Implementation

The genocide has been widely researched and therefore due to lack of space will only be summarily addressed here.[23]

Rwanda has a tradition of pyramidal political–administrative management where orders are spread rapidly and efficiently from top to bottom through intermediary decentralised structures (*préfectures*, *communes*/municipalities, sectors and cells). In the past, these concentric circles have allowed for the inclusion of the entire population in government programmes, for instance in the areas of health and development. The organisers of the genocide have relied on these same structures and mechanisms to launch their extermination campaign against the Tutsi. The first of these concentric circles was an alliance of military and civilians at the central level. As the leading figure in the second track described earlier, Col Bagosora coordinated the actions of unit commanders involved in political assassinations first and the genocide later starting on 7 April. On 8 April, he presided over a decisive meeting

---

[23] In addition to numerous journal articles and reports, the main references include A. Des Forges et al., *Leave None to Tell the Story: Genocide in Rwanda*, New York, Human Rights Watch, 1999; H. Dumas, *Le génocide au village: Le massacre des Tutsi au Rwanda*, Paris, Seuil, 2014; L. A. Fujii, *Killing Neighbors: Webs of Violence in Rwanda*, Ithaca, Cornell University Press, 2009; Guichaoua, *Rwanda, de la guerre au génocide*; J.-P. Kimonyo, *Rwanda's Popular Genocide: A Perfect Storm*, Boulder, Lyne Rienner, 2016; T. Longman, *Christianity and Genocide in Rwanda*, Cambridge, Cambridge University Press, 2010; O. S. McDoom, *The Path to Genocide in Rwanda: Security, Opportunity, and Authority in an Ethnocratic State*, Cambridge, Cambridge University Press, 2021; F. Piton, *Le génocide des Tutsi du Rwanda*, Paris, La Découverte, 2018; F. Reyntjens, *Le génocide des Tutsi au Rwanda*, Paris, Presses Universitaires de France, 2nd ed., 2021; S. Straus, *The Order of Genocide: Race, Power, and War in Rwanda*, Ithaca, Cornell University Press, 2006.

in the Defence Ministry. Only the leaders of the pro-MRND wings of the political parties were invited, while the leaders of the pro-Arusha wings had by then been killed or were in hiding. The speaker of parliament, Théodore Sindikubwabo, was appointed the acting president, and an interim government was put in place with Jean Kambanda of the MDR's 'Hutu Power' wing as the prime minister. Breaking with a long tradition, not a single Tutsi was part of the government, and the RPF was of course not included. The logic was the opposite of that of the Arusha accord. It was presented as a coalition government, but that was just appearance. Although it included members of the same parties as the previous one, in reality it entirely belonged to the MRND or anti-Arusha side, and the most prominent among these members shared the view on the fate that was to be reserved for the Tutsi.

The interim government used the administrative machinery to mobilise the largest number of people possible for the extermination campaign. On 19 April, President Sindikubwabo declared that his team was a 'government of saviours' ready to approach all citizens 'to tell you what it expects of you'. Speeches like this were largely disseminated in order to make people 'more determined to ensure their own safety and to warn trouble makers'.[24] Ministers and high-ranking civil servants did not just direct from above but went to the field, generally in their regions of origin, inciting and encouraging people to actively participate in the genocide, promising rewards for the killers and threatening the waverers. This link between centre and periphery was already seen during the 1963 killings in Gikongoro (cf. Section 5.3).

The next circles were at the prefectoral and local levels.[25] Organisation there was flexible and adapted to the circumstances and depended to some extent on the willingness or ability of officials to fully commit to the violence. Their official position in the hierarchy soon became less important than their implication in the genocidal project. In some places, people without an official function, such as traders, teachers, priests, retired army officers or militia leaders, took effective command in the hunting down and killing of the Tutsi.[26] As is often the case under these circumstances, this moment was also used for individual settling of scores that ignored official hierarchies. An important asset for local mayors was their power to allocate land, often used to promise killers that they would receive the land of their victims. In addition, as mayors were in charge of

---

[24] Letters sent to the prefects by the interior minister on 21 April 1994 (Des Forges et al., *Leave None to Tell the Story*, p. 233).
[25] The local level is well studied in Kimonyo, *Rwanda's Popular Genocide*, and Dumas, *Le genocide au village*.
[26] These local dynamics are described in Straus, *The Order of Genocide*, p. 91.

6.2 The Genocide

the population registry, they had the power to decide over life and death by attesting that someone was Hutu or Tutsi.

The government presented the massacres as a spontaneous popular reaction after President Habyarimana's death and as acts of self-defence against the RPF's military offensive. However, all data show the organised nature of the violence. Developments in the city and *préfecture* of Butare show this very well. Apart from some isolated incidents, the area remained initially calm, thanks to the action of its prefect Jean-Baptiste Habyarimana (the only Tutsi prefect, no kinship link to the deceased president), of other local authorities and some army and *gendarmerie* (national police) officers. Wanting to break Butare's resistance to the genocide, the government dismissed the prefect, who was later assassinated. At the occasion of the inauguration of his successor on 19 April, the interim president and several ministers were present. In their speeches, President Sindikubwabo and Prime Minister Kambanda announced that the 'final war' had started, that the Butare authorities and population had to abandon their 'lax' attitude and that everyone had to begin 'working', a term used to designate the massacre of the Tutsi.[27] These intimidating statements had immediate impact, as the genocide extended to the entire Butare *préfecture* by 22 April. A similar evolution can be seen in Gitarama *préfecture*, where the genocide was imposed on initially recalcitrant local authorities.

While the massacres were not spontaneous but on the contrary organised, there remains the issue of their planning. It must first be noted that the 1948 Convention on the Prevention and Punishment of the Crime of Genocide, the Genocide Convention in brief, does not require planning but the '*intent* to destroy, in whole or in part, a national, ethnical, racial or religious group, as such'. Next, everything depends on the meaning given to the notion of 'planning'. If this refers to a precise place and moment where conspirators met to decide the organisation of a genocide and to prepare its instruments, there is no proof of such conspiracy prior to 6 April 1994. This does not mean that there was no pre-genocide planning, only that it has not been proven. The International Criminal Tribunal for Rwanda (ICTR) came to that conclusion in the Bagosora case when finding that it was 'not satisfied that the Prosecution has proven beyond reasonable doubt that the four Accused conspired amongst themselves or with others to commit genocide before it unfolded on 7 April 1994'.[28]

---

[27] Des Forges et al., *Leave None to Tell the Story*, pp. 457–461.
[28] *The Prosecutor* v. *Théoneste Bagosora et al.*, Case No. ICTR-98-41-T, 18 December 2008, para 2113. The planning thesis was also discussed in detail and rejected in Guichaoua, *Rwanda, de la guerre au génocide*, pp. 443–453.

As said earlier, the absence of planning has no impact on the legal qualification of the crime. The massacre of the Tutsi corresponds without doubt to the definition of the Genocide Convention. Indeed, the Tutsi were the victims of an extermination project, not because of what they did or supposedly did but because of who they were. This is a clear case of the 'destruction, in whole or in part, of an ethnic group, as such'. As for those opposed to the genocidal project, they were generally eliminated, whether they were Hutu or Tutsi.

6.2.3 Means

Several means were put to use to commit the genocide. The first were the militias. During the period of the political transition in 1991–1992, the parties created youth movements. The initial intention was the same as what parties have all over the world, namely to enlarge the party base and recruit future cadres. Among others, those created included the *interahamwe* ('those fighting together') of the MRND, the *inkuba* ('thunder') of the MDR and the *impuzamugambi* ('those with one aim') of the CDR. These youths were increasingly used to accompany public rallies and protect party demonstrators from those of other parties. To that end, some carried sticks and batons. As seen earlier, during the months preceding the genocide some elements of the *interahamwe* received paramilitary training. The distinctions between the youth movements disappeared during the genocide. The *interahamwe* and the *impuzamugambi* operated together, joined by the *inkuba* of the MDR 'Hutu Power' wing. Those who earlier were not part of a youth movement but joined the militias on barrages and in the hunt for Tutsi were all called *interahamwe*, a term that became generic and was no longer limited to the MRND youth. Political rivalries disappeared in favour of the 'common good', which was the extermination campaign.

The media were the second powerful means, particularly the radio widely followed in Rwanda. All along the genocide, both the public Radio Rwanda and the private Radio Télévision des Mille Collines (RTLM) broadcast incitements to massacres and instructions on how to perpetrate them. They warned against 'infiltrators' who massacred the Hutu and called for vigilance. Instructions were relayed on how to conduct 'community labour' (*umuganda*): comb out the bush and marshes, search houses, control waterways and so on. Through pure hate media, RTLM spread the messages of Hutu radicalism: the old irreducible cleavage between the Hutu and Tutsi, the demographic superiority of the Hutu (*rubanda nyamwinshi*, 'the majoritarian people'), the ruse of the Tutsi, their solidarity, their intention to restore the old feudality and repression, the danger they represented for the achievements of the 1959 revolution and, above all, their plan to exterminate the Hutu. Just like the political and administrative authorities, RTLM warned the recalcitrants that they would be severely punished for 'desertion'.[29] However, despite their violent language, the impact of hate radio broadcasts had probably been more limited than has often been assumed, if only because many did not kill for ideological reasons (as shown later).[30]

The third instrument was civilian self-defence. This programme, instituted at the beginning of the war in 1990 in zones close to the front, comprised the organisation of patrols by civilians (called *amarondo*, a kinyarwandisation of the French *ronde*, meaning 'patrol') and the armament of local authorities and army reservists. Scott Straus has observed that this practice involved civilians in the war, thus opening the way for civilian participation in the genocide.[31] These structures were not yet fully in place across the entire country when the war resumed, but on 12 April the government decided to implement the plan to mobilise civilians and put them under the command of retired officers or other military. By the end of May, the plan was fully operational, and it played a central role during the genocide. Civilian self-defence allowed to organise the massacres and to efficiently command, control, supervise and arm civilians. It also served to ensure more discipline and avoid that Hutu killed other Hutu.[32]

6.2.4 Modus Operandi

From the morning of 7 April, barrages were set up all over Kigali. Manned by *interahamwe* but also, as seen earlier, by youths of other parties and by ordinary citizens, they allowed to control movements. Identity cards (which mentioned ethnicity) were checked, Tutsi were stopped and killed, generally by bladed weapons. Those without identity papers were judged on their appearance, and those supposedly corresponding to the 'Tutsi type' suffered the same fate. After a few days, the killings became more systematic and organised. Tutsi were hunted in their homes and taken to official buildings – churches, schools and other public places – where they were massacred at a large scale.

---

[29] On the role of the media see J.-P. Chrétien et al., *Rwanda: Les médias du génocide*, Paris, Karthala, 1995.
[30] McDoom, *The Path to Genocide*, pp. 120–122.
[31] Straus, *The Order of Genocide*, p. 26.
[32] More details on civilian self-defence can be found in Guichaoua, *Rwanda, de la guerre au génocide*, pp. 480–484, 516–521.

The killing of Tutsi rapidly extended to the entire country, except initially to Butare and Gitarama, as discussed earlier.[33] Two modi operandi were generally used. On the one hand, when the killings started, people who felt threatened, mostly Tutsi but also some Hutu, sought refuge in hospitals, schools, churches, stadiums and other public places. Once entrapped and encircled by excited civilians, militia members or military, they were slaughtered mostly by baton, axe or machete, sometimes by grenades or firearms. Each time, hundreds and sometimes thousands of Tutsi were thus killed in a space of one or two days.[34] The second mode targeted the Tutsi individually. They were attacked in their homes, chased on one hill to the next and killed at barrages kept all over the country. The violence was inflicted with great cruelty. Victims were burned alive, thrown dead or fatally wounded in latrines or slowly killed with machetes, which made some pay their assassins to use a firearm. In ethnically mixed households, many were forced to kill the Tutsi members of their own family.

Contrary to the Shoah, the genocide was not an act of specialists using instruments created for this purpose (train convoys, extermination camps, gas chambers, specialised units) but a decentralised action committed by large numbers of ordinary people, a 'popular genocide'.[35] The density of political and administrative structures so typical of Rwanda, a country centralised and decentralised at the same time, gave leaders a rapid and easy access to a population traumatised by war and propaganda. Fujii has shown common characteristics of the massacres throughout the country. First, the perpetrators killed in groups rather than as individuals, and these groups were often larger than physically necessary to harm victims that were generally unarmed and unable to flee. Second, the vast majority of killings were public acts committed in plain daylight and thus observable by all. Third, killers and victims were meeting face to face. The use of bladed weapons belonging to daily rural routine did not allow the physical distance inherent in the use of firearms. Lastly, the killers sang and shouted slogans ('Pawa'[36]), hit empty barrels, blew whistles and were dressed in banana leaves to 'disguise' themselves. In many cases, the rape, torture and mutilation also had a ritual or ceremonial function.[37]

---

[33] Scott Straus provides a list, *commune* by *commune*, of the beginning of the genocide locally (*The Order of Genocide*, pp. 249–255).
[34] Alison Des Forges (*Leave None to Tell the Story*, p. 211) mentions dozens of places where this practice could be observed, though this list is by no means exhaustive.
[35] Kimonyo, *Rwanda's Popular Genocide*.
[36] As seen earlier, this was the kinyarwandisation of the English word 'power'.
[37] Fujii, *Killing Neighbors*, pp. 171–175.

6.2 The Genocide

6.2.5 Dynamics and Motives

A belief held early on that ethnic hatred was the main driving force behind the genocide has been contradicted or at least nuanced by more recent research showing that monocausal explanations cannot account for the complexity of what happened in Rwanda. For instance, Straus argues that three main factors have made the genocide possible: the war, the strength of the state and pre-existing ethnic classifications. The killing of President Habyarimana was a major factor: many of Straus's participants described how his death crystallised a fear that had been diffuse until then and gave renewed force to the propaganda linked to the war. For her part, focalising on individual motivations of local actors, Fujii found that many of her interviewees explained participation in situational terms, not based on identity. 'Circumstances compelled people to do what they did.'[38] Other factors included the legacies of past violence, jealousy and greed, and the 'logic of contamination'.[39]

It is important to note that much of the violence was not ethnic or political. As often in circumstances of war, instability and chaos, this was an occasion to settle scores, seize land or businesses, or eliminate competitors or creditors. There is not much research on this aspect, but a local study shows the diversity of criminal acts and their motives well. Of the twenty-eight persons killed in a sector in the north-west (where the number of Tutsi was very limited), only one was Tutsi. The other twenty-seven victims were Hutu, of whom ten had relatively large land holdings, seven were poor people with virtually no property, five were considered 'trouble makers' and five others were even young men involved in militia.[40] In a similar vein, Fujii's interviewees indicated individual jealousy and greed as important causes of the violence, rather than tensions or animosities between ethnic groups. Greed was part of everyday experience before the genocide, but the context of violence, uncertainty and instability allowed the realisation of criminal projects, even against neighbours and friends.[41]

Like every historical event, the genocide against the Tutsi can therefore not be understood by a monocausal explanation. In a sophisticated analysis based on a large set of data on the micro, meso and

---

[38] Ibid., p. 90.
[39] Ibid., pp. 93–102.
[40] C. André, J.-P. Platteau, *Land Tenure under Unendurable Stress: Rwanda Caught in the Malthusian Trap*, Namur, Cahiers de la faculté des sciences économiques et sociales de Namur, No. 164, 1996. This work shows the increase of land conflicts and social tensions well before the genocide, as well as the links between these pre-existing conflicts and the crimes committed in 1994.
[41] Fujii, *Killing Neighbors*, p. 98.

macro levels, McDoom has proposed a large combination of factors: war, insecurity and fear; demographics and environment; privations and frustrations; racist prejudice; ideological propaganda and myths; political and material opportunism; group effects and collective action; the influence of the state and its elites; dispositions and situations of the perpetrators; impunity; external and international factors – all these elements (and probably more) have conjugated to make possible a crime that was not inevitable.[42]

6.2.6 Number of Victims

The total number of genocide victims is not precisely known, but local and family samples suggest that about three quarters of Tutsi living in Rwanda during the genocide were killed. Admitting that, based on the updated data of the 1991 population census, there were at most 800,000 Tutsi, the number of genocide victims could be as high as 600,000. In a forum published in the *Journal of Genocide Research*, independently from one another the authors arrive at an estimate ranging from 500,000 to 600,000.[43] In 2000, the Rwandan government arrived at the absurdly precise figure of 1,074,017 victims, 94 per cent of whom were said to be Tutsi. This figure is unreliable in light of the demographic reality and the number of Tutsi survivors and Hutu victims.[44] A census conducted soon after the genocide could have clarified this issue. The international community proposed its assistance for such a calculation, but the RPF had not accepted this offer. The absence of a census allowed the RPF to impose its figure, although it was not based on scientific data, as well as to hide the extent of the massacres it itself committed.

6.3 Crimes Committed by the RPF

While the Hutu extremists openly committed genocide, the RPF also was guilty of large-scale massacres that however for a long time escaped media attention and therefore the international public. Already during the first days of the civil war's resumption, the RPF contingent in Kigali had used

---

[42] McDoom, *The Path to Genocide*.
[43] 'Calculating Mortality in the Rwandan Genocide', *Journal of Genocide Research*, Vol. 22, No. 1, 2020, pp. 77–141. Also see L. Reydams, '"More than a Million": The Politics of Accounting for the Dead of the Rwandan Genocide', *Review of African Political Economy*, Vol. 48, No. 168, 2021, pp. 235–256, and McDoom, *The Path to Genocide*, pp. 289–295.
[44] Even the number of survivors is uncertain, as shown by the data proposed by two authors. In his preface to Dumas's book (*Le genocide au village*, p. 1), Stéphane Audouin-Rouzeau arrives at 300,000 survivors, while the figure proposed by Piton (*Le genocide des Tutsi*, p. 210) is 130,000.

6.3 Crimes Committed by the RPF

lists to identify, locate and kill dozens of elite civilians and members of their families. More importantly, it committed massive massacres of civilians in the zones it controlled. A routine practice was the organisation of 'peace meetings' purportedly aimed at providing information or support, a ploy to assemble people who were then indiscriminately killed.[45] Many events of this nature are well documented, and they each time caused hundreds and sometimes thousands to be killed. Civilian massacres were at the time denounced by organisations like Refugees International, Amnesty International and the UNHCR. For instance, a 17 May 1994 Situation Report mentioned one such 'peace meeting', at which 'people were tied together, three by three – men/women/children – and stabbed. The bodies were put on trucks and thrown into the Kagera river.'[46]

Information on crimes committed by the RPF only became available in a piecemeal fashion. Amnesty International noted 'that the RPF closely monitored and controlled movements of foreigners in areas under its control. (...) This ensured that (...) very limited information about abuses by the RPA could be gathered or made public by independent observers.'[47] This was also the experience of Des Forges et al., who noted that the RPF 'was remarkably successful in restricting access by foreigners to certain parts of the country'.[48] The truth nevertheless gradually emerged. In August–September 1994, a UNHCR team led by Robert Gersony visited refugee camps and a quarter of Rwanda's *communes*. Its report, which was never published, found that 'significant areas of Butare Prefecture, Kibungo Prefecture, and the southern and eastern areas of Kigali Prefecture have been (...) the scene of systematic and sustained killing and persecution of their civilian Hutu populations by the RPA. (...) Large-scale indiscriminate killings of men, women, children, including the sick and the elderly, were consistently reported.'[49] Gersony observed that the massacres targeted Hutu without distinction: 'No vetting process or attempt to establish the complicity of the victims in the April 1994 massacres of the Tutsis was reported.'[50] The team estimated that from late

---

[45] This practice was so widespread that people equated *kwitaba inama* (to be called to a meeting) to *kwitaba imana* (to be called to God).
[46] Refugees International, *Rwandan Refugees in Tanzania: New Arrivals Report*, Sitrep #10, 17 May 1994.
[47] Amnesty International, *Rwanda: Reports of Killings and Abductions by the Rwandese Patriotic Army, April–August 1994*, 14 October 1994.
[48] Des Forges et al., *Leave None to Tell the Story*, p. 692.
[49] R. Gersony, UNHCR, 'Prospects for Early Repatriation of Rwandan Refugees Currently in Burundi, Tanzania and Zaire: Summary of UNHCR Presentation before Commission of Experts', Geneva, 10 October 1994, p. 4.
[50] Ibid., p. 8.

April/May to July, and only in the areas mentioned earlier, between 15,000 and 30,000 persons were killed by the RPA.

Later in 1994, UN special rapporteur René Degni-Ségui found cases of summary executions, massacres and forced disappearances and noted that 'in addition to the mass graves for which the RPA is responsible we therefore have all those for which the militia and the Rwandese Armed Forces are responsible, so that it is now difficult to tell them apart'.[51] A month later, a UN commission of experts concluded

> on the basis of ample evidence that individuals from both sides to the armed conflict in Rwanda during the period from 6 April 1994 to 15 July 1994 perpetrated serious breaches of international humanitarian law (and) that ample evidence indicates that individuals from both sides to the armed conflict perpetrated crimes against humanity in Rwanda in the period mentioned above.[52]

The commission remained 'disturbed by ongoing violence committed by some RPF soldiers and recommends that investigation of violations of international humanitarian law and of human rights law attributed to the Rwandese Patriotic Front be continued by the (ICTR) Prosecutor'.[53]

Organised mass killings continued even after the war ended. A mere ten days after the RPF took full control of Kigali, the UNAMIR commander's intelligence officer reported that 'the RPF was running two interrogation centres in Kigali and that summary executions were being conducted all day long'.[54] Former RPA members interviewed by the ICTR Office of the Prosecutor (OTP) mentioned large-scale killings of Hutu. Many were assembled in military installations in Kigali, from where they were taken to Gabiro and Bigogwe camps to be killed. In a number of cases, the victims' bodies were incinerated. One of the former RPA witnesses stated that '[i]t was understood that if there were no Hutu from our side present, we would kill everybody on site (sic)'.[55]

---

[51] United Nations, Economic and Social Council, Commission on Human Rights, *Report on the Situation of Human Rights in Rwanda Submitted by Mr. René Degni-Ségui, Special Rapporteur of the Commission on Human Rights, under Paragraph 20 of Resolution S-3/1 of 25 May 1994*, E/CN.4/1995/70, 11 November 1994, para. 40.

[52] United Nations, Security Council, *Final Report of the Commission of Experts Established Pursuant to Security Council Resolution 935 (1994)*, S/1994/1405, 9 December 1994, paras. 181–182.

[53] Ibid., para. 186.

[54] R. Dallaire, *Shake Hands with the Devil: The Failure of Humanity in Rwanda*, Toronto, Random House Canada, 2003, p. 469.

[55] Witness interview, 28 March 2002, ICTR ref R0000299–302; Witness interview, 18 May 2002, ICTR ref R0000280–283. More witness information is available in a leaked report of a Special Investigations Unit of the ICTR OTP (ICTR, *General Report on the Special Investigations concerning the Crimes Committed by the Rwandan Patriotic Army (RPA) during 1994*, 1 October 2003).

Human Rights Watch documented massacres in Kivumu, Butare, Save, Rango, Kayenzi, Masango and other places where over a thousand people were killed.[56]

While the crimes committed by the RPF have been known for a long time, they were recently documented in detail on the basis of confidential documents of the ICTR OTP and numerous witness interviews, including of former RPA members.[57] While the legal qualification of these crimes is an unsettled issue, the material fact appears indisputable. And yet not a single RPF suspect was prosecuted before the ICTR or any domestic court. This impunity heralded new massive human rights abuse by the RPF in the years following the genocide, in both Rwanda and Zaire/DRC.

6.4 Sequels

6.4.1 The Politics of Justice

After genocide and massive war crimes and crimes against humanity, some form of justice was obviously needed. But 'justice' sounds more neutral than it is: paraphrasing Clausewitz's famous aphorism ('War is the continuation of politics by other means'), one could say that 'lawfare', though less conspicuous than warfare, can be the continuation of war by other means.[58] Transitional justice in Rwanda has been widely researched,[59] and this section can only briefly address its politics at three

---

[56] Human Rights Watch, *The Aftermath of Genocide in Rwanda*, New York, September 1994. Data were updated and complemented in Human Rights Watch, *Rwanda: A New Catastrophe?*, New York, September 1994.

[57] J. Rever, *In Praise of Blood: The Crimes of the Rwandan Patriotic Front*, Toronto, Random House Canada, 2018. Rever concluded that the RPF also committed genocide, this time against the Hutu, thus subscribing to the so-called 'double genocide thesis', a claim that has led to bitter polemics. While acknowledging that the RPF committed mass crimes, most scholars reject the legal qualification of genocide. This position is summarised by Scott Straus, who however leaves a great deal of ambiguity when categorising the killings of the RPF 'in social science terms' as 'mass categorical violence: large-scale, repeated, and systematic violence that targets a specific civilian population group (Rwandan Hutus)', thereby getting very close to the definition of genocide (S. Straus, 'The Limits of a Genocide Lens: Violence against Rwandans in the 1990s', *Journal of Genocide Research*, Vol. 21, No. 4, 2019, pp. 512–513).

[58] J. Meierhenrich, *The Violence of Law: The Formation and Deformation of* Gacaca *Courts in Rwanda*, Cambridge, Cambridge University Press, forthcoming.

[59] Among the wealth of publications, in addition to numerous journal articles, see A. Chakravarty, *Investing in Authoritarian Rule: Punishment and Patronage in Rwanda's Gacaca Courts for Genocide Crimes*, New York, Cambridge University Press, 2016; P. Clark, *The* Gacaca *Courts: Post-genocide Justice and Reconciliation in Rwanda – Justice without Lawyers*, Cambridge, Cambridge University Press, 2010; T. Cruvellier, *Court of Remorse: Inside the International Criminal Tribunal for Rwanda*, Madison, University

levels: domestic justice in Rwanda, in particular before the *gacaca* jurisdictions, the ICTR and the application of universal jurisdiction in third countries. Victor's justice has prevailed at all these levels.

Given the state of its conventional justice system and the huge number of persons detained for their presumed role in the genocide, in 2002 Rwanda launched a gigantic experiment of transitional justice and decided 'to put most of the nation on trial'.[60] The *gacaca* system put in place was very decentralised.[61] In more than 10,000 jurisdictions created at the levels of cells, sectors, *communes* and *préfectures*, justice was to be rendered by *inyangamugayo*, locally elected persons of integrity without legal training. Although the law referred to tradition, apart from their name and local nature, these jurisdictions had nothing traditional. They were modern state institutions applying official law and where state institutions, such as prosecutors' offices, played a central role. At the end of the process in 2012, almost two million cases had been adjudicated and about one million suspects were tried, with an acquittal rate of 14 per cent. The number of people convicted corresponded to more than half the 1994 Hutu male adult population, thus giving the impression that that an entire ethnic group had been collectively criminalised. This unique experiment has generated a great deal of research, which uncovered fundamental flaws: truth was often the victim of Rwandans' ways of telling it and of the government imposing its narrative; the process often led to a decrease rather than an increase in confidence at the local level; state control imposed a vision that was detrimental to individual processes of reconciliation; the population was reluctant to participate and the government had to impose popular involvement; and RPA/RPF crimes were excluded from scrutiny, thus creating frustration and confirming the feeling of victor's justice. Susan Thomson's conclusion on the *gacaca* experience is severe: 'For all the lofty rhetoric about justice and reconciliation, in practice the courts were a formal, state-managed space that served to

---

of Wisconsin Press, 2010; G. Gahima, *Transitional Justice in Rwanda: Accountability for Atrocity*, New York, Routledge, 2013; Human Rights Watch, *Justice Compromised: The Legacy of Rwanda's Community-Based Gacaca Courts*, New York, 2011; B. Ingelaere, *Inside Rwanda's* Gacaca *Courts: Seeking Justice after Genocide*, Madison, University of Wisconsin Press, 2016; K. C. Moghalu, *Rwanda's Genocide: The Politics of Global Justice*, New York–Houndmills, Palgrave Macmillan, 2006; N. Palmer, *Courts in Conflict: Interpreting the Layers of Justice in Post-genocide Rwanda*, Oxford, Oxford University Press, 2019.

[60] L. Waldorf, 'Mass Justice for Mass Atrocity: Rethinking Local Justice as Transitional Justice', *Temple Law Review*, Vol. 79, No. 1, 2006, p. 3.

[61] *Gacaca* literally means 'grass' or 'herbs', reference to a lawn outside where people traditionally used to settle their disputes.

6.4 Sequels

reinforce government authority.'[62] However, there was no single common experience across the country. Ingelaere has shown that the process was inscribed in local social and political dynamics, different from one place to the next. Experiences were multiple, as numerous as the hills of Rwanda.[63]

Created by UN Security Council Resolution 955 on 8 November 1994 to 'prosecute persons responsible for genocide and other serious violations of international humanitarian law committed in the territory of Rwanda and neighbouring States, between 1 January 1994 and 31 December 1994', the ICTR started effectively functioning in mid 1995. Serious problems marred the institution from the beginning, so much so that six years into its operation, the International Crisis Group pointed at 'the mediocre productivity of the judges', 'incompetence in a large part' of the OTP, illegal fee splitting between lawyers and defendants, and internal power struggles.[64]

A problem from day one was the extremely slow pace of procedures. Only in 1998, three years after the ICTR started effectively functioning, were the first three judgments rendered; two of these came after brief trials following guilty pleas. One of the consequences was that suspects spent very long times in pre-trial detention. In an extreme case, between his arrest in 1995 and his judgment in first instance, former mayor Joseph Kanyabashi spent sixteen years in prison and about twenty years until the final decision on appeal. Poor prosecutorial policy was a second sore point. At the beginning, investigations and prosecutions lacked focus, and the OTP went for any suspect, however small, it could find. This considerably delayed the tribunal's work in dealing with suspects ranking high in the hierarchy of genocide. The quality of indictments was poor, as was the way in which the OTP met its burden of proof, a phenomenon judges even complained publicly about.[65] The quality of witness statements, crucial in these cases, which were strongly based on the establishment of facts and where documentary evidence was rare, was an Achilles' heel of the ICTR, and the OTP in particular. Like in the *gacaca* proceedings, false testimonies were frequent, but this did not bother the OTP too much. It indeed appeared more intent on securing convictions than on discovering the truth.

The main flaw of the ICTR was its transformation into an instrument of victor's justice. After prosecutor Carla Del Ponte announced in April

---

[62] Thomson, *Rwanda*, p. 178.
[63] Ingelaere, *Inside Rwanda's* Gacaca *Courts*.
[64] International Crisis Group, *International Criminal Tribunal for Rwanda: Justice Delayed*, Nairobi–Arusha–Brussels, June 2001, pp. 10–13.
[65] 'Judge Yakov Ostrovky Criticisms of ICTR', Arusha, Internews, 13 May 2002.

2002 that she hoped to issue indictments against RPF suspects before the end of the year, the regime reacted by sabotaging the tribunal's work. Staff at the Kigali office were threatened, witnesses were prevented from going to Arusha and Rwandan general prosecutor Gerald Gahima rejected any idea of prosecuting RPF suspects: the RPF saved the nation and any attempt to indict one of its officers would be tantamount to an attack against the nation's unity.[66] By the end of 2002, the Rwandan government had decided that Del Ponte had to go, and it increased the pressure. In late November, it announced that Del Ponte 'has lost the moral authority to prosecute cases linked to the genocide',[67] and on 12 December it asked that she be removed. By the spring of 2003, the OTP Special Investigations Unit had documented some fifteen large-scale massacres committed by the RPF, four of which were ready for indictment. After the US attempted to broker an agreement through which the OTP would renounce further investigation of RPF crimes, the OTP claimed that Rwanda was exercising pressure on the UN Security Council not to renew Del Ponte's mandate. At the end of July, the UN general secretary, with the support of Kigali's allies, the US and the UK, proposed to appoint a separate prosecutor for the ICTR.[68] The Security Council endorsed the proposal, and Rwanda finally got rid of Del Ponte. Her successor, Gambian judge Hassan Bubacar Jallow, abandoned the investigations against RPF/RPA suspects. Despite, in judge Ostrovky's words, 'ample evidence to show that a large number of crimes were committed by the RPF whose leaders today occupy key positions in the government',[69] impunity was to prevail, a fact for which Jallow carries heavy responsibility, as, in his own words, the prosecutor has total discretion in prosecuting or not.[70]

Despite its many shortcomings, the ICTR has contributed to the development of international criminal law, beyond the case of Rwanda. It was the first international court that prosecuted and convicted for genocide. It thus 'gave life to the Genocide Convention for the very first time since that treaty was adopted'.[71] The ICTR also contributed to clarifying and ordering existing norms of international humanitarian law. For instance, as they share a common language, culture and history, the Hutu and Tutsi are no ethnic groups in the narrow sense of the word, a

---

[66] 'Rwanda Questions Usefulness of UN Genocide Court', New York (UN), Reuters, 24 July 2002.
[67] Gouvernement du Rwanda, *Communiqué de presse*, Kigali, 21 November 2002.
[68] Del Ponte was prosecutor for both the ICTR and the ICTY.
[69] 'Judge Yakov Ostrovky' quoted earlier.
[70] H. B. Jallow, 'Prosecutorial Discretion and International Criminal Justice', *Journal of International Criminal Justice*, Vol. 3, No. 1, 2005, pp. 145–161.
[71] Moghalu, *Rwanda's Genocide*, p. 202.

fact that could have prevented the qualification of the crimes committed as genocide. By adopting a broad, 'operational', definition, in its very first judgment the ICTR upheld the charge, among other reasons as 'the Tutsi were conceived of as an ethnic group by those who targeted them for killing'.[72] The same judgment found that rape can be a count of genocide. The ICTR also had a direct impact on Rwandan legislation. Wanting to obtain transfers of cases from Arusha (as well as extraditions from third countries), and realising that the death penalty was an obstacle, the Rwandan government reacted in a pragmatic fashion, abolishing capital punishment in 2007.

At the end of its proceedings in 2015, the ICTR had condemned sixty-two persons and acquitted fourteen. Ten suspects were referred to national jurisdictions, while five fugitives were referred to the International Residual Mechanism for Criminal Tribunals. The cost had been considerable: at an estimated total cost of about US$1.8 billion, this amounts to about US$23 million per person judged.

Finally, a brief mention must be made of trials that have taken place in third countries based on the principle of universal jurisdiction, which allows trying suspects even if the crimes were committed abroad, the perpetrators are foreigners or the victims do not have the citizenship of the country where the procedure takes place. This competence only concerns serious crimes, in particular war crimes, crimes against humanity and genocide. Such cases were tried in Switzerland, Belgium, France, the Netherlands, Canada, Norway, Sweden and Finland. All those prosecuted were condemned to prison sentences of varying terms. These cases had in common with those tried in Rwanda and before the ICTR that only the Hutu suspected of involvement in the genocide were prosecuted, while RPF perpetrators again enjoyed impunity.

6.4.2 Regional Wars

The second sequel of the resumption of the civil war and the genocide was the extraterritorial extension of the Rwandan conflict, followed by that of other civil wars in the region. This extension caused an 'African world war' on the territory of Rwanda's large but weak neighbour, Zaire, in 1994 and the DRC from 1996. Limited to the role of Rwanda, the details will be discussed in the next chapter.[73]

---

[72] *The Prosecutor v. Jean-Paul Akayezu*, No. ICTR-96-4-T, Judgment of 2 September 1998, paras. 170–171.
[73] More on the Congo wars can be found in G. Prunier, *Africa's World War: Congo, the Rwandan Genocide, and the Making of a Continental Catastrophe*, Oxford, Oxford University Press, 2009; F. Reyntjens, *The Great African War: Congo and Regional*

6.5 Conclusion

For Rwanda 1994 was a major critical juncture, in two related respects: the genocide against the Tutsi and the seizure of power by the RPF. These are related yet separate. On the one hand, the RPF could have won a military victory even had the genocide not taken place. Indeed, it started its offensive early in the morning of 7 April before the beginning of the genocide. On the other hand, although the RPF had shown military superiority during the civil war, its victory was not written in the stars. In other words, neither the genocide nor the RPF's seizing power was inevitable. But both occurred, and they have had a fundamental impact: the genocide is a long-lasting trauma for both victims and perpetrators, as well as – paradoxically – a political asset for the RPF, while the change of regime might have created the conditions for new massive violence, as will be discussed in the next chapter.

After the end of the Cold War, political transitions have taken place all over Africa. Although outcomes have diverged, and transitions have failed in some cases, on the whole Africa is more democratic, politically more pluralistic and more respectful of human rights than at the end of the 1980s.[74] In the early 1990s, Rwanda seemed to follow such a course: a new constitution re-introduced multi-party rule, a diverse and free press emerged and political negotiations led to a power-sharing arrangement. However, from being tripolar during the internal democratisation process and the Arusha negotiations with the RPF, the political landscape increasingly became bipolar throughout 1993. Although it could have had a defining political role as the arbitrating force, the opposition fell into the bipolar trap, dividing itself into two competing extremes, one hanging on to power, the other aiming at capturing it. As reminded at the beginning of this chapter, this fatal evolution occurred in the context of ethnic bipolarity exacerbated by the military conflict. This unique combination of a political transition, ethnic bipolarity and civil war caused the transition to fail, while it could otherwise have succeeded as it did elsewhere on the continent.

Geopolitics, 1996–2006, New York, Cambridge University Press, 2009; J. K. Stearns, *Dancing in the Glory of Monsters: The Collapse of the Congo and the Great War of Africa*, New York, Public Affairs, 2011; P. Roessler, H. Verhoeven, *Why Comrades Go To War: Liberation Politics and the Outbreak of Africa's Deadliest Conflict*, London, Hurst, 2016; J. K. Stearns, *The War That Doesn't Say Its Name: The Unending Conflicts in the Congo*, Princeton, Princeton University Press, 2021.

[74] Despite democratic backsliding over the last two decades in Africa and elsewhere in the world.

7 Post-genocide Political Governance

7.1 Two Rwandas

As this chapter is not historical but deals with the contemporary political situation, its style is different from the previous ones and rather reads like a chronicle of current affairs. There are two radically opposed perceptions of post-genocide Rwanda. The one is that of Bono, Pastor Rick Warren, Bill Clinton and Tony Blair, who are just a few of the 'Friends of the New Rwanda', as well as most aid agencies. This view focuses on technocratic/bureaucratic governance and hails economic progress, visionary leadership, reforms in education, health and agriculture, women empowerment and market policies, to name but a few. It is also informed by the regime's genocide credit,[1] as well as by feelings of guilt over international inaction in 1994 (this argument will be discussed later).[2] The other perception is shared by most academic observers of political governance, as illustrated in the edited volume *Remaking Rwanda*.[3] This view focuses on political governance and sees autocratic rule, gross human rights abuse, growing inequality and rural poverty, victimisation of the Hutu majority and injustice. The resulting structural violence may eventually lead to political instability and new conflict. This author belongs to the second school. As is also the case elsewhere in this book, socio-economic development is only tangentially addressed, though this is the area where the current regime has shown remarkable performance, certainly when compared to most other African countries.

---

[1] This refers to the use of the genocide as a political asset, combined with the claim of victim status by the RPF, while not the RPF but the Tutsi living inside the country in 1994 were the victims. As will be seen later, the Tutsi genocide survivors became second-class citizens.

[2] Whenever it is the subject of international criticism, the RPF reminds western countries that they abandoned Rwanda during the genocide and are therefore at least partly responsible for the bloodletting.

[3] S. Straus, L. Waldorf (Eds.), *Remaking Rwanda: State Building and Human Rights after Mass Violence*, Madison, University of Wisconsin Press, 2011.

The RPF has actively pursued its modernising vision. Having inherited a devastated country, the regime achieved rapid recovery, especially after 2000. Economic growth averaged around a robust 8 per cent in most of the post-genocide period. Progress on social indicators such as health and education has been strong. The country has performed well in the World Bank's Ease of doing business rankings. It is also a major contributor to international peacekeeping operations. However, the price of these successes in terms of political repression and the laying of the seeds of future violent conflict is high. It is argued here that the achievements of good bureaucratic/technocratic governance risk being destroyed by the regime's deeply flawed political governance.

Thirty years after having won the civil war and put an end to the genocide against the Tutsi, the ruling RPF has solidly established its hegemony. It has achieved this after eliminating the political opposition and autonomous civil society, massively violating human rights and killing well over a hundred thousand of its own citizens, by abusing the legal and justice systems, and through skilful information and communication management. The focus, in short, has been on maximising the concentration of power in the hands of a small elite. The internal costs on Rwandans are high, and the future is, in consequence, very uncertain. In addition, devastating interventions in eastern Congo have had and continue to have destabilising regional consequences.

7.2 Elections as a Means of Regime Consolidation

From its first days in power, the RPF imposed its view on the country's political dispensation. Despite its formal adherence to the power-sharing formula inscribed in the 1993 Arusha peace accord, it could easily ignore such constitutional limitations, as its victory on the battlefield and the fact that it did not owe much to external forces (except Uganda) gave it a free hand to exercise power as it pleased. It did so all the more willingly since it knew that it would stand no chance in an open political contest. By August 1995, just a year after the RPF's victory, the 'government of national union' ceased to exist. Prime Minister Faustin Twagiramungu of the MDR resigned and left the country along with other members of the cabinet (including Seth Sendashonga, a Hutu minister of the RPF) in protest against the closing of the political landscape, gross human rights violations and partisan appointments in the administration and the judiciary. This was just the tip of the iceberg. Many politicians, civil servants, judges and military officers who had stayed on or who returned after the RPF's victory were threatened or disillusioned, and they fled abroad in increasing numbers from early 1995 on. While those leaving were initially mainly Hutu, they were soon followed by disappointed Tutsi, particularly genocide survivors who felt they were becoming second-class citizens sacrificed by the RPF on the altar of military victory. At the same time, together with the RPF-isation, a 'tutsisation' drive was visible from early on. Although it officially rejected ethnic discrimination and even the notion of ethnicity, the RPF reserved access to power, wealth and knowledge to Tutsi elites. By the end of the 1990s, about two thirds of major positions in the state machinery were occupied by the Tutsi of the RPF, and the military and intelligence services were almost exclusively in their hands (discussed later in the chapter).[4]

As the political transition was to come to an end, the RPF set out to neutralise the opposition parties. The destruction of the MDR, the last party that attempted to maintain some autonomy towards the RPF, started in earnest in 1998. The RPF engineered several splits in the MDR, and members opposed to the 'reformation' of the party were first excluded from parliament and then arrested in early 1999. The MDR was banned altogether in May 2003, just before the first national elections. When former president Bizimungu, after leaving the RPF, attempted to set up a new party in 2001, he was arrested and sentenced to fifteen years in jail. Others suspected of supporting the party were assassinated, 'disappeared' or ended up in prison.[5] Other parties were refused registration. The International Crisis Group concluded that 'the political parties that exist in Rwanda today are only tolerated if they agree not to question the definition of political life drawn up by the RPF'.[6]

The May 2003 constitutional referendum process was criticised by an EU observer mission, which expressed concern over 'control mechanisms (...) that result in restrictions on the freedom of expression, on the freedom of association and on the activities of political parties', as well as over the 'disappearance' of opponents and restrictions on civil society.[7] Nevertheless, presidential and parliamentary elections were held as scheduled. At the presidential poll of 25 August 2003, President Kagame was elected with 95.05 per cent of the vote after a campaign marred by arrests, 'disappearances' and intimidation. The monolithic nature of the political landscape showed clearly in the fact that all parties represented in

---

[4] F. Reyntjens, 'Rwanda, Ten Years On: From Genocide to Dictatorship', *African Affairs*, Vol. 103, No. 2, 2004, pp. 177–210.
[5] Amnesty International, *Rwanda: Number of Prisoners of Conscience on the Rise*, London, 7 June 2002.
[6] International Crisis Group, *Rwanda at the End of the Transition: A Necessary Political Liberalisation*, Nairobi and Brussels, 13 November 2002, p. 2.
[7] Mission d'observation électorale de l'Union Européenne, Référendum constitutionnel, Rwanda 2003, Kigali, n.d.

the transitional parliament supported Kagame's bid. A European observer mission witnessed irregularities and fraud, among others through ballot box stuffing and non-transparent counting procedures.[8] At the direct parliamentary polls for fifty-three MPs, the cartel of the RPF and four small parties obtained 73.78 per cent of the vote, followed by the PSD with 12.31 per cent and the PL with 10.56 per cent. As all parties represented in parliament either joined the RPF list or supported the RPF candidate during the presidential election, all the directly elected MPs were part of one political platform. The EU mission that observed the parliamentary elections reported numerous cases of fraud, intimidation, manipulation of electoral lists, ballot box stuffing, and flawed counting and consolidation procedures.[9] The mission arrived at the paradoxical conclusion that, after the elections, 'political pluralism is more limited than during the transition period'.[10] In reality, the elections returned Rwanda to de facto single-party rule. International reactions to the fraudulent polls were muted, thus reinforcing the RPF in its belief that things would blow over and allowing it to continue a routine of cosmetic elections.

Space forbids offering more than a few illustrations. During the 2008 parliamentary elections, the RPF's machine worked too well: a sample of almost 25 per cent of the votes, collected by an EU observer mission, showed that the RPF obtained 98.39 per cent at the polls. Realising that its score was too 'Stalinist', the RPF lowered it and 'offered' some seats to the PSD and the PL, which were not in the opposition anyway. The official result now became: RPF 78.76 per cent of the votes, PSD 13.12 per cent and PL 7.50 per cent. The EU mission noted other fundamental shortcomings that in themselves would suffice to discredit the entire operation but came to the astonishing conclusion that the polls were 'an important step in the ongoing process to further institutionalise the democratic process in Rwanda'.[11] The EU later ceased to observe elections, but at the 2013 parliamentary polls a Commonwealth Expert Team (CET) noted similar shortcomings. Apart from major irregularities at the polling stations, it found that '[a]s the vote was not traceable through the entire process of tabulation, the CET sees the result as having its credibility compromised'.[12]

---

[8] Mission d'observation électorale de l'Union Européenne, Rwanda: Election présidentielle 25 août 2003. Elections législatives 29 et 30 septembre, 2 octobre 2003. Rapport final, n.d.
[9] Ibid., pp. 36–39.
[10] Ibid., p. 12.
[11] European Union, Election Observation Mission, *Republic of Rwanda: Final Report – Legislative Elections to the Chamber of Deputies*, 15–18 September 2008, 26 January 2009, p. 7.
[12] The Commonwealth, Commonwealth Expert Team, *Rwanda: Legislative Election (Chamber of Deputies)*, 16–18 September 2013, 23 September 2013, p. 20.

7.2 Elections as a Means of Regime Consolidation

In 2010, when some genuine opposition parties sought registration in order to participate in the presidential election, repression was swift and radical. These parties' leaders were arrested and given long prison sentences, and the vice president of one of them was killed. Two of the three remaining independent newspapers, *Umuseso* and *Umuvugizi*, were banned. In late April, the director of *Umuvugizi* fled the country for Uganda after having received repeated death threats. He was followed in exile a month later by his colleague of *Umuseso*. The co-director of *Umuvugizi* was murdered in Kigali on the very day his newspaper's website (whose access was blocked inside Rwanda) published a story about the regime's 'hit squads' operating against exiled opponents in South Africa (see Section 7.5). Two journalists of *Umurabyo* were arrested and sentenced to seventeen and seven years imprisonment.

Now that the opposition candidates were prevented from participating in the presidential polls, the National Electoral Commission registered four contenders – Kagame and three others from parties that belonged to the RPF-led platform. They were no opponents, and they knew (and accepted) that their chances against Kagame were nil. Despite the protests of international human rights organisations and even some signs of concern in the donor community, the polls went ahead on 9 August 2010. The result was predictable: Kagame obtained 93.08 per cent against 5.15 per cent, 1.37 per cent and 0.40 per cent for his three 'opponents'. While technically not compulsory, participation in the vote reached a whopping 98 per cent: Rwandans know very well what is expected of them and the risks involved in 'uncivil' behaviour. The results were strikingly similar in the five provinces: Kagame's score was everywhere between 92.53 per cent and 93.99 per cent of the vote, a spread of under 1.5 per cent. This is understandable in light of the fraud organised at both the local and the national level. In a number of places, local leaders went from door to door to collect voters' cards. They marked the ballot paper, stamped the cards, and informed the electors that they had voted and did not need to go to the polling station. At the national level, a Commonwealth observer team noted lack of transparency in the tabulation procedure: 'It was not possible to ascertain quite where, how and when the tabulation was to be completed',[13] both between the voting stations and the districts and between the districts and the national level.

This was to be Kagame's second and last term in office, but the question whether he would stand for re-election, an option ruled out

---

[13] Commonwealth Secretariat, *Rwanda Presidential Elections 9 August 2010*, Report of the Commonwealth Observer Group, n.d., p. 25.

by article 101 of the constitution, was already launched at the end of 2011. While Kagame himself indicated that he was not interested in a third term, doubts persisted about his genuine intentions, particularly after he indicated that everyone had the right to express themselves on this issue. Things became clear in early 2013, during the RPF's national congress in February and its aftermath. RPF cadres present at the party meeting 'requested President Kagame not to leave office'.[14] An article in the regime's daily suggested that 'a future without Kagame is a future of uncertainties'.[15] A later text paid tribute to Kagame, showed how indispensable he was and advocated his remaining in office after 2017: 'Proponents of uncertain change are either non-Rwandans, misguided Rwandans, or Rwandans who had a hand in our tragic past.'[16] For those who still had doubts, Kagame clarified the issue. In an interview with *The Observer* (London), while confronted with the position of his own justice minister, Tharcisse Karugarama, who stated that it was essential for Kagame to step down in 2017 in order to maintain the primacy of the rule of law, Kagame reacted furiously: 'Why don't you tell him to step down himself? All those years he's been there, he's not the only one who can be the justice minister.'[17] Less than a week later, Karugarama was sacked from the cabinet, a clear sign that the issue was now settled.

In 2015, the regime organised a campaign of 'petitions' addressed to parliament. In early May, the Speaker of the House announced that more than two million petitions in favour of the scrapping of term limits were received.[18] The only dissenting voice came from the non-registered Democratic Green Party, which filed a petition opposing the third term and asking that the duration of terms be reduced from seven to four or five years.[19] During national 'consultations', MPs and senators met only ten individuals, out of a population of eleven million, opposed to a constitutional amendment, which was duly approved by the two houses of parliament. On 18 December 2015, at a referendum following a one-sided campaign, 98.3 per cent of voters approved the amendment. Article 101 as revised maintained the limitation to

---

[14] 'The Task at Hand for RPF Cadres', *The New Times*, 14 February 2013.
[15] 'The Daunting Task Ahead for RPF Cadres', *The New Times*, 14 February 2013.
[16] 'When Citizens Demand Lifting of Presidential Term Limits', *The New Times*, 1 July 2013.
[17] 'Is Kagame Africa's Lincoln or a Tyrant Exploiting Rwanda's Tragic History?', *The Observer* (London), 19 May 2013.
[18] 'Rwanda Set the Ball Rolling in Campaign to Extend Kagame's Rule', *The East African*, 9 May 2015.
[19] 'Green Party dépose au parlement une pétition contre la suppression de la limitation des mandats présidentiels', Kigali, ARI, 18 May 2015.

7.2 Elections as a Means of Regime Consolidation 161

two terms and reduced the duration to five years. However transitional article 172 provided for a fresh seven-year term for the incumbent, in addition to two five-year terms thereafter, thus allowing Kagame to potentially remain in office until 2034.[20] After a campaign marred by intimidation, arrests, disappearances and killings,[21] Kagame was duly elected with 98.79 per cent of the vote. The official turnout was a colossal 98.15 per cent. Criticism by the US and UK governments and international non-governmental organisations (NGOs) were met with the usual defiance: 'These vicious, malicious allegations' were part of 'a deliberately planned and coordinated campaign' aimed at damaging Kagame's reputation.[22]

Rwanda is a strong case of hegemonic authoritarianism, where under the guise of seemingly regular elections in a multi-party context the polls do not perform any meaningful function other than consolidating a dictatorship. It does not even meet Schedler's requirements of electoral authoritarian regimes, where elections are 'minimally pluralistic (opposition parties are allowed to run), minimally competitive (opposition parties, while denied victory, are allowed to win votes and seats), and minimally open (opposition parties are not subject to massive repression, although they may experience repressive treatment in selective and intermittent ways)'.[23] At each election, the National Electoral Commission allocated rather than counted votes. An international scholar generally quite understanding of the regime observed that 'the RPF decided to use a range of heavy-handed tactics to guarantee its electoral success, an approach that has generated widespread resentment'.[24] The international community knew full well that none of Schedler's conditions were present and that every election was deeply flawed, but this issue was never seriously addressed, thus giving the Rwandan regime the (justified) impression that it could proceed unhindered.[25]

---

[20] On this amendment, see F. Reyntjens, 'The Changes Made to Rwanda's Constitution Are Peculiar: Here's Why', *The Conversation*, 28 January 2016.
[21] Human Rights Watch, *Rwanda: Politically Closed Elections*, 18 August 2017; Amnesty International, *Setting the Scene for Elections: Two Decades of Silencing Dissent in Rwanda*, July 2017; Fédération internationale des droits de l'homme, *La démocratie mise sous tutelle au Rwanda: Comment le FPR pérennise sa confiscation du pouvoir et l'accaparement des richesses*, August 2017.
[22] 'How the Western Media Gets It Wrong on Rwanda', *The New Times*, 17 August 2017.
[23] A. Schedler, 'The Logic of Electoral Authoritarianism', in A. Schedler (Ed.), *Electoral Authoritarianism: The Dynamics of Unfree Competition*, Boulder, Lynne Rienner, 2006, p. 3.
[24] P. Clark, 'Rwanda's Recovery: When Remembrance Is Official Policy', *Foreign Affairs*, Vol. 97, No. 1, 2018, p. 41.
[25] More details on the manipulation of the electoral process can be found in Reyntjens, *Political Governance*, pp. 26–56.

7.3 Managing Political Space

The risks involved in the 'democratisation' process entailed the need to eliminate not only the political opposition but civil society as well. Already in the second half of the 1990s, opponents, human rights defenders, journalists, advocates of rural development and NGOs generally were victims of arrests, intimidation, 'disappearances' and assassinations.[26] By 2000, the churches and human rights organisations were under government control,[27] and even the Tutsi survivors' group *Ibuka*, which had become increasingly critical of the government, was neutralised. Its leadership went into exile as a result of death threats and was replaced by RPF faithfuls such as Antoine Mugesera, a member of the RPF central committee. *Ibuka* ceased criticising the regime. The final assault on civil society came in 2004, a year after the definitive elimination of the political opposition, and it was conducted in the same vein. In June 2004, the Parliamentary Commission of Inquiry on Genocidal Ideology recommended the banning of a number of associations 'preaching the ideology of genocide and ethnic hatred'.[28] Among them was the last remaining independent human rights organisation, Liprodhor, as well as a half-dozen other groups, including some involved in the promotion of peasant interests. Human Rights Watch found that 'under such a broad interpretation [of "genocidal ideas"], any opposition to the government can be labelled "a genocide ideology" and its proponents can be severely punished'.[29] Contrary to the MDR a year earlier, it proved unnecessary to formally ban Liprodhor. After parliament sent a list of a dozen Liprodhor cadres to the government with the request that they be arrested and prosecuted, in July most of its leadership fled

---

[26] A survey of these early practices can be found in Front Line Rwanda, *Disappearances, Arrests, Threats, Intimidation of Human Rights Defenders, 2001–2004*, Dublin, 2005. The practice of 'disappearances' reminds of those that occurred at the court under Musinga, mentioned in Chapter 2. One among many examples was the case of Supreme Court judge Augustin Cyiza, considered close to the MDR, who 'disappeared' in April 2003, while a mise en scène tried to make believe that he had fled to Uganda (on this episode, see T. Cruvellier et al., *Augustin Cyiza: Un homme libre au Rwanda*, Paris, Karthala, 2004).

[27] Longman notes continuity: From Christianity's arrival in Rwanda, 'religion was distinguished by two key principles – a cozy relationship between church and state and a practice of playing ethnic politics' (T. Longman, 'Christian Churches in Post-genocide Rwanda: Reconciliation and Its Limits', in M. Girma (Ed.), *The Healing of Memories: African Christian Responses to Politically Induced Trauma*, Lanham–Boulder–New York–London, Lexington Books, 2018, p. 57). On the tight links of the Rwandan Anglican Church with the RPF, see P. Cantrell, *Revival and Reconciliation: The Anglican Church and the Politics of Rwanda*, Madison, University of Wisconsin Press, 2022.

[28] Human Rights Watch, *Rwanda: Parliament Seeks to Abolish Rights Group*, New York, 2 July 2004.

[29] Ibid.

to Uganda and Burundi. Most members of Liprodhor's new board were RPF faithful. Rather than banning it, the RPF took over the organisation, and thus neutralised it.[30]

The media underwent the same fate as civil society generally. Hardly a year after the RPF seized power, Reporters sans frontières (RSF) sounded the alarm and denounced arrests, physical and psychological harassment, and torture of journalists, in addition to the restrictions on the circulation of information.[31] In the words of the editor of the Catholic weekly *Kinyamateka* André Sibomana, the 'turning point' already came in January 1995, with an attack, presumably under the direct orders of then vice president Kagame, on Edouard Mutsinzi, the editor of *Le Messager-Intumwa*.[32] In 2006, Amnesty International cited a list of dozens of journalists who were 'arbitrarily detained, unjustly judged, forced to flee the country, "disappeared" or assassinated' since the RPF came to power.[33] Paradoxically, at a ceremony organised at the occasion of World Press Freedom Day on 2 May 2008, the directors of *Umuseso*, *Rushyashya* and *Umuvugizi* were thrown out of the venue. Information minister (later foreign minister and current general secretary of the Organisation internationale de la Francophonie – OIF) Louise Mushikiwabo indicated that she was to exclude all 'negativist' media outlets from governmental activities.[34]

A book published in 2016 showed the dismal situation of media freedom in a palpable way. Arriving in Kigali in 2012 to train journalists in an international programme, Anjan Sundaram saw his trainees, one after the other, fall prey to the climate of fear created by the regime against critical and even independent voices. They 'disappeared', fled the country, abandoned the profession or started incensing the RPF.[35] No wonder Rwanda year after year scored consistently in the bottom

---

[30] The destruction of Liprodhor is extensively discussed in Front Line Rwanda, *Disappearances*, pp. 45–56.
[31] Reporters sans frontières, *Rwanda: l'impasse? La liberté de la presse après le génocide, 4 juillet 1994–28 août 1995*, n.d. (1995).
[32] While Mutsinzi had been highly critical of the former regime, he also criticised the new one. In an article published shortly before he was assaulted, he called certain elements of the RPA 'the new *interahamwe*'. A witness of the ICTR OTP described the attack on Mutsinzi in detail. He testified that it was organised by Major Steven Balinda and Captain Dan Munyuza, under the direct orders of Kagame, 'to teach a lesson to [Mutsinzi] who had criticised Kagame in his journal'. Kagame reportedly gave orders 'not to kill him, but to cut his tongue, eyes and right hand' (Witness statement 9 February 2002, ICTR ref. R0000232).
[33] Amnesty International, *Rwanda: La liberté de la presse réprimée depuis 12 ans*, London, 3 May 2006.
[34] Reporters sans frontières, *Rwanda: RSF s'inquiète du mépris grandissant du gouvernement envers certains journalistes*, 6 May 2008.
[35] A. Sundaram, *Bad News: Last Journalists in a Dictatorship*, New York, Doubleday, 2016.

twenty to thirty worldwide in RSF's World Press Freedom Index. Scores in Freedom House's Freedom in the World reports are similar.

7.4 Law as a Tool of Control

The way in which the political opposition, civil society and the media were treated epitomised a more general attempt at controlling people and space. One of the tools of that control is the law. A few examples suffice to show this. One of the mechanisms of control was the Consultative Forum for Political Organisations introduced by the 2003 constitution. Dominated by the RPF, it was assigned the task of disciplining political parties and served as a 'means of limiting the range of allowable ideas among politicians'.[36] More importantly, law became a major instrument for redefining collective identities in a way rarely seen elsewhere. For instance, a 2001 law made 'sectarianism', later called 'divisionism', a criminal offense. However, the notion is so broad and vague that a judge interviewed by Human Rights Watch was unable to define it, despite having adjudicated and convicted defendants on divisionism charges.[37] A 2008 law made 'genocide ideology' a criminal offense, but examples given by a Senate report illustrated the scope for political exploitation. For example, 'partisan and unfair political criticism', claims that the RPF is 'a totalitarian regime stifling the opposition, the press, freedoms of association and expression' and references to 'the guilt feelings of the international community that is too lenient on the post-genocide regime' are all punishable.[38] Waldorf noted that the report 'conflates genocide ideology with any ethnic discourse, political criticism, revisionism, and negationism. According to its definition, any mention of alleged RPF war crimes or human rights abuses would constitute "genocide ideology".'[39]

The use of divisionism or genocide ideology related charges is not just a marginal phenomenon affecting a few troublemakers. According to a report on judicial activity in 2007–2008 cited by Human Rights Watch, Rwandan courts initiated 1,304 cases involving genocide ideology during that period. In addition, 243 persons were charged with genocide denial and revisionism.[40] As of August 2009, there reportedly were 912 people

---

[36] USAID, *Rwanda Democracy and Governance Assessment*, November 2002, p. 50.
[37] Human Rights Watch, *Law and Reality: Progress in Judicial Reform in Rwanda*, New York, 2008, p. 34.
[38] République du Rwanda. *Sénat, Idéologie du génocide au Rwanda et stratégies de son éradication*, Kigali, 2006, p. 21. The author of this book is guilty of all these crimes.
[39] L. Waldorf, 'Revisiting Hotel Rwanda, Genocide Ideology, Reconciliation, and Rescuers', *Journal of Genocide Research*, Vol. 11, No. 1, 2009, p. 111.
[40] Human Rights Watch, *Law and Reality*, p. 40.

in prison on genocide ideology charges.[41] Official government statistics quoted by Amnesty International confirmed the widespread impact of charges related to 'divisionism' and 'genocide ideology': during 2007–2009, 1,845 cases were brought before the courts.[42] In these and other fields, accusatory practices made real or imaginary dissenters very vulnerable and imposed loyalty to the RPF.

This desire to control people and space is inspired not just by the need to fend off challenges to the RPF's power or to avert the return of Hutu extremism but also by the way in which the RPF views the population, which it treats with distrust and paternalism. This was well expressed early on by Aloysia Inyumba, an influential RPF leader, when she stated that 'the ordinary citizens are like babies. They will need to be completely educated if we want to move towards democracy.'[43] In other words, democracy will come after re-education, but for the time being, 'a strong, "enlightened" leadership is required'.[44] This leadership can come only from the RPF.

7.5 The RPF Challenged from Within

Strong control by the RPF should however not suggest that it is monolithic. There is anecdotal evidence that debates do occur inside the party, but this is largely invisible to outsiders, as major political decisions are taken not in the cabinet or in parliament but within a small inner circle. On a number of occasions, splits have however been visible. Already in the late 1990s, a number of RPF members left the country and turned into vocal opponents. Kimonyo, who is privy to the 'inside', described the RPF's crisis of internal and external legitimacy in the second half of the 1990s. A unique look behind the curtain relates disagreements, antagonism with the outside world, political defections and the revolt of party officials. Party meetings tackled a number of issues that were seen as deeply problematic: indebtedness of military officers

---

[41] Amnesty International, *Report 2010*, p. 273.
[42] Amnesty International, *Safer to Stay Silent: The Chilling Effect of Rwanda's Laws on 'Genocide Ideology' and 'Sectarianism'*, London, 25 August 2010, p. 19.
[43] J. Corduwener, 'Wederopbouw in Rwanda, met ijzeren hand' ('Reconstruction in Rwanda, with an Iron Fist'), *NRC-Handelsblad*, 27 March 2002. This patronising attitude is also well expressed by a civil servant who used to work at a Ministry in Kigali but had become a local executive secretary: 'I do not like to look at poor people and deal with them. In fact, when I worked in the Ministry, I did not have to look at the poor. (…) It is now in this new function that I'm directly confronted with the poor' (A. Ansoms, 'Re-engineering Rural Society: The Visions and Ambitions of the Rwandan Elite', *African Affairs*, Vol. 108, No. 431, 2009, p. 307).
[44] International Crisis Group, *Rwanda at the End*, p. 5.

to businesspeople, conflicts over the ownership of land and other property, and reprehensible behaviour such as corruption and nepotism. According to Kimonyo, efforts at reformation led to a 'new Rwanda', one born not in 1994 but around 2000.[45]

While these adjustments showed that the RPF is a learning organisation, this did not end intra-regime tensions. In 2010, General Kayumba Nyamwasa, a former chief of army staff and at the time ambassador to India, fled the country and settled in South Africa, from where he openly and virulently attacked Kagame, stating that Rwanda was descending to total dictatorship. Together with other former high officials who had fled during previous years, Kayumba Nyamwasa translated his opposition into political terms. In August 2010, he and Patrick Karegeya (former head of external intelligence), Theogene Rudasingwa (former RPF general secretary and head of the president's office) and Gerald Gahima (former general prosecutor), all of them Tutsi and former RPF leading figures, published *Rwanda Briefing*,[46] which contained a long diatribe against the regime, accusing it of having put in place a totalitarian dictatorship based on terror, of grave human rights violations, of corruption and nepotism, of having committed numerous political assassinations, and – quite remarkable coming from four Tutsi – of having marginalised and excluded the Hutu. In light of the high functions previously exercised by the four 'renegades', as they were called by the regime, this caused grave concern in Kigali, as these men were privy to many regime secrets and might spill the beans on highly embarrassing files, particularly those related to war crimes and the downing of President Habyarimana's plane. Just months later, the four were indicted and judged in absentia. Kayumba Nyamwasa and Rudasingwa were sentenced to twenty-four years in prison, Karegeya and Gahima to twenty years.

In the meantime, they were among the main founders of a new political movement, the Rwanda National Congress(RNC), created in December 2010. Again denouncing the regime, the founders proclaimed their vision for a 'new Rwanda', and they set out to forge alliances with other opposition movements abroad, and even inside Rwanda. More threateningly, they also seemed to establish contacts with armed groups opposed to Kagame in the region, particularly in the DRC and Uganda.

---

[45] J.-P. Kimonyo, *Transforming Rwanda: Challenges on the Road to Reconstruction*, Boulder–London, Lynne Rienner, 2019. The way of dealing with the RPF's internal crisis is also addressed in National Unity and Reconciliation Commission, *History of Rwanda*, pp. 596–610.

[46] https://drive.google.com/file/d/0BzL0v-ZpWCAIMGM1MWVkMTQtMWY0Zi00NjNmLTgxZDgtOTI3NWNkZDhmYTMy/view?hl=en&resourcekey=0-nvB9Ddy4guq9q1whH1nkxA.

Already in June 2010, Kayumba Nyamwasa had been severely injured in an attempt against his life in Johannesburg, and some days later, the assassins attempted to finish him off in his hospital bed. More attempts against his life were made, and in March 2014, South Africa expelled several Rwandan diplomats. In August 2014, a South African court condemned four suspects in absentia for the 2010 attempt. The judge stated that the crime was politically motivated and that the plot came 'from a certain group of people from Rwanda'. Patrick Karegeya was less fortunate than Kayumba Nyamwasa: he was found strangled in a Johannesburg hotel room on New Year's Day 2014. Several Rwandan senior officials came close to admitting that the murder was perpetrated by a government hit squad.[47]

Internal settling of scores went well beyond the highly publicised Kayumba/Karegeya affair, as a few examples show. In 2014, Joël Mutabazi, a former captain of the Republican Guard illegally captured in Uganda in 2013, was condemned to life in prison. Later in the year, retired brigadier general Frank Rusagara, a former permanent secretary of the Ministry of Defence, was arrested, followed during the next days by retired captain David Kabuye and former Republican Guard commander colonel Tom Byabagamba. Other officers were arrested or demoted, but later released and redeployed, a practice that created the insecurity needed to discourage disloyal behaviour. Regular shake-ups in the military leadership served to warn those whose loyalty was in doubt: in Kagame's words, 'we will put you where you belong'.[48] These practices confirmed that, rather than being a coherent and trusting organisation, the RPF is 'a deeply divided, fragile, paranoid party' and that 'Kagame's repressive tactics (…) are less about external threats to his power than about internal RPF pressures'.[49] This atmosphere of intrigue, suspicion and plots reminds of the precolonial royal court discussed earlier.

7.6 Human Rights and Impunity, a Dismal Record

As political rights and freedoms of expression, association and the press were briefly addressed earlier, this section discusses only large-scale violations of the right to life. The RPF/RPA had massively killed civilians inside Rwanda during the period of the genocide and committed large-scale massacres in Zaire/DRC in late 1996–early 1997, as well as

---

[47] On the (attempted) murders in South Africa, see M. Wrong, *Do Not Disturb: The Story of a Political Murder and an African Regime Gone Bad*, New York, Public Affairs, 2021.
[48] 'Kagame Announces New Security Crackdown', *The Chronicles*, 14 November 2019.
[49] P. Clark, 'Rwanda: Kagame's Power Struggle', *The Guardian*, 5 August 2010.

during an insurgency in Rwanda's north-western region in 1997–1998.[50] Massacres in Rwanda abated in October 1994 as a result of warnings by international partners, the US in particular, but smaller scale killings and 'disappearances' continued. In April 1995 thousands of IDPs were killed by the RPA in Kibeho, an event that was to be fatal for the government of national union (as shown in Section 7.2). The scope of the massacre was denied by the Rwandan government, and the international community expressed some concern but did not press the issue.[51] The hardliners in the regime were to remember the lesson of Kibeho very well. They realised that playing hardball towards a pliant international community works, and they replayed Kibeho one-and-a-half years later, this time in Zaire, at an infinitely larger scale.

Following the RPF's victory, close to two million people fled to neighbouring countries. In Zaire (currently the DRC) the remnants of the defeated government army and of the militia guilty of genocide were mingled with civilian populations who lived in camps close to the Rwandan border. The armed elements among them conducted raids inside Rwanda and prepared an invasion. In the absence of international reaction, this imminent security risk was tackled by the RPA, which cleared the camps in the fall of 1996. However, rather than limiting itself to addressing the security threat, the RPA launched a massive extermination campaign of civilian refugees as they trekked westwards, deeper into Zaire. Over one hundred thousand civilians – men, women and children – were massacred by RPA 'search and destroy' units. The most comprehensive report, based on research done on behalf of the UN High Commission for Human Rights, concluded that the vast majority of the 617 listed massacres committed by several armed entities including the RPA were to be classified as war crimes and crimes against humanity. On the issue of genocide, it noted that '[s]everal incidents listed in this report, if investigated and judicially proven, point to circumstances and facts from which a court could infer the intention to destroy the Hutu ethnic group in the DRC in part'.[52] As a result of the massive repatriation, part

---

[50] Details and numerous sources can be found in Rever, *In Praise of Blood*; Reyntjens, *Political Governance*, pp. 98–123. More particularly on crimes committed in Zaire/DRC, see Reyntjens, *The Great African War*, pp. 80–101, 287–290.

[51] Sources on the Kibeho massacre can be found in Reyntjens, *Political Governance*, pp. 105–108. An eyewitness account is T. Pickard, *Combat Medic: An Australian's Eyewitness Account of the Kibeho Massacre*, Wavel Heights, Big Sky Publishing, 2008.

[52] United Nations, Office of the High Commissioner for Human Rights, *Democratic Republic of the Congo, 1993–2003: Report of the Mapping Exercise Documenting the Most Serious Violations of Human Rights and International Humanitarian Law Committed within the Territory of the Democratic Republic of the Congo between March 1993 and June 2003*, Geneva, August 2010, para. 31.

7.6 Human Rights and Impunity, a Dismal Record

voluntary and part forced, of hundreds of thousands of Hutu refugees in late 1996, and of mounting resentment caused by the Rwandan occupation of eastern DRC, the RPA faced a rapidly extending insurgency within Rwanda from early 1997, in the north-west in particular. During brutal counter-insurgency operations, the RPA killed tens of thousands of people, mostly unarmed civilians. Many other people 'disappeared' during this period.[53]

At a lesser scale, a long-standing practice of extrajudicial killings was documented in detail by Human Rights Watch in a major report published in 2017.[54] It documented dozens of extrajudicial executions, enforced disappearances and threats against family members and other witnesses to these crimes. The report was very detailed, containing names and photographs of victims, the identity of responsible state agents and a precise description of events. The (governmental) National Commission for Human Rights rubbished these findings by using lies and manipulation, which Human Rights Watch found easy to document.[55] Just months later, Human Rights Watch published a detailed report on torture and unlawful detentions in illegal military holding sites. To force them to confess or to incriminate others, officials severely tortured or ill-treated detainees, almost all held in illegal incommunicado detention.[56]

While repression hit domestic real or imaginary dissidents, the regime's intelligence and security apparatus was also active abroad. Two former RPF prominent members turned opponents were assassinated in Nairobi, Théoneste Lizinde in 1996 and Seth Sendashonga in 1998. Others were killed because of their knowledge of the RPF's role in downing Habyarimana's plane.[57] Strong indications point at the role of Rwanda in the killing of DRC president Laurent Kabila in Kinshasa in January 2001.[58] The long arm of Kagame is not confined to Africa. In April 2011 MI5 warned the Rwandan high commissioner in London

---

[53] Amnesty International, *Rwanda: Ending the Silence*, London, 25 September 1997; Amnesty International, *Rwanda: Civilians Trapped in Armed Conflict – The Dead Can No Longer Be Counted*, London, 19 December 1997.
[54] Human Rights Watch, *'All Thieves Must Be Killed'. Extrajudicial Executions in Western Rwanda*, July 2017.
[55] Human Rights Watch, *Rwanda: Cover-up Negates Killings*, 1 November 2017.
[56] Human Rights Watch, *'We Will Force You to Confess': Torture and Unlawful Military Detention in Rwanda*, October 2017.
[57] J. Swain, 'The Riddle of the Rwandan Assassin's Trail', *The Sunday Times*, 4 April 2004.
[58] 'Un ex agente de Ruanda implica a su Gobierno en el asesinato de Kabila', *El País*, 21 December 2008; 'Murder in Kinshasa', film by Arnaud Zajtman on Al Jazeera, 28 October 2011. Sources in the Rwandan intelligence apparatus have confirmed to this author that Kigali masterminded Laurent Kabila's assassination.

that the intimidation of supposed opponents in the UK needed to stop.[59] The following month, Scotland Yard warned two British of Rwandan origin that 'the Rwandan Government poses an immediate threat to your life'.[60] Only after the Swedish authorities expelled a Rwandan diplomat did a former journalist, who had gone into hiding, resurface and explain that the Rwandan services 'were after him'.[61]

Even after these practices were condemned internationally, transnational repression increased during the following years.[62] Rwanda found itself in embarrassing company, when Freedom House published a report with six case studies. One of them was Rwanda, alongside China, Russia, Saudi Arabia, Iran and Turkey. The report called Rwandan transnational repression 'exceptionally broad in terms of tactics, targets, and geographical reach', found 'the commitment to controlling Rwandans abroad and the resources devoted to the effort (...) stunning' and claimed that 'the Rwandan government is among the most prolific transnational repression actors worldwide'.[63] Just months later, a group of international media partners published information that Rwanda used the Israeli NSO Group's Pegasus spyware, deployed by authoritarian governments worldwide to monitor the smartphone use of rights activists, journalists, lawyers, opposition members and political leaders.[64] Thorough research by investigative journalist Michela Wrong detailed the regime's worldwide reach of murder, intimidation and surveillance, offering a wider perspective of the deployment of violence inside Rwanda's borders and well beyond.[65]

7.7 A Regional Powerhouse

While before 1994 Rwanda's relations with its neighbours were not conflictual,[66] the post-genocide regime has, at one moment or another,

---

[59] 'Rwandan Wedding Guest Told to Stop Harassing Dissidents in UK', *The Independent*, 19 April 2011.
[60] 'Threats to Life Warning Notice', 12 May 2011. See 'Rwandan Exiles Warned of Assassination Threat by London Police', *The Guardian*, 20 May 2011.
[61] 'Rwandan Journalist Emerges after Month in Hiding', Nairobi, AFP, 17 February 2012.
[62] Human Rights Watch, *Repression across Borders: Attacks and Threats against Rwandan Opponents and Critics Abroad*, 28 January 2014.
[63] Freedom House, *Out of Sight, Not out of Reach: The Global Scale and Scope of Transnational Repression*, February 2021, Case Study Rwanda, pp. 22–26.
[64] Amnesty International, *Massive Data Leak Reveals Israeli NSO Group's Spyware Used to Target Activists, Journalists, and Political Leaders Globally*, 18 July 2021.
[65] Wrong, *Do Not Disturb*.
[66] There have however been occasional hostile exchanges with Burundi, particularly during the Bagaza era in Bujumbura. These were the result of the fact that Rwanda

engaged in hostile behaviour with each of its four neighbours. It twice invaded Zaire/DRC and maintains a covert and sometimes even overt presence there, and it came close to waging a full war with Uganda.[67] As seen earlier, when it invaded Zaire in 1996 hiding behind a proxy rebel movement, Rwanda was addressing a genuine security concern, in the form of the defeated former government army FAR and genocidal militia that had retreated to refugee camps just across the border and posed a threat to the RPF-led regime. Because the new Kabila regime installed in the DRC, as Zaire was renamed in 1997, did not deliver the hoped for cordial relations, Rwanda again intervened in 1998 and continues doing so up to the present day. It has developed an extraordinary degree of military, political and economic control over its huge but weak neighbour.

The Rwandan presence in the DRC continued well after it officially withdrew its troops in application of an accord signed in Pretoria in July 2002. Successive reports by the UN Group of Experts on the DRC showed ongoing support for dissident forces, a fact Rwanda consistently denied against all evidence. Although it had been caught red-handed on several occasions and its major donors had issued serious warnings, Rwanda again took the risk of destabilising eastern DRC in the spring of 2012. Several reports showed that it supplied weapons, ammunition, training and recruits to a new rebel movement, the M23.[68] They documented direct interventions by the Rwanda Defence Force (RDF), as the RPA was renamed, in Congolese territory to reinforce the M23, as well as supporting other mutinies and secessionist politicians. Rwanda again flatly denied the charges, but even its staunch allies had now had it. The US, the UK, the Netherlands, Germany and Sweden suspended aid payments and urged Rwanda to cease its support for the M23 and to withdraw its troops from the DRC. A Force Intervention Brigade (FIB), authorised by the UN Security Council in March 2013 and consisting of South African, Tanzanian and Malawian troops, operating in

---

was Hutu-dominated, while Burundi was Tutsi-dominated, the opposite of the situation today. Regime opponents of both countries have been active on their neighbours' territories.

[67] More details can be found in Prunier, *Africa's World War*; Reyntjens, *The Great African War*; Stearns, *Dancing in the Glory of Monsters*; Roessler, Verhoeven, *Why Comrades Go to War*; Stearns, *The War That Doesn't Say Its Name*.

[68] For instance United Nations, Security Council, *Addendum to the Interim Report of the Group of Experts on the Democratic Republic of the Congo (S/2012/348) concerning Violations of the Arms Embargo and Sanctions Regime by the Government of Rwanda*, S/2012/348/Add.1, 27 June 2012; Human Rights Watch, *D.R. Congo: Rwanda Should Stop Aiding War Crimes Suspect – Congolese Renegade General Bosco Ntaganda Receives Recruits and Weapons from Rwanda*, Goma, 4 June 2012.

support of the Forces armées de la République démocratique du Congo (FARDC), defeated the M23 in October. Its fate was sealed after the US and the UK issued a strong warning to Kagame to stay out of the conflict. For Rwanda, the M23's defeat was a catastrophic outcome. It put an end – or so it seemed – to its last political, military and economic foothold in a region it considered a 'natural' area of influence. After its defeat, the M23 led a dormant life in Rwanda and Uganda, until at the end of 2021, it resumed operations, again with Rwandan support. Like ten years earlier, Rwanda denied any involvement, even after the UN Group of Experts documented in detail in December 2022 the direct intervention of the RDF on the territory of the DRC and its support to the M23.[69]

Rwanda's military interventions have gone well beyond the immediate region. The country became a major contributor to multilateral peacekeeping operations. Beginning with a modest participation in May 2005 by the deployment of one military observer to the UN Mission in Sudan, Rwanda gradually became the third largest contributor to multilateral peacekeeping operations. At the end of the 2010s, more than 6,000 military and police personnel were serving with the UN and the African Union, the majority of them in South Sudan, the Darfur region of Sudan and the Central African Republic. Since the early 2020s, Rwanda has extended its activities outside of multilateral operations, intervening on a bilateral basis at the request of home governments in the Central African Republic and Mozambique. Its political use of military tools is an example of military diplomacy, whereby Rwanda has exploited the capabilities of its military apparatus as a political tool to gain greater international visibility and continental influence.[70] In addition to giving cover for poor domestic governance, human rights abuse and its disruptive role in the region, participation in multilateral operations gave it political leverage in international affairs where it punches well above its weight.[71]

7.8   Information and Communication Management

How did the RPF get away with autocratic rule and major human rights abuse, while these practices were well known internationally? Generally speaking, the regime has been extremely successful in projecting an

---

[69] United Nations, Security Council, *Midterm Report of the Group of Experts on the Democratic Republic of the Congo*, S/2022/967, 16 December 2022.

[70] F. Donelli, 'Rwanda's Military Diplomacy: Kigali's Political Use of the Military Means to Increase Prestige in Africa and Beyond', *Notes de l'Ifri*, Paris, Ifri, April 2022.

[71] 'Rwanda's Ambitions as a Security Provider in Sub-Saharan Africa', International Institute for Strategic Studies, *Strategic Comments*, Vol. 28, No. 23, November 2022.

image of morality, vision and success. One potent instrument was the 'genocide credit' the RPF regime astutely kept alive and exploited. It served several purposes: justifying Tutsi dominance and maintaining the support of many Tutsi, keeping alive the fear of Hutu revenge, and keeping the international community at bay. Reminding that the international community abandoned Rwanda in 1994 and let the genocide happen, that it put an end to genocide, and posing itself as the representative of the victims gave the RPF a nearly unassailable moral high ground. This became and has remained a powerful ideological weapon that allowed to acquire and maintain victim status and to enjoy impunity for its own crimes. Pottier observed that 'those who represent the victims of genocide are not to be challenged'.[72] A US diplomat admitted to the *Washington Post* (14 July 1998) that 'the Americans were terribly manipulated by this government and now we are almost held hostage by it'. However, the argument based on the 'genocide credit' alone does not explain Rwanda's 'donor darling' status. Desrosiers and Swedlund argue that a more complex set of rationales determine donor behaviour towards Rwanda.[73]

The reluctance to speak out extends to international donor agencies, quite a remarkable feat in light of Rwanda's profound aid dependence. Unpleasant information has to be 'sanitised' or framed more positively before sharing it with Rwandan government officials; forms of self-censorship provide a 'positive spin' to troubling information; and international agencies alter or simply do not release reports that might upset Rwandan leaders. An aid official candidly stated: 'You toe the party (RPF) line here. If you don't, you're out. No one wants to look bad before their bosses. So you pretend that everything's OK.'[74] However, a panel put in place by the Organisation of African Unity (OAU) was not fooled: '[The RPF] are masters of shrewd communication strategies. RPF leaders have long understood that they begin with the benefit of the doubt, based on a combination of guilt and sympathy from the world at large. (…) Critics of the government are simply dismissed as genocide sympathisers – a technique that puts a chill on legitimate dissent.'[75]

---

[72] J. Pottier, *Re-imagining Rwanda: Conflict, Survival and Disinformation in the Late Twentieth Century*, Cambridge, Cambridge University Press, 2002, p. 176.

[73] M.-E. Desrosiers, H. J. Swedlund, 'Rwanda's Post-genocide Foreign Aid Relations: Revisiting Notions of Exceptionalism', *African Affairs*, Vol. 118, No. 472, 2019, pp. 435–462.

[74] M. Sommers, *Stuck: Rwandan Youth and the Struggle for Adulthood*, Athens GA–London, University of Georgia Press, 2012, p. 21.

[75] Organisation of African Unity, International Panel of Eminent Personalities to Investigate the 1994 Genocide in Rwanda and the Surrounding Events, *Rwanda: The Preventable Genocide*, Addis Ababa, 7 July 2000, para. 22.36.

One technique of denying harmful information to outsiders, first used in Rwanda and later in Zaire/DRC, was the closure of the conflict scene. Other means were intimidation and infiltration. Without false modesty, Kagame stated that '[w]e used communication and information warfare better than anyone. We have found a new way of doing things', and he confirmed that 'the aim was to let them [NGOs and the press] continue their work, but deny them what would be dangerous for us'.[76] Pottier notes that Kagame's information strategy was 'built around denial' and that the RPF's routine was 'simple but effective: ban outsiders from the battle zone; delay and frustrate their movements; deny any "rumour" of military excesses; withhold information; apply moral argument to shame the international community'.[77]

The monopoly of truth the regime thus successfully gained extended not just to Rwanda's visions and analyses of current affairs, for instance its democratic credentials, its human rights record or its involvement in the DRC, but also to history more generally. In summary, this official history claims that precolonial Rwanda was a unified, harmonious and peaceful society and that ethnicity was artificially introduced by the Belgian administration and the Catholic Church in the context of a divide and rule policy. The RPF put an end to genocide that resulted from divisive politics and restored peace and harmony. Historians find 'a whole set of false propositions and assertions in this narrative', but Vansina understands the reasons for the elaboration of such erroneous propositions: 'the projection of a nostalgic utopia into the past, a past that contrasts with a painful present'.[78] Likewise, Mathys notes that the current regime 'presupposes a harmonious pre-colonial past, and projects the unity of Rwandans into a distant history. (...) This is a chimera.'[79]

Interestingly, this vision of precolonial history is similar to the one promoted under colonial rule. As seen in Introduction and Chapter 1, it presents Rwanda from a central court perspective. This idealised outlook promotes the view of a political system that was centralised, unique, eternal, static, unchallenged, dominant and harmonious. Yet the relationship between the post-genocide and precolonial regimes is ambiguous. While precolonial Rwanda is often presented as a source of inspiration

---

[76] N. Gowing, 'New Challenges and Problems for Information Management in Complex Emergencies: Ominous Lessons from the Great Lakes and Eastern Zaire in Late 1996 and Early 1997', paper presented at Dispatches from Disaster Zones conference, Oxford, 28 May 1998, pp. 4, 15.
[77] Pottier, *Re-imagining Rwanda*, pp. 55, 58.
[78] Vansina, *Antecedents to Modern Rwanda*, pp. 197–198.
[79] Mathys, *Conflicts and Connections*.

7.8 Information and Communication Management

and 'truly Rwandan', its centrepiece, the monarchy, was always rejected by the RPF. Its position was that the last king, Kigeri V Ndahindurwa, could return from exile as an ordinary citizen, a suggestion he rejected. After he died in the US in October 2016, he was buried in Nyanza in January 2017, with only a junior minister attending the funeral.

If history does not suit the regime, a new history is constructed. Observing 'the failure of the human and social sciences that have led to genocide', a conference held in Kigali in 2008 called for 'a new methodology, a new literature, *a new history*'.[80] The regime even succeeded in penetrating international academic work. A book published in 2008 contained a six-page-long preface in which President Kagame was allowed not only to put forward the regime's view on Rwanda's past, present and future but also to propose a strongly worded rebuttal of a chapter by Lemarchand in that very book. Lemarchand was said to be 'mistaken', 'simplistic' and 'wrong': 'The revisionists must receive justice for their crimes against historical truth and the affront of their fraudulent narratives.'[81] As seen earlier, the RPF's narrative is protected by the constitution and by legislation on 'divisionism' and 'genocide ideology'. These broad and ill-defined laws allow the criminalisation of criticism of the government and of legitimate dissent.

One particular aspect of imposing the truth serves a very concrete project. The RPF denies the reality of ethnicity, a denial that is an essential element of the hegemonic strategies of the Tutsi elite. The claim that 'there are no Hutu or Tutsi, we are all Rwandans now' allows to hide the domination by a small group of Tutsi. Collective identities were redefined in a way rarely seen elsewhere, and ethnicity was legislated away. The law reconfigured the ethnic map and entrenched the regime's policing of relations between individuals and groups. De-ethnicisation and reconciliation were imposed in a top-down authoritarian fashion. However, all available fieldwork shows that the regime's narrative merely reflects the public transcript that can be openly expressed but that the narrative and the truth to be found in the hidden transcript – that of most Hutu and of oppressed Tutsi – are very different.[82] For instance,

---

[80] 'Rwanda: Apprendre de l'expérience du génocide rwandais', Kigali, ARI, 23 July 2008 (emphasis added).
[81] P. Kagame, 'Preface', in P. Clark, Z. D. Kaufman (Eds.), *After Genocide: Transitional Justice, Post-conflict Reconstruction and Reconciliation in Rwanda and Beyond*, London, Hurst, 2008, pp. xxi–xxvi.
[82] The fieldwork findings are well rendered in S. Thomson, *Whispering Truth to Power: Everyday Resistance to Reconciliation in Postgenocide Rwanda*, Madison, University of Wisconsin Press, 2013. The reference to hidden and public transcripts is borrowed from J. Scott, *Domination and the Arts of Resistance: Hidden Transcripts*, New Haven, Yale University Press, 1992.

despite the regime's official promotion of women, ethnicity appears more salient than gender in political representation; ethnic ways of seeing the world crowd out gendered ones.[83] In a similar vein, Purdeková and Mwambari note 'the stubborn lingering of racialized distinctions in popular culture',[84] while Mwambari sees vernacular memory practices as 'arenas of resistance against a hegemonic memory that has emerged in post-genocide Rwanda'.[85] In a later book, Mwambari examines how the master narrative has emerged, evolved and been imposed, and explores the plurality of responses to it. This hegemonic master narrative excludes and silences alternative perspectives so that the excluded voice cannot be articulated.[86]

Imposed ethnic amnesia attempts to hide ethnocratic rule. A 2021 survey of senior office holders showed that 166 were Tutsi and 38 were Hutu, or a 81:19 overall ratio. Political elites may claim not to see ethnic differences, but most Rwandans know better in private.[87] During the Youth Connekt Dialogue in June 2013, Kagame invited the Hutu to 'seek forgiveness for those who have killed in their name'. As a follow-up, the government launched the *Ndi Umunyarwanda* (I am Rwandan) programme, following which sessions of demands of forgiveness by Hutu were organised across the country. Among them were several ministers, including Prime Minister Habumuremyi, who thus made themselves politically vulnerable.[88] Coupled with the outcome of the *gacaca* proceedings during which the majority of Hutu males who were adult in 1994 were convicted (see Section 6.4.1), this collective declaration of guilt confirmed, in the words of Minister Nshuti Manasseh, that 'collective guilt means that génocidaire and Hutuism could be translated as synonymous'.[89] The ambiguous nature of dealing with ethnicity and its link to the genocide is clear in the annual commemorations known as *Kwibuka*. While during the rest of the year the state's policy is one of ethnic non-recognition, this 100-day period is characterised by an explicit

---

[83] A. Guariso, B. Ingelaere, M. Verpoorten, 'When Ethnicity Beats Gender: Quotas and Political Representation in Rwanda and Burundi', *Development and Change*, Vol. 49, No. 6, 2018, pp. 1361–1391.

[84] A. Purdeková, D. Mwambari, 'Post-genocide Identity Politics and Colonial Durabilities in Rwanda', *Critical African Studies*, Vol. 14, No. 1, 2021, p. 20.

[85] D. Mwambari, '*Agaciro*, Vernacular Memory, and the Politics of Memory in Post-genocide Rwanda', *African Affairs*, Vol. 120, No. 481, 2021, p. 627.

[86] D. Mwambari, *Navigating Cultural Memory: Commemoration and Narrative in Postgenocide Rwanda*, New York, Oxford University Press, 2023.

[87] F. Reyntjens, 'Rwanda: Ethnic Amnesia as a Cover for Ethnocracy, and Why This Is Dangerous', *The Africa Governance Papers*, Vol. 1, No. 3, 2023, pp. 210–220.

[88] 'Le Premier Ministre regrette son inaction pendant le génocide', Kigali, RNA, 30 November 2013.

[89] 'Trust without Truth?', *The New Times*, 19 July 2013.

acknowledgement and public discussion of ethnic identity. Baldwin notes that such practices have created conditions for a 'survivor nationalism', which exacerbates social tensions and threatens sustainable peace in the long term.[90] In a similar vein, Waldorf observed that efforts to erase ethnic identity are undercut by practices like the 'forced memorialization' in ways that reinforce ethnic divisions.[91]

Final characteristics of Rwandan communication needing mention are two old cultural practices. The first is *ubwenge*, prevalent in all speech, not merely in the political sphere. Rwandans tend to communicate strategically: what counts is not so much the 'truth' in a western sense but rather the usefulness of what is said and how it is said in an insecure and complex setting. Doublespeak is a powerful political and social tool, with speakers using ambiguous ways to convey nuance difficult to grasp for outsiders.[92] In that context, *ubwenge* is a virtue: it refers to 'intelligence resulting in self-controlled public acts. But it also refers to elements of wisdom and trickery, caution, cleverness, prudence. It is the capacity to gain a clear understanding of situations and the capability to surround oneself with a network of profit generating social relations'.[93] This highly developed cultural skill is used as a discursive weapon, both in day-to-day exchanges between Rwandans and in political communication with the outside world. Thus, Kagame uses this verbal asset to inform Rwandans what is expected of them while maintaining his carefully styled international image as a progressive and rational leader.[94]

The second old cultural trait, already mentioned in Chapter 1, is the conviction that Rwanda is special and that Rwandans know best what to do and how to do it. This feeling of superiority can sometimes be irritating, to neighbours and other African countries as well as to international partners. Thus, a European aid official based in Kigali felt that 'the conviction of the Rwandans that they are the best makes them little attentive to other points of view'.[95] When concerns were expressed about

---

[90] G. Baldwin, 'Constructing Identity through Commemoration: *Kwibuka* and the Rise of Survivor Nationalism in Post-conflict Rwanda', *Journal of Modern African Studies*, Vol. 57, No. 3, 2019, pp. 355–375.
[91] L. Waldorf, 'Apotheosis of a Warlord: Paul Kagame', in A. Themnér (Ed.), *Warlord Democrats in Africa: Ex-military Leaders and Electoral Politics*, London, Zed Books, 2017, p. 86.
[92] Thomson, *Rwanda*, p. 229.
[93] B. Ingelaere, '"Does the Truth Pass across Fire without Burning?" Locating the Short Circuit of Knowledge in Postgenocide Rwanda', *Journal of Modern African Studies*, Vol. 47, No. 4, 2009, p. 520.
[94] Thomson, *Rwanda*, p. 233.
[95] 'Le Rwanda, pays du miracle en trompe-l'œil', *Le Temps*, 2 July 2012.

the Rwandan villagisation programme (*imidugudu*) and it was pointed out that such policies had failed in other countries, the director of lands responded, 'Tanzania did it wrong; we'll do it right.'[96] When relations between Uganda and Rwanda were at their lowest in 2001, referring to the size of the Rwandan army, President Museveni expressed concern that it gave Rwanda 'the arrogance to think that they can interfere in the internal affairs of Uganda'.[97] The mantra 'We are the best' is a regular feature in the party's daily *The New Times*.[98]

7.9 Engineering a New Society

The RPF has embarked on a formidable project of political, economic, social and cultural engineering, aimed at radically changing Rwanda and the Rwandans. It involves bold experiments in transitional justice, land tenure and agriculture, re-education, the spiriting away of ethnic identity, knowledge construction, spatial reorganisation (under the form of both villagisation and the redrawing/renaming of territory) and the instauration of pervasive control. The modernisation drive has been extremely fast, indeed too fast for most Rwandans: when the Rwandan government wants something, it wants it immediately, and it sets close and clear deadlines.[99]

As most Rwandans make their living in a subsistence economy, policies with regard to land and agriculture are a good example. A land law adopted in 2005 operated a radical and sudden break with the past, as it aimed at creating a private land market (through a system of registration of individual tenure) and at enlarging holdings (through a system of consolidation). This has led to a sizeable increase in the number of landless peasants and a corresponding rise in absentee landlords, some with very large land holdings. As Tutsi absentee landlords are seen grabbing the land of Hutu peasants, this policy has even caused a dangerous development in light of the problematic history of ethnic relations. Pottier pointed out that the land policy amounted to an

---

[96] S. Straus, L. Waldorf, 'Introduction: Seeing like a Post-conflict State', in Straus, Waldorf, *Remaking Rwanda*, p. 13.
[97] B. Leloup, 'Les rebellions congolaises et leurs parrains dans l'ordre politique régional', in F. Reyntjens, S. Marysse (Eds.), *L' Afrique des Grands Lacs. Annuaire 2001–2002*, Paris, L'Harmattan, 2002, pp. 83–84.
[98] A few examples, just in 2022: 'From Challenger to Incumbent: Rwanda's Journey in Geopolitics', *The New Times*, 19 January 2022; 'Rwanda Is Well, the RPF Knows, but Institution Officials' Feet Must Be Held to the Fire', *The New Times*, 6 May 2022; 'Singapore, Rwanda Is with You All the Way, Minus Plastics, Concrete Jungles', *The New Times*, 29 July 2022.
[99] One of Susan Thomson's sources complained: 'Becoming modern is a real challenge' (Thomson, *Rwanda*, p. 150).

endorsement of widening class differences, reinforced by the 'ethnicisation of landlessness'.[100]

Agricultural policies too attempted to engineer modernity from above. From 2006 the government started to impose the growing of cash crops. Compulsory mono-cropping replaced multi-cropping that shielded peasants from climate or market setbacks. Each region was to plant species supposedly best suited, and this crop selection was accompanied by changes in techniques and modes of cultivation. This authoritarian transformation included a mass rollout of commercial seeds, imported fertilisers and pesticides. As a result of this policy, production rose substantially, but agricultural diversity plummeted, and the price of staple foods on the local markets increased significantly. Imported hybrid seeds imposed on the farmers are expensive and cannot be saved and replanted. So farmers became dependent on a complex supply chain for seeds they used to produce themselves.[101]

Land and agricultural policies were phrased in technical terms: security of tenure, efficient exploitation, plot consolidation, optimal management and productivity. However, beneath these neutral notions lay a risky policy with potentially devastating effects on peasants' lives. Guichaoua summarised the effects of the modernisation drive on rural communities as follows: 'The main result of the new agronomic order imposed without dialogue with the producers is up to now the maintaining of widespread misery, situations of chronic regional famine and the accelerated production of radically pauperised landless farmers. Thus, technocratic and/or security-based decisions are imposed on top of the brutality of social relations, thus disrupting the links with the peasant order.'[102]

Scott found 'a pernicious combination of four elements in (...) large-scale forms of social engineering that ended in disaster': the administrative ordering of nature and society; a high-modernist ideology that believes it is possible to rationally redesign human nature and social relations; an authoritarian government that is 'willing and able to use the full weight of its coercive power to bring these high-modernist designs into being' and 'a prostrate civil society that lacks the capacity to resist these plans'.[103] This is the combination of elements prevailing in post-genocide

---

[100] J. Pottier, 'Land Reform for Peace? Rwanda's 2005 Land Law in Context', *Journal of Agrarian Change*, Vol. 6, No. 4, 2006, p. 533.
[101] M. Milz, 'The Authoritarian Face of the "Green Revolution": Rwanda Capitulates to Agribusiness', *Grain*, 8 August 2011.
[102] A. Guichaoua, 'Transition politique à la rwandaise: d'un totalitarisme à l'autre', *Eins-Entwicklungspolitik Nord-Süd*, 2007, No. 5.
[103] J. Scott, *Seeing Like a State: How Certain Schemes to Improve the Human Condition Have Failed*, New Haven, Yale University Press, 1998, pp. 4–5.

Rwanda. The engineering efforts are in part informed by a strong sense of entitlement among RPF elites who firmly believe that they have it right and that those – even their friends – who criticise them have it wrong.

However, here too the RPF proved to be a learning organisation. Realising the severe side effects of the Green Revolution, particularly for smallholder farmers, and facing mounting grassroots resistance, the government became more flexible in the application of agricultural policies, and policymakers started to engage with contestation. For instance, multi-cropping increasingly emerged as the rule rather than as the exception, and problems related to food security, crop failure and food price inflation were more openly debated in the national media.[104]

7.10 Conclusion

While donors have a nagging feeling that they risk supporting regime policies and behaviour that may lead Rwanda to disaster again, they also, in addition to bureaucratic considerations and foreign policy interests, implicitly accept that authoritarianism is a price worth paying for socioeconomic progress. They feel that their money is well spent in Rwanda (Ethiopia, a country sharing many political characteristics with Rwanda, is another case where this kind of trade-off is visible[105]). Donors did recognise political risks but engaged in wishful thinking, hoping that the Rwandan regime would move in the 'right' direction. The UK, one of the main donors of post-genocide Rwanda, is a good example. In its December 2003 Country Assistance Plan, the Department for International Development (DFID), as it then was, wrote: 'We believe that the government as a whole remains committed to progressively opening up space for legitimate political debate and freedom of expression', but the opposite happened during the following years, and DFID refrained from assessing 'progress'. Eight years later, DFID's Operational Plan 2011–2015 noted 'constraints on rights and freedoms' and saw 'mounting concern that power is too highly centralised, with unpredictable consequences for long term political stability, economic development and human rights', but again continued on a waiting mood without proposing ways of dealing with these concerns.[106]

---

[104] A. Ansoms, 'Expanding the Space for Criticism in Rwanda', *ROAPE Blog*, 12 March 2019; A. Ansoms, 'The End of the New Green Revolution in Rwanda?', *ROAPE Blog*, 11 February 2020.

[105] The case of Ethiopia has recently shown that such systems are not as robust as donors often believe or hope.

[106] On these issues, see Z. Marriage, 'Aid to Rwanda: Unstoppable Rock, Immovable Post', in T. Hagmann, F. Reyntjens (Eds.), *Aid and Authoritarianism in Africa: Development without Democracy*, London, Zed Books, 2016, pp. 44–66.

7.10 Conclusion

Peter Uvin noted early on that donor assessments have differed considerably on 'basic matters such as the current dynamics of the Rwandan conflict, the nature and intentions of the government, the weight of the past in explaining the present, or the nature of the current ethnic, social and economic trends in society'.[107] The lack of clear evidence implied that errors were not just likely but, in the case of Rwanda, potentially very costly, not so much for donors, who only risk losing money, but more so for Rwandans, who risk losing their lives. Some donors have invested large amounts of money and a great deal of political support in Rwanda, and they need to continue supporting the 'model' to avoid its collapse and the loss of their financial and political investment. As elsewhere, donors and recipients need each other: donors need success stories, recipients need money and neither wants to rock the boat. Despite their rhetoric, donors accept 'development without democracy'. Both inside the country and externally, Rwanda's governance style is presented as a necessary trade-off between delivery/development and human rights/democracy, where the latter must yield to the former, at least for the time being.

Next to many differences, there are striking continuities between the pre- and post-genocide regimes. One of these is the nature of the state, which, unlike elsewhere in Africa, is strong and well internalised by citizens. Rwanda is not a colonial creation, and an old state tradition plays an undeniable role in the maintenance of an efficient pyramid-like political and administrative structure. Before as after the genocide, the regimes displayed a strong belief in managing, monitoring, controlling and mobilising the population. However, the current regime goes much further, and the dislocation caused by invasive policies is such that it may prove irreversible when their destructive effects become clear. Another continuity is Rwanda's status of 'donor darling'. Just like Kagame's Rwanda, Habyarimana's was seen as a 'laboratory of development', and 'Rwanda Vision 2020' echoes the five-year development plans in vogue under the second republic. A third, and possibly most important, continuity is the pervasiveness of structural violence. This is expressed in the resentment, frustration, marginalisation, fear and even hatred found by a great deal of field observations among many Rwandans, both ordinary people and elites, Hutu and Tutsi alike. As shown by Uvin with regard to pre-1994 Rwanda, this is a potent breeding ground for renewed, actual, physical violence.[108]

---

[107] P. Uvin, 'Difficult Choices in the New Post-conflict Agenda: The International Community in Rwanda after the Genocide', *Third World Quarterly*, Vol. 22, No. 2, 2001, p. 178.

[108] P. Uvin, *Aiding Violence: The Development Enterprise in Rwanda*, West Hartford, Kumarian Press, 1998.

It is sometimes argued that a degree of authoritarianism is necessary, both because Rwanda is still politically fragile and because progress in socio-economic fields will stave off political demands and tensions. A recent strand in research, challenging what it calls 'naïve liberalism', argues that 'developmental regimes' in Africa are possible so long as they are not required to achieve open and transparent, democratically accountable and comprehensively capable governance.[109] In the case of post-genocide Rwanda, often quoted as an example in the literature, this argument disregards the findings of many researchers with 'thick' knowledge of the country who warn about the risk of a violent backlash caused by heavy-handed and top-down policies based on repression and exclusion. Steven Radelet has convincingly argued that it is the combination of five factors, including 'the rise of more democratic and accountable governments', that provides the basis for the sustainability and expansion of Africa's initial successes. He finds no contradiction between democracy and development. Quite the contrary, his data suggest a strong positive relationship between democratic governance and economic performance in seventeen emerging African countries (Rwanda is one of four exceptions).[110] Also, other African countries manage their divisions in a democratic vein and with respect for human rights.

The argument that political repression is necessary for development is empirically unsustainable. The policies of the Rwandan government are reminiscent of colonial days, when things political were hidden under technocratically driven improvements in infrastructure, health and education. In a similar vein, the RPF regime runs the country like a corporation and seems to believe that Rwandans are no political beings. In the longer run, this is a risky choice. Rwandans have shown to be very resilient, but if structural violence is as widespread as consistent field data suggest, the metaphor that naturally comes to mind is that of a volcano waiting to erupt, thus opening the way for new acute violence that could again affect Rwanda and the entire region.

Viewed from both the *longue durée* and more recent history, the seizure of power by the RPF and the resulting evolution of political governance were path dependent. Linking up with the precolonial past, the RPF

---

[109] This line of thought is well summarised in the Development Regimes in Africa project, which builds on the findings of the Tracking Development project and the Africa Power and Politics Programme. A synthesis can be found in D. Booth et al., *Developmental Regimes in Africa: Initiating & Sustaining Developmental Regimes in Africa – Synthesis Report*, London, ODI, 2015.

[110] S. Radelet, 'Success Stories from "Emerging Africa"', *Journal of Democracy*, Vol. 21, 2010, pp. 87–101. This article is based on Radelet's book *Emerging Africa: How 17 Countries Are Leading the Way*, Washington, DC, Center for Global Development, 2010.

7.10 Conclusion

privileged military solutions and used a performant armed force – based in part on experience in its Ugandan years – to capture power, which was its aim since the 1990 attack. During the civil war and after taking power, the maintenance of military norms and ethos motivated the military's centrality and penetration of all society's sectors, economically, politically, socially and institutionally, with the ultimate aim of retaining power.[111] Contrasting three 'high conflict' cases (Burundi, Rwanda and Uganda) with two 'low conflict' cases (Kenya and Tanzania) in East Africa, Cheeseman et al. have traced the way in which domestic conflict has undermined three key elements of the democratisation process: the quality of political institutions, the degree of elite cohesion and the nature of civil–military relations.[112]

---

[111] A. Purdekova, F. Reyntjens, N. Wilén, 'Militarisation of Governance after Conflict: Beyond the Rebel-to-Ruler Frame – The Case of Rwanda', *Third World Quarterly*, Vol. 39, No. 1, 2018, pp. 158–174.

[112] N. Cheeseman, M. Collord, F. Reyntjens, 'War and Democracy: The Legacy of Conflict in East Africa', *Journal of Modern African Studies*, Vol. 56, No. 1, 2018, pp. 31–61.

Conclusion

At first sight, it may look like three fundamental ruptures occurred in modern Rwandan history: colonisation, starting towards the end of the nineteenth century; the revolution of 1959–1961 followed by independence in 1962; and the 1994 genocide against the Tutsi followed by the seizure of power by the RPF. Of course, these are major breaks with the past, and they have been presented as such both by the players themselves and by historians. However, there are also striking continuities spanning the entire period, from the mid nineteenth century to the 2020s. These include the concentration of power, intra-regime conflict, ethnicity and the nature of the state. Another characteristic – the pervasiveness of the military institution and of military ethics – disappeared during colonial days and the first two republics but resurfaced from 1994 onwards, thus resuming continuity after a century-long interval.

The period covered by this book was marked by continuity more than by change. An obvious continuity throughout the four periods is the concentration of power. The precolonial kingdom became increasingly centralised, particularly from the latter part of the eighteenth century. The areas under central court control were embedded in a pyramid structure, where regional authorities were dependants of the *mwami* and below them were the chiefs who represented him. In a much larger territorial expanse, authoritarian centralisation continued in colonial days in two ways. On the one hand, indirect rule reinforced and stabilised the power of the court and the chiefs. On the other, the Belgian colonial administration was itself authoritarian and, like the indigenous one, ignored such principles as the separation of powers and the rule of law. The elective principle and checks and balances were introduced less than two years before independence. Hence it is not surprising that, in Rwanda like elsewhere in Africa, the political elites that inherited the state practised 'business as usual' and continued colonial modes of governance. In this respect, there is not much of a break between colonial rule, the de facto single-party first republic, the de jure single-party second republic and the de facto single-party regime in post-genocide Rwanda.

Conclusion 185

The pre- and post-genocide regimes have fundamentally shared the same authoritarian concern with power and control. Both visions promoted an understanding of state–society relations that stressed respect for authority, hierarchy and Rwandans' place as followers of their 'enlightened' and 'benevolent' leaders. Presenting themselves as harbingers of an 'improved' or 'new' Rwanda, both leaderships have claimed to be best able and willing to guide the country along the right path to peace, security, ethnic unity and development.[1] Likewise, looking through the lens of surveillance, Purdeková finds that 'the Rwandan state of today (...) closely resembles its much maligned predecessor'. The oversight structures and techniques have intensified over time, from the precolonial and colonial days, through the first and second republics, up to the present day: 'striking continuities are evident across historical epochs, despite claims of decisive and even revolutionary breaks with the past'.[2]

Intra-regime conflict is the second continuity. The authoritarian nature of the successive regimes might suggest that they were monolithic, but they were not. Internal strife within the royal court and among ruling elite circles was common in precolonial days. Most successions to the throne were contested and led to bitter and often violent infighting, and even to civil war. Factions fought each other through false or true accusations of conspiracy, manipulation, torture and murder. Internal struggles continued during the first years of German rule, and they only came to an end when the Germans succeeded in imposing law and order the harsh way, at the same time preventing Musinga's overthrow. Nevertheless, the Germans realised that powerful factions continued to contend within the court and that 'beneath the veneer of absolutism was political turmoil that could lead to civil war'.[3] It took military expeditions, the burning of entire villages and summary executions to 'pacify' the country, a situation that was only achieved in 1912.[4] From 1916, Belgian rule no longer needed military force to prevent intrigues from destabilising the country, but they did not disappear. During the entire reign of Musinga, until his removal by the Belgians in 1931, factions at the court continued jostling for power, influence and wealth.[5]

---

[1] M.-E. Desrosiers, S. Thomson, 'Rhetorical Legacies of Leadership: Projections of "Benevolent Leadership" in Pre- and Post-genocide Rwanda', *Journal of Modern African Studies*, Vol. 49, No. 3, 2011, pp. 429–453.
[2] A. Purdeková, '"Mundane Sights" of Power: The History of Social Monitoring and Its Subversion in Rwanda', *African Studies Review*, Vol. 59, No. 2, 2016, p. 80.
[3] Louis, *Ruanda-Urundi*, p. 126.
[4] Ibid., pp. 145–156.
[5] Des Forges, *Defeat Is the Only Bad News*.

Regime infighting resumed after independence. The gradual narrowing of the MDR-Parmehutu's power base through the elimination of important constituencies eventually led to the downfall of the first republic. A similar phenomenon occurred under the second republic. The north took power in 1973, but Gisenyi and Ruhengeri *préfectures* soon fell out with each other, followed by a split between the Bushiru and Bugoyi regions inside Gisenyi. Hardly seven years after the birth of the second republic, this conflict led to major intra-regime tensions. After an episode where pamphlets were published with a virulence never seen in a country that usually exhibits a great deal of discretion and restraint, a number of regime leaders – among them the powerful director of the intelligence service – were arrested in 1980. Fearing a similar fate, others fled the country.

The RPF had also fallen prey to intense struggle, which pitted factions against each other from the first days of the invasion, when three high-ranking officers, including the military commander Gen. Fred Rwigema, were killed in an apparent internal settling of scores. Much of the infighting is largely invisible to outsiders, as the debate on major issues takes place within a small inner circle. On a number of occasions, however, splits have been apparent. Already in the late 1990s, a number of RPF members left the country and turned into vocal opponents. This evolution became more pronounced after 2000, and it took a radical turn in 2010 when four leading figures who fled abroad published a document called *Rwanda Briefing*, which contained a long diatribe against the regime.

While a predominantly ethnic reading skews historical understanding, there is no way of escaping the fact that the third major continuity is the salience of ethnicity, although it has had different political implications depending on the period. Political ethnicity emerged in the nineteenth century. The distinction between ethnic groups, which earlier referred to political positions and economic and military occupations, became institutionalised. With the introduction around 1870 of the *uburetwa* labour obligation, to which only the Hutu were submitted, two hierarchical social categories came into being. From indications of a situation of class or dependency or occupation, 'Hutu' and 'Tutsi' became absolute categories.[6] From the 1870s, the awareness of ethnic distinction spread in areas under the rule of the royal court and led to several revolts. While some of these Hutu movements targeted the court, others were aimed at the Tutsi as such. The 1897 insurrection showed that the population was conscious of a divide between the two ethnic groups.[7]

---

[6] Vansina, *Antecedents to Modern Rwanda*, p. 136.
[7] Ibid., pp. 136–139.

Colonial rule further institutionalised and rigidified ethnicity. Inspired by the Hamitic Hypothesis, Belgium first entrenched Tutsi rule but switched sides in the 1950s when democratisation and independence came to the fore. Although there were underlying social, political and economic grievances, the revolution of 1959–1961 took place under an almost exclusively ethnic banner. Hutu elites dominated the first two republics, under which an overt ethnic narrative (*rubanda nyamwinshi* – 'the majoritarian people') and practice (such as a quota system) prevailed. Upon assuming power, the RPF set out to pursue a policy of de-ethnicisation. However, the denial of ethnicity is an essential element of the hegemonic strategies of the Tutsi elite. The claim that 'there are no Hutu or Tutsi, we are all Rwandans now' allows them to hide a Tutsi ethnocracy. Collective identities were redefined in a way rarely seen elsewhere, and ethnicity was legislated away. The law reconfigured the ethnic map and entrenched the regime's policing of relations between individuals and groups. However, de-ethnicisation and reconciliation were imposed in a top-down authoritarian fashion, and all available fieldwork shows that the regime's narrative merely reflects the public transcript and that the hidden transcript – that of most Hutu and of oppressed Tutsi – is very different.[8]

The final strong continuity lies in the nature of the state, which, unlike in much of Africa, is strong and well internalised by citizens. Rwanda is not a colonial creation, and an old state tradition plays an undeniable role in the maintenance of an efficient pyramid-like political and administrative structure. Today's Rwandan Leviathan is highly centralised and hierarchical, and – contrary to the precolonial one – the modern state reaches every inch of the territory and every citizen.[9] Echoing the situation in colonial days and under the two previous republics, a mere two years after the extreme human and material destruction in 1994, the state had been rebuilt. Rwanda was again administered from top to bottom, territorial, military and security structures were in place, the judicial system was re-established and tax revenues were collected and spent. Within a short time the regime was able to establish total control over state and society. Before as after the genocide, the regimes displayed a strong belief in managing, monitoring, controlling and

---

[8] The differences between the two transcripts have often been highlighted with regard to post-genocide Rwanda; see for example J. Burnet, *Genocide Lives in Us: Women, Memory, and Silence in Rwanda*, Madison, University of Wisconsin Press, 2012; Thomson, *Whispering Truth to Power*.

[9] The metaphor of a Leviathan comes from Straus (*The Order of Genocide*, pp. 201–223), who details how and why the Rwandan state is qualitatively different from most of the rest of Africa.

mobilising the population, and they used the state in projects of economic and social engineering. Ideally all citizens are agents of development who march together under the stewardship of forward-looking and enlightened leaders.

But change also occurred in some important respects. Discontinuities can be most prominently seen in two areas: the dominant role of the military, both as an institution and as a source of ethics, and diverging approaches to the issue of ethnicity. In precolonial days, the military institution was central to the state structure. Not just the army as an institution but military values more generally were pervasive. The recruitment and indoctrination of *intore* were strong instruments to spread these values across the entire elite and to promote the glorification of a warrior ethos. The centrality of the army and its values disappeared for a full century, during colonial days and the two pre-1994 republics. Of course, the armies lost their military function as the European powers imposed *Pax Germanica/Belgica*, but the *itorero* training continued, in which military skills alongside history, etiquette, poetry, dance and the use of words were still taught to young Tutsi. *Itorero* eventually disappeared as a military institution and became limited to the teaching and practice of music and dance, until the RPF gave it new substance.

The role of the military was limited between independence and 1994. The army was small, was not involved in a single external war or in domestic keeping of order and played no significant role in politics. Even after the army took power in 1973, civilians dominated the political system just years after the coup. There were no references to the military institution or warrior values in the two 'Hutu republics' ideologies. Rather the ethical reference was that of the hard working peasant. In this ideology of rural romanticism, only the Hutu were the real peasants, while the Tutsi belonged to a feudal class.[10]

Militarisation returned almost overnight under RPF rule, and the continuity with the precolonial era was explicitly affirmed. After 'warrior nationalism' was actively promoted in the Tutsi diaspora,[11] both the army as an institution and military values have been actively promoted since the RPF took power. Institutionally, this shows in the fact that the army and the intelligence services became the pillars of the regime and that a small circle of officers, mainly coming from the Ugandan diaspora, takes all important decisions in an opaque way, whereby the government

---

[10] P. Verwimp, *Peasants in Power: The Political Economy of Development and Genocide in Rwanda*, Dordrecht, Springer, 2013.

[11] T. Riot, N. Bancel, P. Rutayisire, 'Un art guerrier aux frontières des grands lacs: Aux racines dansées du Front Patriotique Rwandais', *Politique Africaine*, No. 147, 2017, pp. 109–134.

only deals with the day-to-day management of administrative affairs and parliament is a mere rubber stamp. Beyond the institutional aspect, military ethos and values permeate the entire Rwandan society. Again with reference to the precolonial past, the *ingando* re-education camps and *itorero* training disseminate military values, in addition to the teaching of history and the advocacy of national unity.[12] Of course, the past is not the only reason for this militarisation. The circumstances in which the RPF seized power made the building of strong security forces a pragmatic necessity. There is thus a mix of tradition and modernity, with tradition reinforcing the dictates of a rational reliance on military strength.[13] Militarisation has effects beyond Rwanda's borders, which can be seen in the regime's behaviour towards the region. While the former regimes never threatened neighbouring countries and generally maintained friendly relations with them, the RPF has engaged in large-scale military and economic adventures beyond its borders, in particular in the DRC, and, acting as a regional power, has become a menace to its neighbours. In an apparent revival of *Urwanda ruratera, ntiruterwa* and *ku-aanda*, wars were waged directly with the DRC and Uganda and indirectly with Tanzania and Burundi.

Though the salience of ethnicity can be seen throughout the four periods, the role played by it and the use made of it are another break. The awareness of the division between the Tutsi and Hutu spread during the second half of the nineteenth century. Functions in the court and the chiefly apparatus were reserved for Tutsi, and only Hutu were subjected to *uburetwa*. The segregation showed clearly in *itorero*, which was almost exclusively reserved for the Tutsi, while the few Hutu and Twa were placed in a separate sub-group within the corps. David Newbury sees a confirmation of the hierarchical nature of the kingdom in the emergence, under Rujugira's reign, of two strata in the military organisation: *intore* (elite warriors) and *ingabo* (commoner warriors).[14] Even under German rule, Ruhamiriza recalls: 'There were one hundred and fifty of us, almost all Tutsi. There were a few Hutu, but not more than ten. In any case the Hutu children were at one side in the dances; they were in separate quarters, and we did not eat with them or drink milk together with them.'[15]

---

[12] Analyses of *ingando* and *Itorero* can be found in A. Purdeková, *Making Ubumwe: Power, State and Camps in Rwanda's Unity-Building Process*, Oxford–New York, Berghahn Books, 2015; M. Sundberg, *Training for Model Citizenship: An Ethnography of Civic Education and State-Making in Rwanda*, London, Palgrave Macmillan, 2016; Purdeková, Reyntjens, Wilén, 'Militarisation of Governance'.
[13] I thank René Lemarchand for having drawn my attention to this hybridity.
[14] Newbury, *The Land beyond the Mists*, 323.
[15] Codère, *The Biography of an African Society*, p. 53.

Ethnicity was made explicit, and further institutionalised and rigidified under the Belgian administration, whose support for the Tutsi hierarchy ended only in the late 1950s in a pre-revolutionary context. It then became important for the Tutsi elites to stress the 'centuries-old' national unity and to deny the reality of ethnic discrimination. Ethnocratic rule thus attempted to hide itself under the guise of ethnic amnesia, a discourse that can be seen again after 1994.

In opposition, the ethnic card was explicitly played in the first and second republics. The historical narrative claimed that the Twa were the first inhabitants of Rwanda, supposedly followed around 1000–500 BCE by the Hutu, who settled there during the great 'Bantu' migration coming from Cameroon. The Tutsi were claimed to have arrived just some centuries ago. They could therefore be labelled foreign invaders. Despite the wide popular acceptance of this chronology of human settlement,[16] there is no scientific evidence to support it. However, this reading of history gave rise to the claim that Rwanda was the land of the Hutu and to the conflation of democracy with Hutu rule. Just as the Hutu had been before the revolution, the Tutsi were the victims of discrimination and even of genocidal violence, particularly at the end of 1963 and of course in 1994. Many fled the country, and by the end of the 1980s over half a million Tutsi lived in exile. Although their situation improved after the seizure of power by Habyarimana in 1973, when regional cleavages became more prominent, they remained second-class citizens. A quota system limited their access to education and jobs, and governments would typically include a single token Tutsi. The continuing notion of the 'majority people' was coupled with the fear of the return of 'feudal' days, a threat that in the eyes of many Hutu materialised in 1990–1994.

After seizing power, the RPF resumed the narrative of Tutsi elites in the 1950s. Ethnicity was said to have been introduced by the colonial rulers practising a policy of divide and rule, and the country now reverted to the harmony that characterised Rwanda before colonial days. There are no longer Hutu, Tutsi and Twa but only Rwandans. National unity and reconciliation are imposed top-down and the de-ethnicisation project is supported by legislation on 'divisionism' and 'genocide ideology', and by prosecutions under these laws. In 2013, the programme 'Ndi Umunyarwanda' ('I am Rwandan') was launched.[17] As it is clear

---

[16] Interestingly, even the Tutsi court historian Alexis Kagame adhered to this narrative, albeit in a book written after the revolution, that is under 'Hutu' rule (Kagame, *Un abrégé de l'ethno-histoire*, pp. 22–28).

[17] Strangely enough in a context of fighting ethnicity, under the same programme, President Kagame asked all Hutu to implore forgiveness for a genocide committed in their name.

that Tutsi elites exercise a disproportionate share of power in politics, the military and intelligence services, the central and local administrations, and the (parastatal) economy, this ethnic amnesia in reality serves to hide the reality of a Tutsi ethnocracy. Thus a formal quota system under the Hutu republics is replaced by an informal one under the Tutsi republic, again a return to precolonial reality.

Clearly the continuities of this *longue durée* outweigh the ruptures. Rwanda was, and is, a violent society.[18] Wars with neighbouring countries and unruly regions were frequent, as were violent confrontations within ruling elites. Scores of people, both elite and ordinary citizens, were killed until the early days of German occupation, and again from 1959 onwards, with the 1994 genocide of the Tutsi as a tragic climax. Throughout the entire period, central political power has been almost absolute, and it was reinforced and extended during early colonial rule. Indeed, today's Rwanda is in large part a creation of colonisation: rule of the *mwami* was spread to parts of the country that previously were not incorporated in the Nyiginya kingdom, the current borders were consolidated during the early years of colonial rule, and political and administrative management were homogenised across entire current-day Rwanda.

The tradition of a strong state dates back to *mwami* Rujugira, almost 250 years ago, and continues up to the present day. Contrary to what can be seen in many other African countries, the state is pyramidal, hierarchical, centralised and strongly internalised by citizens. Its political culture exhibits enduring characteristics: in a context of strong respect for authority and discipline, leaders succeed in managing, monitoring, controlling and mobilising the population. In apparent contrast to this monolithic image, intra-regime elite conflict is considerable, and has been a recurrent source of often violent conflict. Since the late eighteenth century, not a single head of state has been succeeded in a constitutional, peaceful fashion.

The salience of ethnicity has been and remains another defining factor, although it has played out in different ways depending on the political dispensation of the time. Simply put, under Tutsi rule, ethnic amnesia is used to hide ethnocracy by Tutsi elites, while under Hutu rule, ethnic belonging is highlighted to justify ethnocracy by Hutu elites claiming to represent the popular majority. In both cases, this practice

---

[18] This book has dealt with politics and violence at the macro level, but Rwandan society is also replete with everyday violence at the micro level. De Lame noted that '[b]rutality seemed to be one of the rare cures for the boredom of rural life' and that '[t]he collective exercise of physical force in combat is a measure of virility in Rwandan culture' (de Lame, *A Hill among a Thousand*, p. 489).

has been and is used to relegate the other group to a subordinate status in the political dispensation and in social and economic life. It is important to stress that these are elite policies. Throughout the entire period studied in this book, the gap between the elites and the people has been and remains wide. Just like the court and chiefly culture was disconnected from the daily lives of the vast majority of Rwandans in precolonial days, the RPF leadership's urban and cosmopolitan lifestyle is miles apart from that of ordinary citizens, both Hutu and Tutsi. Likewise, during the 'Hutu Republics', besides the Hutu, Tutsi and Twa, a 'fourth ethnic group', that of a small bi-ethnic bourgeoisie, accumulated wealth and privileges.[19]

A final determining continuity is the pervasiveness of the military institution and of warrior ethics and values. What is particularly striking is the re-emergence of this characteristic in 1994, after it had virtually disappeared during colonial days and the two 'Hutu republics'. After that century-long gap, it reappeared almost seamlessly. This is well rendered by the RPF's military historian Brig. Gen. Frank Rusagara, who wrote that 'the RDF [Rwanda Defence Force] today not only ensures security for all, but provides a model of national unity and integration that continues to inform Rwanda's socio-political and economic development'.[20] Beyond the institution, military values are disseminated throughout the entire society by the widespread use of means like *ingando* and *itorero*. In the eyes of the elite in power today, the period from 1895 and 1994 had been a century-long interlude during which the country was ruled by colonial and neo-colonial (and ethnically sectarian) usurpers. The 1962 independence day is no longer celebrated, as the country is claimed to have regained independence only in 1994.

In today's Rwanda, constant references to history, whether factually true or not, are used as a tool of legitimation. The idealised glorification of the precolonial era supports the political objectives and strategies of the current rulers. Therefore, the *longue durée* is not just a historical and epistemological issue but very much a concrete contemporary political stake, hence the efforts of the RPF to impose and tightly police its narrative. The problem is that the public and the hidden transcripts often do not tally. Jessee and Watkins show this when confronting the 'Tutsi' and 'Hutu' readings of the monarchy. For the former, the kings were benevolent; for the latter they were bloody tyrants. Divergent versions on this and other themes align with people's own experiences,

---

[19] Vidal, *Sociologie des passions*.
[20] Rusagara, *Resilience of a Nation*, back cover.

received knowledge and political preferences. History in Rwanda is highly politicised and polarised and is considered a dangerous subject by most ordinary Rwandans.[21] In a political context where the hidden transcript cannot be publicly expressed, alternative narratives encode subtle resistance to the official history.[22]

---

[21] E. Jessee, S. Watkins, 'Good Kings, Bloody Tyrants, and Everything in Between: Representations of the Monarchy in Post-genocide Rwanda', *History in Africa*, Vol. 41, 2014, pp. 35–62.

[22] E. Jessee, 'The Danger of a Single Story: Iconic Stories in the Aftermath of the 1994 Rwandan Genocide', *Memory Studies*, Vol. 10, No. 2, 2017, p. 148; Thomson, *Whispering Truth to Power*.

Bibliography

Referenced Archives

Africa Archive
Ministry of Foreign Affairs
Rue des Petits Carmes 15
1000 Brussels
diplomatie.belgium.be/en/archives/heritage/africa-archive

Archives of the White Fathers
Via Aurelia 269
Rome
peresblancs.org/activités/ailleurs/a-rome-pisai

Derscheid Collection
University of Florida
ufdc.ufl.edu/collections/DERSCHEID

Amnesty International, *The Republic of Rwanda: A Spate of Detentions and Trials in 1990 to Suppress Fundamental Rights*, October 1990.
Amnesty International, *Rwanda: Ending the Silence*, London, 25 September 1997.
Amnesty International, *Rwanda: Civilians Trapped in Armed Conflict. The Dead Can no Longer Be Counted*, London, 19 December 1997.
Amnesty International, *Rwanda: Number of Prisoners of Conscience on the Rise*, London, 7 June 2002.
Amnesty International, *Rwanda: La liberté de la presse réprimée depuis 12 ans*, London, 3 May 2006.
Amnesty International, *Safer to Stay Silent: The Chilling Effect of Rwanda's Laws on 'Genocide Ideology' and 'Sectarianism'*, London, 25 August 2010.
Amnesty International, *Setting the Scene for Elections: Two Decades of Silencing Dissent in Rwanda*, July 2017.
Amnesty International, *Massive Data Leak Reveals Israeli NSO Group's Spyware Used to Target Activists, Journalists, and Political Leaders Globally*, 18 July 2021.
André, C., Platteau, J.-P., *Land Tenure under Unendurable Stress: Rwanda Caught in the Malthusian Trap*, Namur, Cahiers de la faculté des sciences économiques et sociales de Namur, No. 164, 1996.
Ansoms, A., 'Re-engineering Rural Society: The Visions and Ambitions of the Rwandan Elite', *African Affairs*, Vol. 108, No. 431, 2009, pp. 289–309.

Ansoms, A., 'Expanding the Space for Criticism in Rwanda', ROAPE Blog, 12 March 2019.
Ansoms, A., 'The End of the New Green Revolution in Rwanda?', ROAPE Blog, 11 February 2020.
Bachmann, K., *A History of Rwanda: From the Monarchy to Post-genocidal Justice*, London–New York, Routledge, 2023.
Baldwin, G., 'Constructing Identity through Commemoration: Kwibuka and the Rise of Survivor Nationalism in Post-conflict Rwanda', *Journal of Modern African Studies*, Vol. 57, No. 3, 2019, pp. 355–75.
Barahinyura, S. J., *1973–1988: Le Général-Major Habyarimana – Quinze ans de tyrannie et de tartuferie au Rwanda*, Frankfurt am Main, Editions Izuba, 1988.
Bayart, J. F., Constantin, F., Coulon, C., Martin, D., 'Par le canal du scrutin. Comment dépouiller les élections africaines?', in Centre d'étude de l'Afrique noire, *Aux urnes l'Afrique! Elections et pouvoir en Afrique noire*, Paris, Pedone, 1978, pp. 1–24.
Bézy, F., *Rwanda 1962–1989, bilan socio-économique d'un régime*, Louvain, Institut d'Etudes du Développement, 1990.
Booth, D. et al., *Developmental Regimes in Africa: Initiating and Sustaining Developmental Regimes in Africa. Synthesis Report*, London, ODI, 2015.
Bourgeois, R., *Banyarwanda et Barundi*, Vol. 2, *La coutume*, Brussels, Institut royal colonial belge, 1954.
Burnet, J., *Genocide Lives in US: Women, Memory, and Silence in Rwanda*, Madison, University of Wisconsin Press, 2012.
'Calculating Mortality in the Rwandan Genocide', *Journal of Genocide Research*, Vol. 22, No. 1, 2020, pp. 77–141.
Callaghy, T. M., *The State–Society Struggle: Zaire in Comparative Perspective*, New York, Columbia University Press, 1984.
Cantrell, P., *Revival and Reconciliation: The Anglican Church and the Politics of Rwanda*, Madison, University of Wisconsin Press, 2022.
Capoccia, G., Kelemen, R. D., 'The Study of Critical Junctures: Theory, Narrative, and Counterfactual in Historical Institutionalism', *World Politics*, Vol. 59, 2007, pp. 341–69.
Chakravarty, A., *Investing in Authoritarian Rule: Punishment and Patronage in Rwanda's Gacaca Courts for Genocide Crimes*, New York, Cambridge University Press, 2016.
Cheeseman, N., Collord, M., Reyntjens, F., 'War and Democracy: The Legacy of Conflict in East Africa', *Journal of Modern African Studies*, Vol. 56, No. 1, 2018, pp. 31–61.
Chemouni, B., 'La recherche sur l'État rwandais en débat', *Politique africaine*, No. 160, 2020, pp. 7–34.
Chrétien, J.-P., 'Les fratricides légitimés', *Esprit*, 1976, pp. 822–34.
Chrétien, J.-P., 'Pluralisme démocratique, ethnismes et stratégies politiques: La situation du Rwanda et du Burundi', in Conac, G. (Ed.), *L'Afrique en transition vers le pluralisme politique*, Paris, Economica, 1993, pp. 139–47.
Chrétien, J.-P. et al., *Rwanda. Les médias du génocide*, Paris, Karthala, 1995.
Chrétien, J.-P., *The Great Lakes of Africa: Two Thousand Years of History*, New York, Zone Books, 2003.

Clark, P., Kaufman, Z. D. (Eds.), *After Genocide: Transitional Justice, Post-Conflict Reconstruction and Reconciliation in Rwanda and Beyond*, London, Hurst, 2008.
Clark, P., 'Rwanda: Kagame's Power Struggle', *The Guardian*, 5 August 2010.
Clark, P., *The Gacaca Courts: Post-genocide Justice and Reconciliation in Rwanda – Justice without Lawyers*, Cambridge, Cambridge University Press, 2010.
Clark, P., 'Rwanda's Recovery: When Remembrance Is Official Policy', *Foreign Affairs*, Vol. 97, No. 1, 2018, pp. 35–41.
Classe, L. P., 'Pour moderniser le Ruanda', *L'Essor colonial et maritime*, No. 489, 4 December 1930.
Classe, L. P., 'Un triste Sire!', *L'Essor colonial et maritime*, No. 494-495, 21–25 December 1930.
Codère, H., *The Biography of an African Society: Rwanda, 1900–1960*, Tervuren, Royal Museum for Central Africa, 1973.
Collins, B., *Rwanda 1994: The Myth of the Akazu Genocide Conspiracy and Its Consequences*, New York, Palgrave Macmillan, 2014.
Commonwealth Expert Team, *Rwanda: Legislative Election (Chamber of Deputies), 16–18 September 2013*, 23 September 2013.
Commonwealth Secretariat, *Rwanda Presidential Elections 9 August 2010, Report of the Commonwealth Observer Group*, n.d.
Corduwener, J., 'Wederopbouw in Rwanda, met ijzeren hand' ('*Reconstruction in Rwanda, with an Iron Fist*'), NRC-Handelsblad, 27 March 2002.
Cruvellier, T. et al., *Augustin Cyiza: Un homme libre au Rwanda*, Paris, Karthala, 2004.
Cruvellier, T., *Court of Remorse: Inside the International Criminal Tribunal for Rwanda*, Madison, University of Wisconsin Press, 2010.
Dallaire, R., *Shake Hands with the Devil: The Failure of Humanity in Rwanda*, Toronto, Random House Canada, 2003.
'Décolonisation et indépendance du Rwanda et du Burundi', *Chronique de politique étrangère*, 1963, pp. 439–718.
de Heusch, L., *Le Rwanda et la civilisation interlacustre*, Brussels, Université Libre de Bruxelles, Institut de Sociologie, 1966.
de Lacger, L., *Ruanda*, Kabgayi, Imprimerie de Kabgayi, 1959.
de Lame, D., *A Hill among a Thousand: Transformations and Ruptures in Rural Rwanda*, Madison, University of Wisconsin Press, 2005.
Des Forges, A. et al., *Leave None to Tell the Story: Genocide in Rwanda*, New York, Human Rights Watch, 1999.
Des Forges, A. L., *Defeat Is the Only Bad News: Rwanda under Musinga, 1896–1931*, Madison, University of Wisconsin Press, 2011.
Desrosiers, M.-E., *Trajectories of Authoritarianism in Rwanda: Elusive Control before the Genocide*, Cambridge, Cambridge University Press, 2023.
Desrosiers, M.-E., Thomson, S., 'Rhetorical Legacies of Leadership: Projections of "benevolent leadership" in Pre- and Post-genocide Rwanda.' *Journal of Modern African Studies*, Vol. 49, No. 3, 2011, pp. 429–53.
Desrosiers, M.-E., Swedlund, H. J., 'Rwanda's Post-genocide Foreign Aid Relations: Revisiting Notions of Exceptionalism', *African Affairs*, Vol. 118, No. 472, 2019, pp. 435–62.
Desrosiers, M.-E., Russell, A., 'Histories of Authority in the African Great Lakes: Trajectories and Transactions', *Africa*, Vol. 90, No. 5, 2020, pp. 952–71.

de Vleeschauwer, A., *Belgian Colonial Policy*, New York, Belgian Government Information Center, 1943.
de Wolf, R., Ntashamaje, A., Reyntjens, F., *Projet de constitution de la République Rwandaise: Rapport présenté à Monsieur le Président de la République*, Kigali, July 1978.
d'Hertefelt, M., 'Les élections communales et le consensus politique au Rwanda', *Zaïre*, 1960, pp. 403–38.
d'Hertefelt, M., 'Stratification sociale et structure politique au Rwanda', *La Revue Nouvelle*, 1960, pp. 449–62.
d'Hertefelt, M., *Les clans du Rwanda ancien*, Tervuren, Musée royal de l'Afrique centrale, 1971.
d'Hertefelt, M., de Lame, D., *Société, culture et histoire du Rwanda: Encyclopédie bibliographique 1863–1980/87*, Tervuren, Musée royal de l'Afrique centrale, 1987.
Donelli, F., 'Rwanda's Military Diplomacy: Kigali's Political Use of the Military Means to Increase Prestige in Africa and Beyond', *Notes de l'Ifri*, Paris, Ifri, April 2022.
Doornbos, M., *Not all the King's Men: Inequality as a Political Instrument In Ankole, Uganda*, The Hague, Mouton Publishers, 1978.
Dumas, H., *Le génocide au village: Le massacre des Tutsi au Rwanda*, Paris, Seuil, 2014.
European Union, Election Observation Mission, *Republic of Rwanda: Final Report – Legislative Elections to the Chamber of Deputies, 15–18 September* 2008, 26 January 2009.
Fallers, L., 'The Predicament of the Modern African Chief: An Instance from Uganda', *American Anthropologist*, 1955, pp. 290–305.
Fédération internationale des droits de l'homme, *La démocratie mise sous tutelle au Rwanda. Comment le FPR pérennise sa confiscation du pouvoir et l'accaparement des richesses*, August 2017.
Fisher, J., 'Writing about Rwanda since the Genocide: Knowledge, Power and "Truth"', *Journal of Intervention and Statebuilding*, Vol. 9, No. 1, 2015, pp. 134–45.
Freedom House, *Out of Sight, Not out of Reach. The Global Scale and Scope of Transnational Repression*, February 2021.
Front Line Rwanda, *Disappearances, Arrests, Threats, Intimidation of Human Rights Defenders, 2001–2004*, Dublin, 2005.
Fujii, L. A., *Killing Neighbors: Webs of Violence in Rwanda*, Ithaca, Cornell University Press, 2009.
Gahama, J., *Le Burundi sous administration belge*, Paris, Karthala, 1983.
Gahima, G., *Transitional Justice in Rwanda: Accountability for Atrocity*, New York, Routledge, 2013.
Gasana, J., *Rwanda: du parti-Etat à l'Etat-garnison*, Paris, L'Harmattan, 2002.
Gersony, R., 'Prospects for Early Repatriation of Rwandan Refugees Currently in Burundi, Tanzania and Zaire: Summary of UNHCR Presentation before Commission of Experts', Geneva, UNHCR, 10 October 1994.
Gordon, N., *Murders in the Mist*, London, Hodder and Stoughton, 1993.
Gowing, N., 'New Challenges and Problems for Information Management in Complex Emergencies. Ominous Lessons from the Great Lakes and Eastern

Zaire in Late 1996 and Early 1997', paper presented at Dispatches from Disaster Zones conference, Oxford, 28 May 1998.

Gravel, P. B., *Remera: A Community in Eastern Rwanda*, The Hague, Mouton Publishers, 1968.

Guariso, A., Ingelaere, B., Verpoorten, M., 'When Ethnicity Beats Gender: Quotas and Political Representation in Rwanda and Burundi', *Development and Change*, Vol. 49, No. 6, 2018, pp. 1361–91.

Guichaoua, A., *Le problème des réfugiés rwandais et des populations banyarwanda dans la région des Grands Lacs africains*, Geneva, UNHCR, May 1992.

Guichaoua, A., (Ed.), *Les crises politiques au Burundi et au Rwanda (1993–1994)*, Paris, Karthala, 1995.

Guichaoua, A., 'Transition politique à la rwandaise: d'un totalitarisme à l'autre', *Ein-Entwicklungspolitik Nord-Süd*, 2007, No. 5, pp. x–xvi.

Guichaoua, A., *Rwanda, de la guerre au génocide: Les politiques criminelles au Rwanda (1990–1994)*, Paris, La Découverte, 2010.

Hailey (Lord), *Native Administration in the British African Territories*, London, H.M.S.O., 1950–1953.

Hanssen, A., *Le désenchantement de la coopération: Enquête au pays des mille coopérants*, Paris, L'Harmattan, 1989.

Harroy, J.-P., *Rwanda: De la féodalité à la démocratie 1955–1962*, Brussels, Hayez, 1984.

Heyse, T., *Le mandat belge sur le Ruanda-Urundi*, Brussels, La Renaissance de l'Occident, 1930.

Historique et chronologie du Ruanda, s.l., s.d., 1955.

Human Rights Watch, *The Aftermath of Genocide in Rwanda*, New York, September 1994.

Human Rights Watch, *Rwanda: A New Catastrophe?*, New York, September 1994.

Human Rights Watch, *Rwanda: Parliament Seeks to Abolish Rights Group*, New York, 2 July 2004.

Human Rights Watch, *Law and Reality: Progress in Judicial Reform in Rwanda*, New York, 2008.

Human Rights Watch, *Justice Compromised: The Legacy of Rwanda's Community-Based* Gacaca *Courts*, New York, 2011.

Human Rights Watch, *D.R. Congo: Rwanda Should Stop Aiding War Crimes Suspect – Congolese Renegade General Bosco Ntaganda Receives Recruits and Weapons from Rwanda*, Goma, 4 June 2012.

Human Rights Watch, *Repression across Borders. Attacks and Threats against Rwandan Opponents and Critics Abroad*, 28 January 2014.

Human Rights Watch, *'All Thieves Must Be Killed'. Extrajudicial Executions in Western Rwanda*, July 2017.

Human Rights Watch, *Rwanda: Politically Closed Elections*, 18 August 2017.

Human Rights Watch, *'We Will Force You to Confess'. Torture and Unlawful Military Detention in Rwanda*, October 2017.

Human Rights Watch, *Rwanda: Cover-Up Negates Killings*, 1 November 2017.

Ibingira, G. S., *African Upheavals since Independence*, Boulder, Westview Press, 1980.

ICTR, 'General report on the Special Investigations concerning the crimes committed by the Rwandan Patriotic Army (RPA) during 1994', 1 October 2003.

Ingelaere, B., '"Does the Truth Pass across Fire without Burning?" Locating the Short Circuit of Knowledge in Postgenocide Rwanda', *Journal of Modern African Studies*, Vol. 47, No. 4, 2009, pp. 507–28.
Ingelaere, B., *Inside Rwanda's Gacaca Courts: Seeking Justice after Genocide*, Madison, University of Wisconsin Press, 2016.
International Crisis Group, *International Criminal Tribunal for Rwanda: Justice Delayed*, Nairobi–Arusha–Brussels, June 2001.
International Crisis Group, *Rwanda at the End of the Transition: A Necessary Political Liberalisation*, Nairobi–Brussels, 13 November 2002.
Jallow, H. B., 'Prosecutorial Discretion and International Criminal Justice', *Journal of International Criminal Justice*, Vol. 3, No. 1, 2005, pp. 145–61.
Jamoulle, M., 'Notre mandat sur le Ruanda-Urundi', *Congo*, 1927, pp. 477–96.
Jentgen, P., *Les frontières du Ruanda-Urundi et le régime international de tutelle*, Brussels, Académie royale des sciences coloniales, 1957.
Jessee, E., 'The Danger of a Single Story: Iconic Stories in the Aftermath of the 1994 Rwandan Genocide', *Memory Studies*, Vol. 10, No. 2, 2017, pp. 144–63.
Jessee, E., Watkins, S., 'Good Kings, Bloody Tyrants, and Everything in between: Representations of the Monarchy in Post-Genocide Rwanda', *History in Africa*, Vol. 41, 2014, pp. 35–62.
Johnson, C., *Revolutionary Change*, Stanford, Stanford University Press, 1982.
Kabwete Mulinda, C., Nkaka, R., 'The Political Vision of the Rwandan Kingdom', *Rwanda Journal of Arts and Humanities*, Vol. 2, No. 2, 2017, pp. 59–75.
Kagambirwa, W., *Les autorités rwandaises face aux pouvoirs européens à Nyanza (1900–1946)*, Butare, Université Nationale du Rwanda, mémoire de licence, 1979.
Kagame, A., *Les milices du Rwanda précolonial*, Brussels, Académie royale des sciences d'outre-mer, 1963.
Kagame, A., *Un abrégé de l'ethno-histoire du Rwanda*, Butare, Editions universitaires du Rwanda, 1972.
Kagame, A., *Un abrégé de l'histoire du Rwanda de 1853 à 1972*, Butare, Editions universitaires du Rwanda, 1975.
Kajeguhakwa, V., *Rwanda: De la terre de paix à la terre de sang, et après?*, Paris, Editions Remi Perrin, 2001.
Kimonyo, J.-P., *Rwanda's Popular Genocide: A Perfect Storm*, Boulder, Lynne Rienner, 2016.
Kimonyo, J.-P., *Transforming Rwanda: Challenges on the Road to Reconstruction*, Boulder–London, Lynne Rienner, 2019.
Lagarde, F., *Colonialisme et révolution: Histoire du Rwanda sous la Tutelle*, Paris, L'Harmattan, 2017.
La position internationale de la Belgique, Brussels, Imprimerie du Moniteur belge, 1934.
Latham-Koenig, A. L., 'Ruanda-Urundi on the Threshold of Independence', *The World Today*, 1962, pp. 288–95.
Lavroff, D. G., *Les partis politiques en Afrique noire*, Paris, P.U.F., 1970.
Lebart, G., Mupangu, 'La "politique indigène" de la Belgique au Ruanda-Urundi', *La Revue Nouvelle*, 1960, pp. 462–82.

Leloup, B., 'Les rebellions congolaises et leurs parrains dans l'ordre politique régional', in Reyntjens, F., Marysse, S. (Eds.), *L'Afrique des grands lacs: Annuaire 2001–2002*, Paris, L'Harmattan, 2002, pp. 79–114.

Lemarchand, R., 'L'influence des systèmes traditionnels sur l'évolution politique du Rwanda et du Burundi', *Revue de l'Institut de Sociologie*, 1962, pp. 333–57.

Lemarchand, R., *Rwanda and Burundi*, London, Pall Mall Press, 1970.

Lemarchand, R., 'The Coup in Rwanda', in Rotberg, R. I., Mazrui, A. A. (Eds.), *Protest and Power in Black Africa*, New York, Oxford University Press, 1970, pp. 877–923.

Lemarchand, R., 'Rwanda', in Lemarchand, R. (Ed.), *African Kingships in Perspective: Political Change and Modernization in Monarchical Settings*, London, Frank Cass, 1977, pp. 67–92.

Le président Kayibanda vous parle, Kigali, 1964.

'Le sort des Tutsi au Rwanda', *Remarques Africaines*, No. 418, 16–31 March 1973.

Leurquin, P., *Le niveau de vie des populations rurales au Ruanda-Urundi*, Louvain-Paris, Nauwelaerts, 1960.

Lijphart, A., *Democracies: Patterns of Majoritarian and Consensus Government in Twenty-One Countries*, London–New Haven, Yale University Press, 1984.

Linden, I., *Church and Revolution in Rwanda*, Manchester, Manchester University Press, 1977.

Logiest, G., *Mission au Rwanda: Un blanc dans la bagarre Tutsi-Hutu*, Brussels, Didier Hatier, 1988.

Longman, T., *Christianity and Genocide in Rwanda*, Cambridge, Cambridge University Press, 2010.

Longman, T., 'Christian Churches in Post-Genocide Rwanda: Reconciliation and Its Limits', in Girma, M. (Ed.), *The Healing of Memories: African Christian Responses to Politically Induced Trauma*, Lanham–Boulder–New York–London, Lexington Books, 2018, pp. 55–76.

Louis, W. R., *Ruanda-Urundi 1884–1919*, Oxford, Clarendon Press, 1963.

Lugan, B., *Histoire du Rwanda: De la préhistoire à nos jours*, s.l., Bartillat, 1997.

Lugard (Lord), *The Dual Mandate in British Tropical Africa*, first edition Edinburgh–London, William Blackwood, 1922, fifth edition London, Frank Cass, 1965.

Mamdani, M., *When Victims Become Killers: Colonialism, Nativism, and the Genocide in Rwanda*, Princeton NJ, Princeton University Press, 2001.

Maquet, J.-J., *Le système des relations sociales dans le Ruanda ancien*, Tervuren, Musée royal de l'Afrique centrale, 1954.

Maquet, J.-J., *The Premise of Inequality in Ruanda: A Study of Political Relations in a Central African Kingdom*, London, Oxford University Press, 1961.

Maquet, J. J., Naigiziki, S., 'Les droits fonciers dans le Ruanda ancien', *Zaïre*, 1957, pp. 340–59.

Marriage, Z., 'Aid to Rwanda: Unstoppable Rock, Immovable Post', in Hagmann, T., Reyntjens, F. (Eds.), *Aid and Authoritarianism in Africa: Development without Democracy*, London, Zed Books, 2016, pp. 44–66.

Marysse, S., de Herdt, T., Ndayambaje, E., *Rwanda: Appauvrissement et ajustement structurel*, Brussels-Paris, Institut Africain/CEDAF-L'Harmattan, Cahiers Africains, No. 12, 1994.

Mathys, G., 'Bringing History Back In: Past, Present, and Conflict in Rwanda and the Eastern Democratic Republic of Congo', *Journal of African History* Vol. 58, No. 3, 2017, pp. 465–87.

Mathys, G., 'Lines through the Lake: Why the Congo-Rwanda Border Can't Be Redrawn', *African Arguments*, 2 May 2023.

Mathys, G., *Conflicts and Connections: Making the Histories of the Lake Kivu Region*, Cambridge, Cambridge University Press, forthcoming.

Mbonimana, G., 'Christianisation indirecte et cristallisation des clivages ethniques au Rwanda (1925–31)', *Enquêtes et Documents d'Histoire africaine*, 1978, pp. 125–63.

McDoom, O. S., *The Path to Genocide in Rwanda: Security, Opportunity, and Authority in an Ethnocratic State*, Cambridge, Cambridge University Press, 2021.

MDR-Parmehutu, *Manifeste-Programme, Statuts, Résolutions*, Gitarama, Secrétariat exécutif national, s.d.

Mecklenburg, Duke of, *In the Heart of Africa*, London, Cassell, 1910.

Meek, C. K., *Land Law and Custom in the Colonies*, London, Oxford University Press, 1949.

Meierhenrich, J., *The Violence of Law: The Formation and Deformation of Gacaca Courts in Rwanda*, Cambridge, Cambridge University Press, forthcoming.

Milz, M., 'The Authoritarian Face of the "Green Revolution": Rwanda Capitulates to Agribusiness', *Grain*, 8 August 2011.

Minani, F., 'Evolution des institutions rwandaises', in *Les constitutions et les institutions administratives des Etats nouveaux*, Compte-rendu de la 33ème session de l'Incidi, Brussels, 1965, pp. 207–28.

Ministère des Affaires étrangères, *Toute la vérité sur le terrorisme 'Inyenzi' au Rwanda*, Kigali, 1964.

Minnaert, S., 'The White Fathers and Rwandan Society during the German Colonial Period', in Bachmann, K., Bar, J. (Eds.), *German Colonialism in Africa*, Berlin, Peter Lang, 2023, pp. 157–96.

Mission d'observation électorale de l'Union Européenne, *Référendum constitutionnel, Rwanda* 2003, Kigali, n.d.

Mission d'observation électorale de l'Union Européenne, *Rwanda: Election présidentielle 25 août 2003. Elections législatives 29 et 30 septembre, 2 octobre 2003. Rapport final*, n.d.

Moghalu, K. C., *Rwanda's Genocide: The Politics of Global Justice*, New York–Basingstoke, Palgrave Macmillan, 2006.

Morris, H. F., 'Sir Philip Mitchell and "Protected Rule" in Buganda', *Journal of African History*, 1972, pp. 305–23.

Morris, H. F., Read, J. S., *Indirect Rule and the Search for Justice*, Oxford, Clarendon Press, 1972.

Munyangaju, A., *L'actualité politique au Rwanda*, s.l., s.ed., 1959.

Munyantwali, E., 'La politique d'équilibre dans l'enseignement', in *Les relations interethniques au Rwanda à la lumière de l'agression d'octobre 1990. Genèse, soubassements et perspectives*, Ruhengeri, Editions universitaires du Rwanda, 1991, pp. 300–7.

Munyarugerero, F.-X., *Réseaux, pouvoirs, oppositions: La compétition politique au Rwanda*, Paris, L'Harmattan, 2003.

Murego, D., *La révolution rwandaise 1959–1962: Essai d'interprétation*, Louvain, Publications de l'Institut des sciences politiques et sociales, 1976.
Mwambari, D., '*Agaciro*, Vernacular Memory, and the Politics of Memory in Post-genocide Rwanda', *African Affairs*, Vol. 120, No. 481, 2021, pp. 611–28.
Mwambari, D., *Navigating Cultural Memory: Commemoration and Narrative in Postgenocide Rwanda*, New York, Oxford University Press, 2023.
Muzungu, B., *Histoire du Rwanda pré-colonial*, Paris, L'Harmattan, 2003.
Mworoha, E., *Peuples et rois de l'Afrique des lacs: Le Burundi et les royaumes voisins au XIXe siècle*, Dakar–Abidjan, Les Nouvelles Editions Africaines, 1977.
Nahimana, F., *Le Rwanda: Émergence d'un État*, Paris, L'Harmattan, 1993.
National Unity and Reconciliation Commission, *History of Rwanda: From the Beginning to the End of the Twentieth Century*, Kigali, 2016.
Ndagijimana, A., *L'Afrique face à ses défis: Le problème des réfugiés rwandais*, Geneva, Arunga, 1990.
Newbury, C., *The Cohesion of Oppression: Clientship and Ethnicity in Rwanda, 1860–1960*, New York, Columbia University Press, 1988.
Newbury, C., 'Rwanda: Recent Debates over Governance and Rural Development', in Hyden, G., Bratton, M. (Eds.), *Governance and Politics in Africa*, Boulder–London, Lynne Rienner, 1992.
Newbury, D., *The Land beyond the Mists: Essays on Identity and Authority in Precolonial Congo and Rwanda*, Athens, Ohio University Press, 2009.
Newbury, D., 'Editor's Introduction', in Des Forges, A. L. (Ed.), *Defeat Is the Only Bad News: Rwanda under Musinga, 1896–1931*, Madison, University of Wisconsin Press, 2011, pp. xxiii–xxxvi.
Newbury, D., Newbury, C., 'Bringing the Peasants Back In: Agrarian Themes in the Construction and Corrosion of Statist Historiography in Rwanda', *The American Historical Review*, Vol. 105, No. 3, 2000, pp. 832–77.
Ntezimana, E., 'Coutumes et traditions des royaumes hutu du Bukunzi et du Busozo', *Etudes Rwandaises*, No. 2, April 1980, pp. 15–39.
Ntezimana, E., 'L'arrivée des Européens au Kinyaga et la fin des royaumes hutu du Bukunzi et du Busozo', *Etudes Rwandaises*, June 1980, pp. 1–29.
Office de l'information et des relations publiques pour le Congo Belge et le Ruanda-Urundi, *Le Ruanda-Urundi*, Brussels, 1959.
Organisation of African Unity, International Panel of Eminent Personalities to Investigate the 1994 Genocide in Rwanda and the Surrounding Events, *Rwanda: The Preventable Genocide*, Addis Ababa, 7 July 2000.
Pagès, A., *Un royaume hamite au centre de l'Afrique*, Brussels, Institut Royal Colonial Belge, 1933.
Palmer, N., *Courts in Conflict: Interpreting the Layers of Justice in Post-Genocide Rwanda*, Oxford, Oxford University Press, 2019.
Paternostre de la Mairieu, B., *Le Rwanda: Son effort de développement*, Brussels–Kigali, A. De Boeck-Editions rwandaises, 1972.
Pauwels, M., 'Le Bushiru et son Muhinza ou roitelet hutu', *Annali Lateranensi*, 1967, pp. 205–322.
Perham, M., 'Some Problems of Indirect Rule in Africa', *Journal of the African Society*, 1934, Supplement to No. 2 of April 1934.

Perraudin, A., *Un évêque au Rwanda: Témoignage*, Saint Maurice, Editions Saint Augustin, 2003.

Pickard, T., *Combat Medic: An Australian's Eyewitness Account of the Kibeho Massacre*, Wavel Heights, Big Sky Publishing, 2008.

Piton, F., *Le génocide des Tutsi du Rwanda*, Paris, La Découverte, 2018.

Piton, F., 'Dans les plis de l'ethnie: Pouvoirs et société au nord du Rwanda (1930–1961)', Doctoral thesis, Université de Paris, 2020.

Pottier, J., *Re-imagining Rwanda: Conflict, Survival and Disinformation in the Late Twentieth Century*, Cambridge, Cambridge University Press, 2002.

Pottier, J., 'Land Reform for Peace? Rwanda's 2005 Land Law in Context', *Journal of Agrarian Change*, Vol. 6, No. 4, 2006, pp. 509–37.

Prezidansi ya Repubulika, *Ingingo z'ingenzi mu mateka y'u Rwanda. Imyaka cumi y'isabukuru y'ubwingenge 1.7.1962–1.7.1972*, Kigali, Ibiro by'amakuru muli Prezidansi ya Repubulika, 1972.

Prunier, G., 'Eléments pour une histoire du Front patriotique rwandais', *Politique africaine*, No. 51, October 1993, pp. 121–38.

Prunier, G., *The Rwanda Crisis: History of a Genocide*, New York, Columbia University Press, 1995.

Prunier, G., *Africa's World War: Congo, the Rwandan Genocide, and the Making of a Continental Catastrophe*, Oxford, Oxford University Press, 2009.

Purdeková, A., *Making Ubumwe: Power, State and Camps in Rwanda's Unity-Building Process*, Oxford–New York, Berghahn Books, 2015.

Purdeková, A., '"Mundane Sights" of Power: The History of Social Monitoring and Its Subversion in Rwanda', *African Studies Review*, Vol. 59, No. 2, 2016, pp. 59–86.

Purdeková, A., Mwambari, D., 'Post-genocide Identity Politics and Colonial Durabilities in Rwanda', *Critical African Studies*, Vol. 14, No. 1, 2021, pp. 19–37.

Purdeková, A., Reyntjens, F., Wilén, N., 'Militarisation of Governance after Conflict: Beyond the Rebel-to-Ruler Frame – The Case of Rwanda', *Third World Quarterly*, Vol. 39, No. 1, 2018, pp. 158–74.

Radelet, S., *Emerging Africa: How 17 Countries Are Leading the Way*, Washington, DC, Center for Global Development, 2010.

Radelet, S., 'Success Stories from "Emerging Africa"', *Journal of Democracy*, Vol. 21, 2010, pp. 87–101.

Ramsay, 'Uha, Urundi und Ruanda', *Mitteilungen aus den Deutschen Schutzgebieten*, 1897, pp. 177–81.

Raporo ya komisiyo y'ubugenzuzi y'inteko nkuru y'amategeko muwa 1968, Kigali, 29 October 1968.

Refugees International, *Rwandan Refugees in Tanzania. New Arrivals Report*, Sitrep #10, 17 May 1994.

Rennie, J. K., 'The Precolonial Kingdom of Rwanda: A Reinterpretation', *Transafrican Journal of History*, Vol. 2, No. 2, 1972, pp. 11–54.

Reporters sans frontières, *Rwanda: l'impasse? La liberté de la presse après le génocide, 4 juillet 1994–28 août 1995*, 1995.

Reporters sans frontières, *Rwanda: RSF s'inquiète du mépris grandissant du gouvernement envers certains journalistes*, 6 May 2008.

République rwandaise, Commission spéciale sur les problèmes des émigrés rwandais, *Le Rwanda et le problème de ses réfugiés*, Kigali, May 1990.

République du Rwanda, *Sénat, Idéologie du génocide au Rwanda et stratégies de son éradication*, Kigali, 2006.

Rever, J., *In Praise of Blood: The Crimes of the Rwandan Patriotic Front*, Toronto, Random House Canada, 2018.

Reydams, L., '"More than a Million": The Politics of Accounting for the Dead of the Rwandan Genocide', *Review of African Political Economy*, Vol. 48, No. 168, 2021, pp. 235–56.

Reyntjens, F., 'La nouvelle constitution rwandaise du 20 décembre 1978', *Penant*, 1980, pp. 117–34.

Reyntjens, F., *Pouvoir et droit au Rwanda: Droit public et évolution politique, 1916–1973*, Tervuren, Musée royal de l'Afrique centrale, 1985.

Reyntjens, F., 'La deuxième république rwandaise: évolution, bilan et perspectives', *Afrika Focus*, No. 3–4, 1986, pp. 273–98.

Reyntjens, F., 'Cooptation politique à l'envers: les législatives de 1988 au Rwanda', *Politique Africaine*, No. 34, 1989, pp. 121–6.

Reyntjens, F., *L'Afrique des Grands Lacs en crise: Rwanda, Burundi – 1988–1994*, Paris, Karthala, 1994.

Reyntjens, F., *Rwanda: Trois jours qui ont fait basculer l'histoire*, Paris, L'Harmattan, 'Cahiers Africains' No. 16, 1995.

Reyntjens, F., 'Rwanda, Ten Years On: From Genocide to Dictatorship', *African Affairs*, Vol. 103, No. 2, 2004, pp. 177–210.

Reyntjens, F., *The Great African War: Congo and Regional Geopolitics, 1996–2006*, New York, Cambridge University Press, 2009.

Reyntjens, F., *Political Governance in Post-Genocide Rwanda*, New York, Cambridge University Press, 2013.

Reyntjens, F., 'The Changes Made to Rwanda's Constitution Are Peculiar – Here's Why', *The Conversation*, 28 January 2016.

Reyntjens, F., *The RPF Did It: A Fresh Look at the 1994 Plane Attack That Ignited Genocide in Rwanda*, Antwerp, IOB Working Paper, 2020-5.

Reyntjens, F., *Le génocide des Tutsi au Rwanda*, Paris, Presses Universitaires de France, 2nd ed., 2021.

Reyntjens, F., 'Rwanda: Ethnic Amnesia as a Cover for Ethnocracy, and Why This Is Dangerous', *The Africa Governance Papers*, Vol. 1, No. 3, 2023, pp. 210–20.

Riot, T., Bancel, N., Rutayisire, P., 'Un art guerrier aux frontières des grands lacs: Aux racines dansées du Front Patriotique Rwandais', *Politique Africaine*, No. 147, 2017, pp. 109–34.

Roberts-Wray, K., *Commonwealth and Colonial Law*, London, Stevens, 1966.

Roessler, P., Verhoeven, H., *Why Comrades Go to War: Liberation Politics and the Outbreak of Africa's Deadliest Conflict*, London, Hurst, 2016.

Rouquié, A., 'La dynamique des élections sans risque ou la voie africaine de l'Etat', in Centre d'étude de l'Afrique noire, *Aux urnes l'Afrique! Elections et pouvoir en Afrique noire*, Paris, Pedone, 1978, pp. 217–28.

Rumiya, J., *Le Rwanda sous le régime du mandat belge (1916–1931)*, Paris, L'Harmattan, 1992.

Rusagara, F., *Resilience of a Nation: A History of the Military in Rwanda*, Kigali, Fountain Publishers Rwanda, 2009.
Rutabuzwa Buranga, *Rwanda et Burundi: les nouveaux sorciers*, Paris, author's edition, 1979.
Ryckmans, P., 'Le problème politique du Ruanda-Urundi', *Congo*, 1925, pp. 407–13.
Ryckmans, P., *Dominer pour servir*, Brussels, Albert Dewit, 1931.
Sanders, E. R., 'The Hamitic Hypothesis: Its Origin and Functions in Time Perspective', *Journal of African History*, 1969, pp. 521–32.
Saucier, J.-F., 'The Patron–Client Relationship in Traditional and Contemporary Southern Rwanda', New York, Columbia University, PhD thesis, 1974.
Schedler, A., 'The Logic of Electoral Authoritarianism', in Schedler, A. (Ed.), *Electoral Authoritarianism: The Dynamics of Unfree Competition*, Boulder, Lynne Rienner, 2006, pp. 1–23.
Scott, J., *Domination and the Arts of Resistance: Hidden Transcripts*, New Haven, Yale University Press, 1992.
Scott, J., *Seeing Like a State: How Certain Schemes to Improve the Human Condition Have Failed*, New Haven, Yale University Press, 1998.
Sebasoni, S., *Les origines du Rwanda*, Paris, L'Harmattan, 2000.
Segal, A., 'Rwanda: The Underlying Causes', *Africa Report*, April 1964, pp. 3–6.
Segal, A., *Massacre in Rwanda*, London, Fabian Research Series Pamphlet 240, 1964.
Smith, P., *Le récit populaire au Rwanda*, Paris, Armand Collin, 1975.
Sommers, M., *Stuck: Rwandan Youth and the Struggle for Adulthood*, Athens GA–London, University of Georgia Press, 2012.
Stanley, H. M., *Through the Dark Continent*, London, Sampson Low, Marston, Searl & Rivington, 1878.
Stearns, J. K., *Dancing in the Glory of Monsters: The Collapse of the Congo and the Great War of Africa*, New York, Public Affairs, 2011.
Stearns, J. K., *The War That Doesn't Say Its Name: The Unending Conflicts in the Congo*, Princeton, Princeton University Press, 2021.
Straus, S., *The Order of Genocide: Race, Power, and War in Rwanda*, Ithaca, Cornell University Press, 2006.
Straus, S., 'The Limits of a Genocide Lens: Violence against Rwandans in the 1990s', *Journal of Genocide Research*, Vol. 21, No. 4, 2019, pp. 504–24.
Straus, S., Waldorf, L., 'Introduction: Seeing Like a Post-conflict State', in Straus, S., Waldorf, L. (Eds.), *Remaking Rwanda: State Building and Human Rights after Mass Violence*, Madison, University of Wisconsin Press, 2011, pp. 3–21.
Straus, S., Waldorf, L. (Eds.), *Remaking Rwanda: State Building and Human Rights after Mass Violence*, Madison, University of Wisconsin Press, 2011.
Sundaram, A., *Bad News: Last Journalists in a Dictatorship*, New York, Doubleday, 2016.
Sundberg, M., *Training for Model Citizenship: An Ethnography of Civic Education and State-Making in Rwanda*, London, Palgrave Macmillan, 2016.
Swain, J., 'The Riddle of the Rwandan Assassin's Trail', *The Sunday Times*, 4 April 2004.

Sylla, L., *Tribalisme et parti unique en Afrique noire*, Abidjan–Paris, Université nationale de Côte d'Ivoire-Presses de la Fondation nationale des sciences politiques, 1977.

Tanner, R. E. S., 'The Belgian and British Administration in Ruanda-Urundi and Tanganyika', *Journal of Local Administration Overseas*, 1965, pp. 202–11.

Thomson, S., *Whispering Truth to Power: Everyday Resistance to Reconciliation in Postgenocide Rwanda*, Madison, University of Wisconsin Press, 2013.

Thomson, S., *Rwanda: From Genocide to Precarious Peace*, New Haven–London, Yale University Press, 2018.

Tilly, C., 'War Making and State Making as Organized Crime', in Evans, P. B., Rueschemeyer, D., Skocpol, T. (Eds.), *Bringing the State Back In*, New York, Cambridge University Press, 1985, pp. 169–91.

United Nations, Economic and Social Council, Commission on Human Rights, *Report on the Situation of Human Rights in Rwanda Submitted by Mr. René Degni-Ségui, Special Rapporteur of the Commission on Human Rights, under Paragraph 20 of Resolution S-3/1 of 25 May 1994*, E/CN.4/1995/70, 11 November 1994.

United Nations, Office of the High Commissioner for Human Rights, *Democratic Republic of the Congo, 1993–2003. Report of the Mapping Exercise Documenting the Most Serious Violations of Human Rights and International Humanitarian Law Committed within the Territory of the Democratic Republic of the Congo between March 1993 and June 2003*, Geneva, August 2010.

United Nations, Security Council, *Final Report of the Commission of Experts Established Pursuant to Security Council Resolution 935 (1994)*, S/1994/1405, 9 December 1994.

United Nations, Security Council, *Addendum to the Interim Report of the Group of Experts on the Democratic Republic of the Congo (S/2012/348) concerning Violations of the Arms Embargo and Sanctions Regime by the Government of Rwanda*, S/2012/348/Add.1, 27 June 2012.

United Nations, Security Council, *Midterm report of the Group of Experts on the Democratic Republic of the Congo*, S/2022/967, 16 December 2022.

USAID, *Rwanda Democracy and Governance Assessment*, November 2002.

Uvin, P., *Aiding Violence: The Development Enterprise in Rwanda*, West Hartford, Kumarian Press, 1998.

Uvin, P., 'Difficult Choices in the New Post-Conflict Agenda: The International Community in Rwanda after the Genocide', *Third World Quarterly*, Vol. 22, No. 2, 2001, pp. 177–89.

Uwizeyimana, L., 'La politique d'équilibre ethnique et régional dans l'emploi', in *Les relations interethniques au Rwanda à la lumière de l'agression d'octobre 1990. Genèse, soubassements et perspectives*, Ruhengeri, Editions universitaires du Rwanda, 1991, pp. 308–22.

Vanderlinden, J., *La République rwandaise*, Paris, Berger-Levrault, 1970.

Van Leeuw, C., *L'administration territoriale au Congo Belge et au Ruanda-Urundi. Fondements institutionnels et expérience vécue 1912–1960*, Dissertation Licence en Philosophie et Lettres (Histoire), Louvain-la-Neuve, Université catholique de Louvain, 1981.

Van Overschelde, A., *Un audacieux pacifique: Monseigneur Léon Paul Classe, apôtre du Rwanda*, Namur, Grands Lacs, 1948.

Vansina, J., *Antecedents to Modern Rwanda: The Nyiginya Kingdom*, Madison, University of Wisconsin Press, 2004.

Verwimp, P., *Peasants in Power: The Political Economy of Development and Genocide in Rwanda*, Dordrecht, Springer, 2013.

Vidal, C., 'Anthropologie et histoire; le cas du Ruanda', *Cahiers internationaux de sociologie*, Vol. 43, 1967, pp. 143–57.

Vidal, C., 'Alexis Kagame entre mémoire et histoire', *History in Africa*, Vol. 15, 1988, pp. 493–504.

Vidal, C., *Sociologie des passions (Côte d'Ivoire, Rwanda)*, Paris, Karthala, 1991.

Waldorf, L., 'Mass Justice for Mass Atrocity: Rethinking Local Justice as Transitional Justice', *Temple Law Review*, Vol. 79, No. 1, 2006, pp. 1–88.

Waldorf, L., 'Revisiting Hotel Rwanda, Genocide Ideology, Reconciliation, and Rescuers', *Journal of Genocide Research*, Vol. 11, No. 1, 2009, pp. 101–25.

Waldorf, L., 'Apotheosis of a Warlord: Paul Kagame', in Themnér, A. (Ed.), *Warlord Democrats in Africa: Ex-military Leaders and Electoral Politics*, London, Zed Books, 2017, pp. 68–94.

Wallis, A., *Stepp'd in Blood: Akazu and the Architects of the Rwandan Genocide against the Tutsi*, Winchester–Washington, Zero Books, 2019.

Wheare, K. C., *The Constitutional Structure of the Commonwealth*, Oxford, Clarendon Press, 1960.

White, C. M. N., 'Indirect Rule', in Apthorpe, R. (Ed.), *From Tribal Rule to Modern Government*, 13th conference proceedings, Lusaka, Rhodes-Livingstone Institute for Social Research, 1959, pp. 195–202.

Wrong, M., *Do Not Disturb: The Story of a Political Murder and an African Regime Gone Bad*, New York, Public Affairs, 2021.

Yeld, R., *Implications of Experience with Refugee Settlement*, E.A.I.S.R. conference paper, Kampala, Makerere University, 1962.

Index

abanyabutaka, 11, 57
abanyamukenke, 11, 57
Abarashi, 110
abatware b'ingabo, 11, 57
abiru, 12, 53–54, 81, 87
Afrika, E., 102
agriculture, 178–179
akazi, 65–66
akazu, 123, 132
Amnesty International, 147, 163, 165
Amselle, J.-L, 20
Angola, 33
Aprosoma (Association pour la promotion sociale des masses), 80, 82, 84–87, 90, 95, 98–99
Aredetwa, 87
armies, 8–9, 83
Arusha peace accord, 132, 135, 140, 156
Association des éleveurs du Ruanda-Urundi, 80
authoritarianism, 57, 71, 94, 180, 182, 184–185, 187
autochthony, 96

Bachmann, K., 4
Bagosora, Th., 138–139, 141
Bahutu Manifesto, 107
Bakiga, 111
Baldwin, G., 177
Banyenduga, 111
Baumann, O., 24
Belgian Congo, 32, 35–36
Berlin, 24, 29
Bézy, F., 122
Bigogwe, 148
bipolar identities, 128, 135
Birara, J., 116–117
Bizimana, A., 136
Bizimungu, P., 157
Blair, T., 155
Bono, 155
Booh-Booh, J.-R, 138

bourgeoisie, 122, 192
Britain, 33–34, 170, 180
Bruguière, J.-L., 137
Buberuka, 48
Buganda, 46, 49
Bugesera, 48, 103, 132, 136
  attack, 102
Bugoyi, 20, 23–24, 45, 116–117, 186
Bukunzi, 45, 47–48
Bumbogo, 48
Bunyabungo, 8
Burabyo, D., 102
bureaucratisation, 56, 60, 62, 65, 71
Buregeya, B., 117
Burundi, 16, 103, 135
Busanza, 23
Bushi, 8, 16, 29
Bushiru, 15, 23, 45–48, 116–117, 186
Busoga, 62
Busozo, 45, 47–48
Butare, 141, 144
Bwanakweri (chief), 79
Byabagamba, T., 167

Capoccia, G., 2
Catholic Church, 80
Catholic seminaries, 79
Central African Republic (CAR), 172
centralisation, 184, 187
Cheeseman, N., 183
chiefs, 43, 56–58, 60–61
Chrétien, J.-P., 17, 21–22, 111, 120
Christianisation, 61
civil society, 123, 125, 156, 162
civil war, 30, 128, 130, 185
civilian killings, 167
civilian self-defence, 103, 143
clans, 23, 56
Classe (Monsignor), 44, 52, 55–56
Clausewitz, C. von, 149
Clinton, B., 155

208

Index

Coalition pour la défense de la République (CDR), 133, 142
Comité pour la paix et l'unité nationale (CPUN), 112, 114, 116
Committee of public salvation, 110
Communauté économique des pays des grands lacs (CEPGL), 121
constitution 1961, 88
constitution 1962, 88, 94, 96, 126
constitution 1973, 112
constitution 1978, 114, 126
constitution 1991, 129
constitution 2003, 157, 164
constitution 2015, 160
Consultative Forum for Political Organisations, 164
continuities, 181, 184–185, 191
corvée labour, 64–65
counter revolution, 83
counter-elites, 79, 93
coup d'état, 107, 110, 112, 117, 188
critical junctures, 2, 30–31, 51, 72, 93, 154

D'Hertefelt, M., 7
De Clerck, J.-F., 33, 37, 42–43, 49
de Lacger, L., 7
de Lame, D., 122
Degni-Ségui, R., 148
Del Ponte, C., 151–152
Democratic Christian Party (Parti démocrate-chrétien – PDC), 129
Democratic Green Party, 160
democratisation, 74–75, 88, 91, 128, 162
Des Forges, A. L., 20, 24, 42, 147
Desrosiers, M.-E., 1–2, 104, 121, 124, 126, 173
developmental regimes, 182
Dialogue, 123
Division spéciale présidentielle (DSP), 131
divisionism, 164–165, 175, 190
donors, 180–181
Dorsinville, M., 103–104
Democratic Republic of the Congo (DRC), 149, 167–168

economic regress, 124
elections, 75–76, 85–86, 156–159, 161
engineering, 178, 188
Ethiopia, 180
ethnicity, 2–3, 20–21, 30, 42, 45, 48, 50–51, 56–57, 63, 72, 76, 78, 80, 82, 84, 91, 93, 100, 103, 110–111, 116, 119–120, 126, 128, 131, 135, 174–176, 179, 186–191
ethnocracy, 127, 157, 166, 173, 175–176, 187, 190–191

exceptionalism, 177
extraterritorial repression, 159, 167, 169

Fallers, L., 62
Forces armées de la République démocratique du Congo (FARDC), 172
Force Intervention Brigade (FIB), 171
Forces armées rwandaises (FAR), 131
Fossey, D., 123
Franck, L., 39–41, 43
Freedom House, 170
Fujii, L. A., 144–145

Gabiro, 148
gacaca, 150–151, 176
Gahama, J., 68
Gahima, G., 152, 166
Garde nationale, 102, 107, 109
Gasana, J., 122, 126, 136
genocide, 93, 104, 137, 168, 190–191
  credit, 155, 173
  denial, 164
  dynamics and motives, 145
  ideology, 162, 164–165, 175, 190
  means, 142
  modus operandi, 143
  organisation, 141
  planning, 141
  popular, 144
  survivors, 157
  victims, 146
German East Africa, 24, 27, 29, 33, 35
German policy, 26, 34
Gersony, R., 147
Gihanga, 6
Gikongoro, 103–104
Gisaka, 24, 35, 39, 45, 48
Gisenyi, 186
Gisimba, Chr., 102
Gitarama, 88, 109, 111, 141, 144
  congress, 88
  constitution, 88, 94
  coup d'etat, 87
Gitera, J., 82, 98
Gordon, N., 123
Green Revolution, 180
Groupe scolaire of Astrida, 61, 79
Guichaoua, A., 135, 179

Habumuremyi, P. D., 176
Habyarimana, J., 107, 110, 115–118, 120–121, 124–128, 131, 137, 141
Habyarimana, J.-B., 141
Hailey (Lord), 70
Hamitic Hypothesis, 47, 49, 54, 63, 187

Hanssen, A., 122
Harroy, J.-P., 74, 80–83, 92
hegemony, 156, 161, 176
hidden transcript, 175, 187, 192–193
human rights, 97, 156, 167
Human Rights Watch, 149, 162, 164, 169
Hutu, 40, 64–66
 burdens, 59, 65–66
 elites, 67
 masses, 63
 propaganda, 142
 protection, 63

ibikingi, 59, 77
Ibingira, G. S., 100
Ibuka, 162
ibwami, 58–59, 83
Ijwi, 29, 32
ikoro, 11, 64
Imandwa, 24
imidugudu, 178
impuzamugambi, 142
indirect rule, 26, 30–31, 36, 39–41, 50, 52, 55, 57, 68, 70, 72, 85, 90, 184
 contradictions, 69–70, 73, 91
 information and communication management, 156, 172
ingabo, 83, 189
ingando, 189, 192
Ingelaere, B., 151
inkotanyi, 130
inkuba, 142
inner circle, 165, 186
insurrections, 20–21, 23
interahamwe, 136, 142–143
interim authorities, 84–85, 92
interim government, 138, 140
internal self-government, 75, 85, 87–88, 92
International Criminal Tribunal for Rwanda (ICTR), 141, 148–149, 151
International Crisis Group, 151, 157
international donors, 173
international peacekeeping, 156
International Residual Mechanism for Criminal Tribunals (MICT), 153
International status, 28, 33
intore, 9, 188–189
intra-regime conflict, 185, 191
inyenzi, 99–100, 102, 104, 119, 126, 131
Inyumba, A., 165
itorero, 9, 188–189, 192

jacquerie, 82, 91–92, 111
Jallow, H. B., 152

Jessee, E., 192
Johnson, Ch., 73

Kabare, 19
Kabila, L., 169, 171
Kabuye, D., 167
Kagame, A., 3, 7, 10–11, 14, 16–19, 24, 27–28, 53
Kagame, P., 157, 159–161, 163, 166, 174–175, 177
Kagenza, A., 118
Kamarampaka, 90
Kambanda, J., 140–141
Kandt, R., 15
Kanguka, 123
Kangura, 123
Kanjogera, 19, 24
Kanyabashi, J., 151
Kanyarengwe, A., 112, 116–117
Karegeya, P., 166
Karinda, C., 102
Karugarama, Th., 160
Kayibanda, G., 87, 90, 99, 103–104, 107, 110–112, 121, 126
Kayumba Nyamwasa, F., 166
Kelemen, R. D., 2
Kibeho killings, 168
Kibuye, 132, 136
Kigeri Ndahindurwa, 81, 87, 99, 175
Kigeri Rwabugiri, 8, 12–14, 16–22, 24, 27, 29–30, 64
Kigwa, 6
Kimonyo, J.-P., 165
kings, 42–44, 54, 58–59
Kinyaga, 22, 45, 47, 50
Kinyamateka, 123, 125, 163
Kwibuka, 176

la relève, 74
Lake Kivu, 32–33
land, 178–179
Lavigerie (Cardinal), 25, 61
Lavroff, D. G., 94
Le Messager-Intumwa, 163
League of Nations, 34–35
Lemarchand, R., 3, 66, 77, 89, 175
Liberal Party (*Parti libéral* – PL), 129
Linden, I., 22, 66
Liprodhor, 162
Lizinde, Th., 116–117, 169
Logiest, G., 74, 83–84, 86–87, 89, 91, 98
longue durée, 4–6, 182, 191–192
Louis, Wm. R., 15, 26, 28
Lugan, B., 4
Lugard (Lord), 69

Index

M'Bokolo, E., 20
M23, 171–172
Makuza, A., 110
Mamdani, M., 121, 126
Manasseh, Nshuti, 176
mandate, 34–36, 39, 53
Mandement de carême, 80
Manifeste des Bahutu, 80
Mapping Report, 168
Maquet, J. J., 11, 14
Mathys, G., 17, 22, 174
Mayuya, S., 118
Mbarubukeye, A., 107, 109–110
Mbonimana, G., 61
Mbonyumutwa, D., 82, 87, 107
McDoom, O. S., 146
MDR-Parmehutu, 86–87, 89–90, 95, 98–100, 105–107, 110, 113, 129
Mecklenburg (Duke of), 26
media, 142, 163
migration, 66
militarisation, 9, 29–30, 188–189
militarism, 8
military, 9, 11, 183, 188, 192
military campaigns, 32
military diplomacy, 172
military ethos, 101
militia, 142, 144
Mise au point, 80
missions, 25, 49
Mitchell (Governor), 69
Mitterrand, F., 125, 128
modernisation, 178–179
monarchy, 87, 97, 175
monetary economy, 76
Morris, H. F., 69
Mortehan, G., 55
Mouvement démocratique progressiste, 80–81
Mouvement démocratique républicain (MDR), 85, 129, 142, 157
Mouvement Révolutionnaire National pour le Développement (MRND), 114, 119, 124–125, 142
Mouvement social muhutu, 80, 82
Mozambique, 172
Mpirikanyi, M., 102
Mugesera, A., 162
Mugesera, L., 136
Mulera, 45
Mulindahabi, C., 106–107
multipartyism, 125
Munyangaju, A., 123
Muramutsa, J., 107
Mushikiwabo, L., 163
Mutabazi, J., 167
Mutara, 45
Mutara Rudahigwa, 52, 54, 59, 80, 92, 98
Mutsinzi, E., 163
Mwambari, D., 176
Mwima coup d'état, 81, 92
Mworoha, E., 14, 16, 18, 23

National Commission for Human Rights, 169
National Electoral Commission (NEC), 161
National Resistance Army (NRA), 130
National Synthesis Commission, 125, 129–130
National Unity and Reconciliation Commission (NURC), 4
Ndabarasa, 10
Ndadaye, M., 135
Ndahiro, M., 102
Ndasingwa, L., 138
Ndazaro, L., 102
Ndi Umunyarwanda, 176, 190
Ndorwa, 45, 48
Ndungutse, 27–28, 48
Newbury, C., 1, 5, 14, 22, 50, 89, 92, 122
Newbury, D., 1, 3, 5, 14, 16–19, 22, 30, 89, 92, 189
Ngango, F., 138
Nkeramugaba, A., 103
Nsekalije, A., 116
Ntaryamira, C., 137
Ntezimana, E., 17
Ntsibura, 8
Nyabingi cult, 20
Nyatanyi, P., 107
Nyiginya kingdom, 7–9, 14, 20, 22, 47

Organisation commune africaine et malgache (OCAM), 121
Office of the Prosecutor (OTP) (ICTR), 148, 151–152
Organisation pour l'aménagement et le développement du bassin de la rivière Akagera (OBK), 121
Ostrovky, Y., 152

Pagès, A., 7
parliamentary elections, 89–90, 98, 115
parliamentary report 1968, 106
Parmehutu (Parti du mouvement de l'émancipation des Bahutu), 82, 84–85
Parsons, T., 62
path dependency, 2, 30–31, 51, 71, 126, 182
peacekeeping operations, 172

Pegasus spyware, 170
Perham, M., 59, 62
peripheral regions, 15, 45, 50, 65, 191
Perraudin (monsignor), 74
Piton, F., 20
plane attack, 137, 166
political emancipation, 77, 85, 89
political opposition, 133
   elimination, 156–157, 162
political parties, 81
political regime, hybridity, 97
political space, limits, 162
political transition, 128, 157
Postiaux, L., 53
Pottier, J., 173–174, 178
press freedom, 125
Preud'homme, A., 83
protection treaty, 37
public law, 35–36, 67–68, 85, 88
public transcript, 187, 192
Purdeková, A., 176, 185

queen mother, 12–13, 17–19, 24, 30, 42, 53
quota system, 120–121, 190

Radelet, S., 182
Rassemblement démocratique rwandais (RADER), 79, 81, 84–85, 87, 98, 102
Radio Télévision des Mille Collines (RTLM), 142
Ramsay (captain), 24–25
rebellions, 19, 21, 27
referendum, 37–38, 90, 114
refugees, 93, 130–131, 168
Refugees International, 147
regime consolidation, 156
regime infighting, 186
regional conflicts, 112, 105, 108, 116–117, 170, 190
religion, 43
Renkin, J., 32, 37
Rennie, J. K., 7
Reporters sans frontières (RSF), 163
repression, 156, 159
resistance, 65
revisionism, 164
revolution
   accelerators, 73, 80
   conditions, 73
   premises, 74
Rouquié, A., 115
royal drum, 12–13, 19
Rucunshu coup d'état, 19, 24–25, 27–28, 30

Rudasingwa, Th., 166
Ruganzu Ndori, 8, 47
Ruhamiriza, 189
Ruhengeri, 186
Ruhengeri prison, 102, 113
Ruhinankiko, 19
Rujugira, 8, 10, 17, 189, 191
Rukeba, F., 102
Rukiga, 48
Rusagara, F., 9, 167, 192
Rushyashya, 163
Russell, A., 1–2
Rutarindwa, 18–19, 25
Rutsindintwarane, J., 102
Ruyaga, 48
Rwagafilita, P. C., 117
Rwagasana, M., 102
Rwanda Briefing, 166
Rwanda Defence Force (RDF), operations in the DRC, 171
Rwanda National Congress (RNC), 166
Rwanda Patriotic Front (RPF), 2, 93, 126, 130–131
   attack, 130
   cells, 136
   crimes, 132, 146, 150, 152
   internal conflicts, 165, 167, 186
   offensive, 133
   vision, 156
Rwigema, F., 186
Ryckmans, P., 41, 57, 70

Sandrart (lieutenant), 25
Schedler, A., 161
schools, 49, 60, 79, 118
Scott, J., 179
Service central des renseignements (SCR), 124
Sebasoni, S., 9
sectarianism, 164
Segal, A., 104
Sendashonga, S., 156, 169
Serubuga, L., 117
Sibomana, A., 125, 163
Sindikubwabo, Th., 140–141
single party rule, 90, 98, 100, 114, 124, 158
Social Democrat Party (Parti social-démocrate – PSD), 129
Society of Nations, 36
South Africa, 159, 166–167, 171
Speke, J. H., 49
Stanley, H. M., 24
Strategies of tension, 135
Straus, S., 143, 145
structural violence, 155, 181–182

Index

Sundaram, A., 163
superiority (sense of), 15, 177
Sweden, 170
Swedlund, H. J., 173

taxation, 28, 64–66
territorial administrators, 68
territorial reorganisation, 59
terrorism, 18, 23, 29, 92, 101, 136
Thomson, S., 150
Tombeur (general), 32, 39
torture, 169
transitional broad based government (*gouvernement de transition à base élargie* – GTBE), 134
transitional national assembly (*Assemblée nationale de transition* – ANT), 134
transnational repression, 170
Treaty of Versailles, 34
trust territory, 77
Trusteeship Council, 78
Tutsi, 40, 92, 100, 132
  arrests, 132
  discrimination, 119, 127
  divisions, 61
  extermination, 139
  killings, 132, 140, 144
  massacres, 100, 102–103
  political exclusion, 120
  political monopoly, 48, 50–51, 54
  refugees, 93, 100, 119
Twagiramungu, F., 156

ubuhake, 8, 11, 66, 76–77, 108
ubukonde, 91, 108–109
uburetwa, 21, 27, 30, 64–66, 186, 189
ubwenge, 177
ubwiru, 12, 19, 43
Uganda, 16, 45, 167, 183
umuganda, 142
umuganura, 43
umuhinza, 46–47
Umurabyo, 159
Umuranga, 123

Umuseso, 159, 163
umutware, 57
umutware b'ingabo, 57
Umuvugizi, 159, 163
UN Group of Experts on the DRC, 171–172
UN High Commission for Human Rights, 168
Union nationale ruandaise (UNAR), 81–87, 89–90, 95, 98–100, 102–104
UN High Commission for Refugees (UNHCR), 131, 147
United Nations, 75, 77, 88
United Nations Assistance Mission for Rwanda (UNAMIR), 134, 137, 148
universal jurisdiction, 153
Uvin, P., 181
Uwilingiyimana, A., 138

Vansina, J., 3, 8–10, 14, 18, 21, 23, 174
victor's justice, 151, 153, 173
Vidal, C., 7
violence, 13–14, 20, 29–30, 93, 191
Voisin, Ch., 54, 61
von Götzen (count), 24

Waldorf, L., 164, 177
war crimes, 168
Warren, R., 155
wars, 16, 30
Washington refugee conference 1988, 120
Watkins, S., 192
Weberian norms, 62–63, 70
White Fathers, 25, 44, 49, 56
White, C. M. N., 69
Wilson, W., 37
witnesses, 151
Wrong, M., 170

Yuhi Musinga, 17, 19–20, 24–28, 30, 35, 37–38, 42–44, 47, 49, 52–53, 60, 70, 185

For EU product safety concerns, contact us at Calle de José Abascal, 56–1°, 28003 Madrid, Spain or eugpsr@cambridge.org.

www.ingramcontent.com/pod-product-compliance
Ingram Content Group UK Ltd.
Pitfield, Milton Keynes, MK11 3LW, UK
UKHW020442250925
463284UK00026B/1231